ST. MARY'S COLLEGE OF MARYLAND LIBRARY
ST. MARY'S CITY, MARYLAND

S0-BQZ-910

4.50 Princeton U. 8-67 (Griffin)

POLITICAL REALISM AND THE CRISIS OF WORLD POLITICS

An American Approach to Foreign Policy

———◦•◦———

BY KENNETH W. THOMPSON

PRINCETON, NEW JERSEY
PRINCETON UNIVERSITY PRESS
1960

Copyright © 1960 by Princeton University Press

ALL RIGHTS RESERVED

L.C. Card: 60-5758

Printed in the United States of America by
Princeton University Press, Princeton, New Jersey

22039

DEDICATED
TO THE MEMORY OF
MY FATHER

PREFACE

THIS little volume has its origins and growth in the author's experiences over a decade of study, teaching, and writing. During this period, an important trend of thinking on foreign policy has emerged within the United States. It is an approach which expresses deep and grave misgivings concerning the main currents of popular and public writing and thinking on international relations. It represents a reaction against a viewpoint dominated by legalistic and moralistic points of emphasis. It carries its own religious and moral commitments but places these commitments in the context of the harsh realities and difficult choices of international politics. Few public figures or aspiring political leaders have openly espoused the new approach, particularly during the years of their public service. Nevertheless, many of them, perhaps more than they know, have been influenced by insights embedded in the new tradition. For the most part, political realism has engendered controversy and debate rather than widespread consensus or agreement. Its spokesmen have sometimes felt constrained to qualify their loyalty even to the beliefs of others writing and thinking within the same tradition. It is not a mark of popularity to carry the name political realist. A full understanding of the underlying philosophy of this approach is needed, however, if American statesmen and scholars are to advance public understanding and awareness of the realities of international life and close the gap between what leaders feel and do and what the people imagine they do. Therefore the central aim I have had in mind is a careful explication, first, of the origins of political realism as an approach to American foreign policy, and, secondly, of its implications for the major unsolved fundamental problems of America's relations with the rest of the world.

The immediate stimulus for the writing of the book was the invitation to deliver the Riverside Memorial Lectures in the winter of 1958. These lectures, devoted each year to an examination of the relation between Christian principles and the broad concerns of American society, gave me an opportunity for the development of some of the major themes around which the book took shape. The aims and purposes of the Lectureship have been stated as follows: "The Riverside Lectures express the conviction of The Riverside Church [New York City] that the Christian Faith and academic disciplines need to understand each other at the level of their most significant developments, and that the lines of communication and conversation need to be kept open by scholars in the sciences, humanities, and religion." I am especially indebted to Mr. James Livingston and Dr. Gordon Chamberlin for their continued interest and encouragement. In the preparation and revision of the manuscript, I have had the benefit of the wise counsel and patient help of Miriam Brokaw and Herbert Bailey.

That a study of political realism can be associated with an inquiry into the relevance of ethics for international affairs should not be surprising. The political realists whose writings I have described and analyzed are almost without exception men whose concern with the moral dilemmas of modern life has driven them to attempt to establish a philosophy of international relations. Each of them has tried to be positive while avoiding naïveté, moral though shunning moralism, and systematic without excluding the ambiguities and uncertainties of international life. I am particularly indebted to certain individual scholars like Hans J. Morgenthau, Reinhold Niebuhr, and George F. Kennan, who, while bearing no responsibility for the shortcomings or inadequacies of my own writings, have been a source of inspiration and guidance. If this volume serves to underscore some of the fundamental issues with which these writers have been concerned and which remain crucial problems in the years ahead, it may have contributed to the continuing dialogue on the principles of American foreign policy. If this dialogue is maintained free of the unnatural restraints or untimely restrictions that self-acknowledged sources of authority or conformity seek to impose on every generation, the future of the Republic will be brighter and more hopeful. Each successive generation of observers and interpreters carries the heavy burden of appraising and, if necessary, correcting or enlarging the reach and grasp of those who have gone before. I see the contribution of the political realists in this light. I am confident that each of them would point to the unfinished tasks of broadening and deepening the realist tradition. In the end, I conceive my study as a primer or introduction to the main currents of a single challenging approach to the perplexing issues of contemporary foreign policy. I could wish that younger scholars in particular might draw from the broad outlines and unsolved problems of this approach an agenda for vigorous reflection and research. My own hope and intent for the future would be to find a place among those who, in William James's well-chosen phrase "stubbornly attempt to think clearly," wherever the evidence may lead them. In this respect, political realism is an invitation to seek the truth and not a termination of free inquiry. It provides a framework and not a doctrine, a set of hypotheses rather than a list of answers. The pages that follow have been written in this spirit and I would profoundly hope might be read this way, however emphatic or outspoken I have been at certain points in explanation or analysis.

K.W.T.

November 1959

CONTENTS

PART ONE

AMERICAN FOREIGN POLICY:
THEORISTS AND PRACTITIONERS

CHAPTER 1

MAIN CURRENTS OF AN
AMERICAN APPROACH TO INTERNATIONAL
POLITICS: PHILOSOPHERS, COLUMNISTS,
AND POLICY PLANNERS

Interests . . . not ideas dominate directly the actions of men. Yet the "images of the world" created by these ideas have very often served as switches determining the tracks on which the dynamism of interests kept the actions moving.—MAX WEBER

IN THESE TURBULENT AND UNCERTAIN TIMES, any honest mind approaching the problems of world politics is tormented by a sense of inadequacies and limitations. It is true that we know more about the world in which we live than we did a century or two ago. Statistics are better, and knowledge of the past is more complete. We have better birth rates, death rates, and emigration rates. Through the public press and democratic institutions men have a greater stake in their government; the elemental factors responsible for the growth and prosperity of nations are better understood and controlled. Yet, although knowledge is greater, the factors that must be assessed have increased in number and complexity to a bewildering degree. In place of the isolated rivalries of the past, we are facing struggles that involve directly or indirectly the whole habitable globe. Our problems have become so vast, their solution so painful and doubtful, and the weight of contingencies so overwhelming that even for the wisest statesman foreign policy is at least three-fourths guesswork. Moreover, for all our statistics, historical and economic knowledge, and responsible governments, we have had little success in foreseeing future events, let alone coping with present ones.

Failures in political prophecy are, of course, nothing new. History records countless examples of decisive political developments that caught even the most experienced observers by complete surprise. In the eighteenth century neither Benjamin Franklin nor Frederick the Great appear to have anticipated the approaching French Revolution, yet both were constant observers of the course of French affairs. Nor did someone as active in revolutionary politics as Madame Roland make a single allusion before 1789, in her voluminous correspondence, to the impending downfall of the French monarchy. Napoleon was confident that "Europe will be either Cossack or Republican," and Pitt prophesied that the end of the Papacy was in sight.

Political prophecies concerning foreign states have most often fallen short of the mark. The knowledge that people possess of the social and political conditions of another country is almost always so imperfect, superficial, and cribbed and confined by parochialism that popular generalizations tend to go widely astray. In 1760 Rousseau predicted that in twenty years England would be ruined and have lost her liberty. The statesmen of Europe joined philosophers such as Rousseau in proclaiming England a decadent and second-class power, a sort of insular Poland, selfish, faction-torn, without nerve and consistency, and destined probably to fall under Russia's domination. The illusion that England was fast declining was shared by Joseph II of Austria, Frederick II of Prussia, and Catherine II of Russia. These erroneous estimates provided the basis for momentous policies which affected the future of the world. In much the same way the Kaiser and Hitler underestimated both Britain and America and chose courses that changed the history of the West and of the rest of the world as well.

If these experiences carry any lesson for the present, it is that future events may be decisively shaped by the estimates of Britain or Russia or India or China presently being made as a basis for contemporary foreign policies.

Fortunately we also find in history examples of leaders who pierced the veil of the future, who foresaw the course of history more clearly than their contemporaries. We find philosophers and statesmen who were attuned to the larger forces and impending issues that now are seen as the major factors that determined the future. Burke saw with a clarity greater than his contemporaries the potential strength of the American Colonies, the rise of the peoples of India, and the irrepressible dynamism of the French Revolution. His world view was faulty in many respects but, because he saw the truth of a few essential principles, his writings cast a golden shaft of light into the dark corners of the future.

Polybius predicted the rise of the Roman Empire and its unifying role throughout the Mediterranean world and foresaw the signs and causes of its eventual decline. De Tocqueville anticipated the race problem in America, the coming of the "War Among the States," and forecast the appearance of those recurrent and perennial problems of democracy such as the tyranny of public opinion, the decrying of personal excellence and superior virtue, and the intolerances of patriotism. At the same time he had the wisdom to confess the shortcomings of "all the ingenious and erroneous systems with the aid of which men had tried to explain a present which was not yet clearly seen and to predict a future which was not seen at all." Karl Marx predicted that the seizure of Alsace-Lorraine by Prussia in 1871—which Bismarck also viewed with misgivings—would throw France into the arms of Russia and force Germany to confront the combined strength of the Slavs and the Latins.

More recently, in March 1936, Mr. Winston Churchill warned Britain and a world not yet prepared to heed his words: "For four hundred years the foreign policy of England has been to oppose the strongest, most aggressive, most dominating Power on the continent and particularly to prevent the low countries falling into the hands of such a power." And he asked: ". . . which is today the power which is strongest, and which seeks in a dangerous and oppressive sense to dominate. Today, for this year, probably for part of 1937, the French Army is the strongest in Europe." But no one feared France. He concluded: "Therefore, it seems to me that all the old conditions present themselves again, and that our national salvation depends upon our gathering once again all the forces of Europe to contain, to restrain, and if necessary to frustrate, German domination."[1] However, in the same debate before the House of Commons, Neville Chamberlain saw little in the "necessarily excessive" figures on German rearmament, and for the moment his appraisal won public acceptance.

As we reflect on these prophecies, the question arises, why were some philosophers and statesmen, like Burke, Churchill, and de Tocqueville, more prescient and farsighted than others? What accounts for their greater wisdom? What part is the outgrowth of reason, and how much is the result of the instinctive and acquired knowledge that civilization accords its keenest observers? Perhaps the most compelling of possible answers is one offered by Mr. Churchill, who has many times pointed to the importance of an organizing theory: "Those who are possessed of a definite body of doctrine and of deeply rooted convictions upon it will be in a much better position to deal with the shifts and surprises of daily affairs."[2] Accordingly, political prediction, insofar as it rests at all upon an intellectual process, is little more than historical generalization which varies according to the knowledge and acumen of the prophet. In one sense the "right" political prediction is no more than the outcome of a powerful and creative mind play-

[1] Winston Churchill, *The Second World War: The Gathering Storm*, Vol. I (Boston: Houghton Mifflin Co., 1948), pp. 207-09.
[2] *Ibid.*, p. 210.

ing on a situation. Despite modern ingenuity in contriving devices to replace superior human judgment, no substitute has yet been found for practical wisdom, nor a Univac to replace unique moral and intellectual endowments. It may not be stretching a point to say that Rembrandt and Picasso are to the minor painters what Thucydides and Churchill are to the minor philosophers and statesmen.

On the other hand, it is fair to ask whether these heroic figures are unique in every respect or whether they embrace certain common approaches, concerns, and qualities.[3] This much can be asserted: In political theory in general, at least in Western civilization, and in the theory of international politics in particular, the lasting contributions have come from men who resisted the fateful divorce of theory from practice. We are tempted to ask if there is not a fundamental and inescapable link between men's grasp of the relationships between theory and practice in international politics and the enduring value of their views. In any event, from Machiavelli to Clausewitz, from Admiral Mahan to Hugh Gibson and George F. Kennan, we note a fruitful relationship between their direct struggles with the intractable facts of political behavior and their evaluation of these facts. It would appear that political prognosis thrives on political practice, however this practice may be experienced and however the hazards and perils of a too-passionate involvement or commitment are met. Perhaps a parallel can be drawn with the medical sciences, where research and practice are intimately related and where the experimenter is never far removed from the patient's bedside. Medical scientists take for granted the link between human problems and research. The case, then, for political science—conceived as a pure science of human behavior or as the worship of apparently irrelevant abstractions unrelated to

[3] This question is indeed a long one, crying out for much study and research. There is a surprising dearth of literature on the problem, although the sociological writings of men like Philip Selznick and the writings on political theory of men like Hans J. Morgenthau touch on the problem.

7

life's problems or of towering objectivity in social affairs—may in the end prove to be based on a false conception of the nature of science itself.

The question still remains, of course, whether we can distill from past international politics as viewed by some of our wisest interpreters a body of common principles or a core of residual truths reflecting the essence of their approach. Fundamentally this is the question which has been asked either explicitly or by implication for more than two decades by the philosophers, columnists, and policy planners who comprise the subject of the present article. This question may conceivably escape man's reach. Nevertheless a few of the pointers that have guided our school of writers along the way can be set down at the outset and reexamined throughout the course of this study.

First of all, great students of international politics have brought to their task a lively sense of history. We do well to remind ourselves of this, however obvious it may seem, for modern man, in his impatience to confront and solve present-day problems, is by instinct suspicious if not contemptuous of this approach. How often one hears that history never repeats itself, or that no one ever learns anything from history! How frequently do the words "let the dead past bury itself" or "change is the first law of the universe" resound in both scholarly and public discourse! This conviction may stem partly from an incurable faith in progress and in the upward march of mankind. Most of us shared the vague expectation that the First World War and more recently the Second World War were to usher in a new era, replace old ideals with new, establish the human family on a more amicable basis, and eliminate once and for all the poisonous emotions infecting past international relations. Few if any observers saw these tragic events as a fatal retrogression from which we could recover only by long and painful struggles. More basically, however, the rejection of history involves the substitution of spurious and simple-minded interpretations for the onerous demands of a patient search for meaning among the complexities of the past.

It is said that Sir Neville Henderson, Britain's Ambassador in Berlin from 1937 to 1939, felt that his reading of *Mein Kampf* on board ship when he was returning home from Latin America fully prepared him for observing developments in Germany. He apparently believed that the underlying appeal of German militarism, the legacy of Bismarck and Frederick the Great, and Germany's historic objectives were of little immediate importance. His illusion is traced in *Failure of a Mission*. It is instructive to contrast these views with the cogent analysis, informed by history, of Sir Eyre Crowe of the British Foreign Office, which offered a rational basis for policies that might have prevented a world war. More recently an American Secretary of State declared that the only prerequisite for understanding Soviet foreign policy is the reading of Stalin's *Problems of Leninism*—as if this could explain Soviet tactics toward Yugoslavia, Sino-Russian rivalries, or Soviet ties with anti-revolutionary dictatorships in the Middle East.

Great social groupings, classes, and nations tend within broad limits to react in similar ways to similar situations. History in terms of these recurrent patterns provides the ground on which more intricate and individual patterns of social conduct can be worked out. Mr. Churchill's firm grasp of world politics was rooted in history. His conception of the Grand Alliance was based on the lessons of the coalition that resisted Louis XIV. His historical masterpiece, *Marlborough: His Life and Times*, was written during the decade of "The Gathering Storm," about which he warned not ex post facto but as the first signs of dark clouds were appearing on the horizon. As Marlborough was the linchpin of the first Grand Alliance that thwarted the French attempt to dominate Eu-

9

rope, so Churchill played a parallel role in marshalling resistance to Germany's expansion.

There is, of course, no one plot in history, despite the best efforts of philosophers to find one, nor can history provide a detailed roadmap to guide men from one point to the next. H. A. L. Fisher, in the Preface to his *History of Europe*, holds up a warning sign when he declares: "I can see only one emergency following upon another as wave follows wave . . . only one safe rule for the historian: that he should recognize in the development of human destinies the play of the contingent and the unforeseen." However, his scorn for grand designs and theories fixes primarily upon one form and philosophy of history. This is the philosophy of progress. In criticism of the theory of progress he writes: "The fact of progress is written plain and large on the pages of history; but progress is not a law of nature. The ground gained by one generation may be lost by the next. The thoughts of men may flow into the channels which lead to disaster and barbarism."

While there is no one plot in history, there *are*, nonetheless, rhythms, patterns, and repetitions. Otherwise there could be no understanding nor valid generalization. Thucydides, despising contemporary renown, asked only that his History of the Peloponnesian War be considered not "as an essay which is to win the applause of the moment, but as a possession for all time." For he said: "If it be judged useful by those inquirers who desire an exact knowledge of the past, as an aid to the interpretation of the future, which in the course of human things must resemble, if it does not reflect it, I shall be content." In the same spirit, was it not Sir Walter Raleigh who said that "the end and scope of all history . . . [is] to teach us by example of times past such wisdom as may guide our desires and actions"? Different types of studies have their special virtues, but the greatest Western minds would probably join with Bacon, who declared that "Histories make men wise."

One lesson of history is expressed in the saying that you may drive out history with a pitchfork but it always comes back. In England, Cromwell and the army sought to make a drastic break with the past by scrapping the time-honored monarchical form of government. With the death of Cromwell traditional forms came sweeping back and the monarchy was restored. Sorel, in his great work *L'Europe et la Révolution Française*, traces the continuity of French policy during the Revolutionary and Napoleonic periods with that of the Ancien Régime. Today in the Soviet Union the absence of political freedom, the ever-present secret police, and the unquestioning acceptance of an authoritarian regime are reminders of Tsarist Russia. The sharp break between past and future foreseen by some liberal historians can hardly be supported by the record. Listen to these words: "It is probable . . . that the resumed march of Russia towards her age-long objectives, towards an Atlantic port, in the Baltic and the Balkans, towards a Mediterranean outlet, in the Middle and Far East, will occupy important pages in what is to come of twentieth century history."[4] They were written by a British historian in 1944. Precisely a decade before the Polish and Hungarian revolutions of 1956, George F. Kennan predicted uprisings in the Soviet empire in about ten years. The grounds for his prediction were a knowledge of Russian history and of the anatomy of totalitarian regimes.

The second quality worth mentioning in a survey of philosophers and statesmen who speak with a singular timelessness is the assumption by most of them that an understanding of political phenomena, whether international or domestic, is inseparable from a clear picture of human nature. This view, it must be said, runs counter to much of present-day thought. Social scientists are disposed to argue that man is a bundle of contradictory impulses and that his behavior must be tested

[4] A. L. Rowse, *The Use of History* (London: Hodder & Stoughton Ltd., 1946), pp. 26-27.

11

and analyzed experimentally before we can say anything at all. Political institutions and procedures preoccupy the scholar as more manageable units of study. Yet the question with which Reinhold Niebuhr began the Gifford Lectures in the spring of 1939 returns to haunt us: "Man has always been his most vexing problem. How shall he think of himself?"[5] This is the starting point for all serious philosophers, whatever the answer they give. Moreover, even philosophers who pride themselves on freedom from any controlling view of man more often than not embrace implicit assumptions that shape their conclusions. Alexander Hamilton, in seeking the cause of conflict among states, concluded: "To presume a want of motives for such contests would be to forget that men are ambitious, vindictive and rapacious."[6] Other philosophers, who assume that men are by nature cooperative and virtuous, view the international system as cast in another mold. Therefore, writers who claim to be entirely free from presuppositions about man carry a heavier baggage of assumptions than they know; and the gravest problems arise from theories of the world founded upon a conception of man that is concealed and for this reason never examined.

A third condition of the theories of the prophetic political philosophers derives from their attitude toward human progress. One view is the Enlightenment conception, that man's history is essentially an upward spiral, with each generation becoming wiser, better, and more prosperous than the last. Another view is espoused by millennial Christians and liberals or Marxist secularists alike; it is an article of faith for them all that man is corrupted and depraved but that he awaits one decisive event which will bring "a new heaven and a new earth." In the past men have been selfish, grasping, and evil;

[5] Reinhold Niebuhr, *The Nature and Destiny of Man: A Christian Interpretation*, Vol. 1 (New York: Charles Scribner's Sons, 1945), p. 1.
[6] Alexander Hamilton, James Madison, and John Jay, *The Federalist*, ed. Max Beloff (Oxford: Basil Blackwell, 1948), p. 20.

with one blinding act they will be transfigured from mortal men to members of a classless society—progress indeed!

But more prevalent by far is the theory of progress that sees man transforming himself through newer, more rational institutions. In *Essays on the Social Gospel*, Adolf Harnack declares: "Retrogression is no longer possible for us; and shame upon those who desire it."[7] This is probably less pernicious than other determinist creeds. Yet in the end it is equally mischievous because it suggests that progress is waiting at the other end of a charter, a constitution, or a court judgment. The United Nations was presented by some of its American champions as an organization that would do away with alliances, balance of power, and bitter rivalries among states—in other words, this novel institution would overnight create a new form of international behavior. The world would be done with blocs, security guarantees, and regional arrangements except as they might spring from the new international organization. How prophetic were these disciples of progress? Newspaper dispatches and headlines give the answer. NATO, SEATO, the Eisenhower Doctrine, the Baghdad Pact, the Warsaw Pact, and the bilateral security arrangements between the United States and more than forty countries.

One must hasten to add that a rejection of these extravagant views of progress does not imply a denial of progress as such. It is progress as perfectibility that is questioned. History is the record of significant human advances, but of advances marred by retreat and retrogression. More often than not, progress is the half-step, the partial advance which is accepted when the ultimate goal is beyond reach. This truth is one that wise men perceive, and in perceiving make their contribution to progress.

Finally, the enduring philosophies of international politics possess a viable, workable concept of politics. It is politics that

[7] Adolf Harnack and Wilhelm Herrmann, *Essays on the Social Gospel* (New York: G. P. Putnam's Sons, 1907), p. 7.

presents the statesman with his severest test on the international scene; it is politics that demands meaningful analysis and generalization. Yet it is politics, on the international no less than on the national scene, that suffers the worst calumnies, contempt, and abuse. Many of our leaders want not so much to understand politics as to eliminate it. An American President proclaims that politics is one thing he doesn't care much about; others contrast the high principles of the statesman with the low tactics of the politician. Professor Carl Becker pointed out that "the term politics has taken on a certain unsavory meaning, as when we say 'playing politics' or 'it's only politics.' In international relations playing politics, otherwise known as 'the diplomatic game,' has recently become a little more unsavory or even sinister, by being described as 'power politics.' "[8]

If politics is anything, however, it is compromise, the adjustment of divergent interests, and the reconciliation of rival moral claims. Politics calls for the highest moral stamina if men are to stand on the uncertain terrain where to act may be to act unjustly, where there are few if any absolutes, and where success, for better or for worse, is the most common criterion. Henry Ward Beecher observed that not that which men do worthily but that which they do successfully is what history makes haste to record. Success in politics, just as success in business, is contingent on an understanding of its principles or "laws." This understanding has been achieved by men whose predictions ring true; lack of understanding is the cause of the failure of those whose words are foolishness today.

I. THE PHILOSOPHERS

If it is true that the words of some academic scribbler lie behind most policies that are eventually hammered out in the public forum, we need make no apology for studying the ap-

[8] Carl L. Becker, *How New Will the Better World Be?* (New York: Alfred A. Knopf, 1944), p. 76.

proach of the philosophers. Scholars are often accused of living in ivory towers and of divorcing themselves from the realities around them. Bacon said in his *On the Advancement of Learning*: "Philosophers make imaginary laws for imaginary commonwealths, and their discourses are as the stars which give little light because they are so high." However, the academician in American universities and colleges has frequently proved himself capable of developing sound approaches to a greater degree than the man of affairs. Professor Bernard Brodie has written: "We political scientists have learned a great deal these past fifteen or twenty years . . . Hitler and the war he brought us were a great educating influence on the subjects of politics and the use of power."

The intellectual journey of twentieth-century American scholars and philosophers must be plotted along four relatively distinct lines. During one phase, prior to and through World War I, diplomatic historians enjoyed what amounted to a virtual monopoly. What most distinguished this period was a high level of historical accuracy and faithful attention to the canons of historiography. Historians conceived as their first duty the forswearing of every temptation to generalize in sweeping and unqualified terms about their observations. Their sole aim was to record a story in all its fullness and essential simplicity. The price paid for this rigorous, objective, and non-generalized approach was the absence of anything corresponding to a theory of international relations. Moreover, the criticism was voiced that this approach provided public opinion and the general citizenry with no guideposts for understanding and action.

In consequence, during the truce between the two wars there grew up an overriding concern to discover the means for studying the immediate present. In place of the detached and highly specialized techniques of diplomatic history, an approach that has been called the current-events point of view emerged. The "bible" for the study of international relations

15

became *The New York Times,* and the function of the teacher became that of interpreting and explaining the immediate significance of current events. This approach occasioned a flurry of popular interest which, however, proved premature, resting as it did on weak and unstable foundations. This version of scholarship cast the teacher in the role of a pundit, and made of specialists little more than advocates and special pleaders. As a result, the areas that might have been exploited from the earlier study of diplomatic history were left largely untouched, and the study of the present was pursued without any of the ordering principles that might have been drawn from past experience. Each scholar became a spokesman for his own brand of international legislation or reform. Some discussed, off the cuff, free trade versus protectionism; others, international monetary reform; still others, new ways and means of transforming international organization. But none attempted to relate postwar political problems with issues of an earlier day. To have done this would have been antiquarian and would have proved that the scholar was at odds with his times.

Even scholarly leaders like President Woodrow Wilson inveighed against using studies of the Congress of Vienna as background for the Paris Peace Conference, a proposal made by the British. The light that Talleyrand or Metternich might have thrown on foreign policy was ruled out of order. The approach became little more than a day-by-day exercise in proposing and disposing of each major or minor world problem as it presented itself. Furthermore, the absence of a firm methodological foundation for studying these events led to a grand and extravagant conception of what international studies should encompass. Anything foreign was relevant; everything, from the anthropology of primitive tribes to the phenomenon of xenophobia, was equally important. In these terms an informed discussion of the Olympic Games was as appropriate as one on the latest move in German diplomacy. However engaging this concept was in theory and however appropriate for group discussion, it could scarcely lead to any carefully conceived approach to the relevant problems upon which war and peace might hinge. Someone has said that this was an era of letters to Congressmen, to editors, and to interest groups, without more than a line or two of scholarly monographs. The idea that scholars and their public could influence foreign policy was spawned during this period, and strengthened by the tendencies inherent in a third and overlapping phase of international studies.

Throughout these years, if any dominant philosophy was giving content to the current events approach, and direction and purpose to research, it was that of international law and organization. Inaugurated shortly after World War I, this approach set two goals for its disciples. Students were to discover the ends and objectives toward which international society should tend, and then labor faithfully to attain them. Not without reason the purpose of the first chair in international politics at the University of Wales was defined as "the study of those related problems of law and . . . of ethics which were raised by the projects of a League of Nations." Through indoctrination of ideas and information regarding the League, international studies were to perform an educational and transforming function. Critics were to say of this mode of thinking that in no other field had scholars become captive to such a degree of emotions and wishful thinking.

The success and failures of this period in international relations resulted essentially from three of its characteristics. First, the era was dominated by a spirit of boundless optimism. Second, the research and academic interests as well as the special qualification of scholars lay overwhelmingly in international law and organization. Third, a tendency was everywhere apparent to draw moral judgments in favor of every international venture at the expense of any national experience. The spirit of optimism and the conception of progress undoubtedly derived from the philosophy of the Enlightenment and from its stepchild, the peace movement of the nineteenth century. Powerful industrial figures like Mr. Ginn, the publisher, and Mr. Andrew Carnegie, the steel magnate, approached international problems with a confidence born of their breathtaking successes in private enterprise. The Carnegie Endowment in its prescription for abolishing "the foulest blot on our civilization" hinted that war was only one in a series of problems which American ingenuity would soon efface. Mr. Carnegie himself instructed the Trustees of the Carnegie Endowment for International Peace: "When . . . war is discarded as disgraceful to civilized man, the Trustees will please then consider what is the next most degrading evil or evils whose banishment . . . would most advance the progress, elevation and happiness of man. . . ."

The heavy concentration of scholarship and scholars on international law and organization can readily be documented. Of the twenty-four scholars who held the rank of professor of international relations by 1930, eighteen devoted themselves exclusively to this specialization. Throughout this period a tendency persisted to equate peace with government, and war with power politics and the balance of power. When international politics and its enduring practices and techniques was studied at all, it was by the diplomatic historian within the limits of his interests and outlook. The experiences of the nineteenth century in easing international tensions were considered inappropriate subjects for serious inquiry. Instead, technical and procedural problems, organizational reforms, and improvements of international government preoccupied almost every scholar.

Finally, an implicit if unstated assumption underlay the selection of almost every subject of inquiry: everything international was good, and everything national was bad. Hence selected for study were such good and constructive international experiments as the League of Nations, and such dubious

18

national policies as imperialism and integral nationalism. Passed over for study was the "bad," or at least morally ambiguous, internationalism of the Third International and the "good" quest for a legitimate national security. Indeed one of the illnesses from which the study of international relations still suffers is the cult of internationalism, with its own moral evaluations arrived at through a simple dichotomy of good internationalism and bad nationalism. This is ironic indeed when one reflects that nationalism has become a principal ally of the West in the strivings of Soviet satellites to be more than puppets in a scheme for world domination or of the new nations to carve out independent destinies free of communist control.

Following World War II, a tendency that began in the years immediately before the war came to the forefront. The study of international politics replaced the study of international organization as the central point of reference in international relations. An approach was made to recurrent world problems not with a view to praise or condemn but to understand them. In a survey published in 1947 for the Council of International Relations, President Grayson Kirk of Columbia University, then Professor of International Relations, found that international politics had become the basic introductory field of study almost everywhere throughout the country. In place of examining the structure and organization of international society, scholars were turning to the underlying forces and trends that mold and shape the behavior of nation states.

The aim was to study international politics in the same way that domestic politics had been studied for almost a generation. Much as studies of American government and politics had moved from examination of the Constitution and basic statutes to practical politics and pressure groups, so international studies became concerned with the underlying tendencies in the foreign policies of separate nation states and the forms and techniques through which the various national policies of states could be compromised and adjusted on the international plane. Instead of beginning with international society, the new line of inquiry emphasized the study of *national* goals and objectives as a logical point of departure. Just as no one would imagine for one moment that policy on the domestic scene is a given quantity but must be sought in the adjustment of rival claims of political parties and pressure groups, so international policy, say within the United Nations, must be studied as the result of the pressures and claims of nations on the international scene. When taken from this point of view, the practices and policies of international organization are no longer abstract considerations. Instead they are conceived within the framework of the aims and purposes of nations, their points of conflict, and their areas of compatibility and incompatibility. In this way, the historic policies of England, the United States, or the Soviet Union become objects of greater interest than isolated studies of international government divorced from international politics as such. International organization finds its proper place when it is approached as a forum within which national rivalries are adjusted through partly novel and partly historic political processes.

What this has done in practice has been to tie the study of international relations to political science. Without this core international relations had tended to ride off in all directions; with it came for the first time a chance of discovering relevant and general principles by which citizens and statesmen might be guided. Political science assumes that rivalry among individuals and groups for political power and the ways power and authority are exercised is a subject for study; in the same way international politics assumes that the struggle for influence and power can be examined systematically.

International politics has become the focal point of present-day research and teaching partly because of the march of events in the 1930's. It was ushered in largely because of the failure of earlier viewpoints to conform even accidentally with the facts of the interwar period. The crises that followed in rapid succession from Mukden Bridge in 1931 to the present found both students and teachers emotionally and intellectually unprepared. The widespread belief that the new formal institutions would quickly modify international conduct bore little resemblance to actual events. The relations of civilized nations which were to have been modified by the League of Nations progressively deteriorated as the European balance of power was threatened by Germany and Italy. It was no minor constitutional defect of the League but rather the political conditions under which it operated that was the primary cause of its breakdown. Only by a realistic assessment of international phenomena could the League's decline and fall have been anticipated. The clue to the basic point of departure in international politics as distinguished from international organization may be found in the way the United Nations is evaluated. Formerly the League had been at the center of the majority of the studies; now world politics is the focal point of all studies, including those dealing with the functions of the United Nations. The rivalries occasioning international tensions are now generally assumed at a critical point to be political in character. As a result the political scientist has moved to the center of international studies. The concern of international politics today is threefold—with the forces and influences which bear on the conduct of foreign policy everywhere, with the techniques and machinery used to execute foreign policy, and with the novel institutions and traditional practices used to adjust conflicts among nations. Fundamental and persistent forces of world politics, such as nationalism, imperialism, and the balance of power, have belatedly become proper subjects for study, and the basic drives underlying foreign policies of states, such as the search for security and power, are the elements of this new approach. If one is asked for a short definition of international politics it may be called the study of rivalry among nations and the conditions and institutions which ameliorate or exacerbate these relationships.

This approach to international relations is not, of course, the product of a single mind nor even of a single school comparable to, for example, the Vienna School in psychoanalytic theory. No Freud stands at the center, with critics and interpreters, glossators, and revisionists ranged around him. Professional journals like *The American Political Science Review, World Politics,* and *The Review of Politics* have given opportunities to emerging specialists, but the best writings are rather widely scattered in both political and religious, popular and scholarly periodicals. Admittedly it is hazardous to claim special credit for certain scholars to the exclusion of others who may be equally creative and thoughtful. However, it must nevertheless be said that the decisive role, while not perhaps as significant as that of Keynes in economics or Clausewitz in military strategy, has unquestionably been played by a few men. Their backgrounds are surprisingly diverse. One is a theologian, Reinhold Niebuhr; another an English historian, E. H. Carr; the third, a man who worked in the shadowy area where considerations of geography and foreign policy collide, Nicholas J. Spykman; and the last a political theorist, Hans J. Morgenthau. The one tie that binds this group together is their concern with the comprehensive study of theory and practice in international politics. Other scholars, to be sure, have concerned themselves with methodology or concrete problems in the field. A few extraordinarily able columnists and practitioners, about whom we shall have more to say, have grappled with fundamental issues. However, the little group we have singled out is distinguished by its attention to the over-all problem of working out a general framework for approaching contemporary problems. Each has rejected the seductive comforts and temptations of scholarship divorced from the harsh and stubborn problems confronting policymakers. For example it is possible to say what these men believe or have believed about the cold war, Soviet objectives, or international organization. Surprisingly, many of their contemporaries are curiously silent on present-day problems; this is perhaps no more than an unconscious reaction to the heavier emphasis of an earlier day on current affairs, although it may also result because abstract methodology is less controversial in this age of conformity.

The diplomatist and historian George F. Kennan has called Reinhold Niebuhr "the father of all of us." The writings of this remarkable theologian over a period of more than forty years come to more than 1,500 articles and book reviews and sixteen major volumes. In a field he calls his avocation a torrent of comment has issued forth on contemporary social and political problems. The political philosopher John H. Hallowell of Duke University best captures the essential quality of Niebuhr's contribution in the following words: "Dr. Niebuhr's analyses make the impact they do upon modern minds because they 'ring true.' . . . We are attracted to his analysis because it confirms what history and our personal experience confirms. He makes explicit what we have been unable before to articulate but what we have felt to be true." The gradual unfolding of his ideas, Niebuhr tells us, came not so much through study as through the pressure of world events. As the scientist's hypotheses are adjusted to experimental findings, Niebuhr's concepts and ideas have kept pace with the lessons of current history. *Moral Man and Immoral Society*, written in the early thirties, represented a breaking through of fact and experience which forced him to abandon Christian absolutism. He tells us that before World War I he was "a young man trying to be an optimist without falling into sentimentality." When the war ended and the full tragedy had been revealed he "had become a realist trying to save himself from cynicism." Above and beyond his engaging ability to revise his point of view in the face of events, he very early perceived the issue between the philosophies of realism and idealism as well as the perils and excesses inherent in the two points of view.

Perhaps Niebuhr's chief contribution to the substance of international politics can be found in his bold and fearless attacks on the most widely held illusions, such as the misconception that institutions in and of themselves would reshape international society. In the 1937 Report of the Advisory Committee on International Relations of the Social Science Research Council, Professor James Shotwell spoke of "new forms arising which . . . will modify the entire relationship of civilized nation." Others saw the millennium in the signing in 1928 of the Pact of Paris renouncing war. Even though Niebuhr's idealism was at its high point between 1928 and 1935, when the beginning of the Ethiopian War initiated its rapid decline, he had already pointed out in July 1929, when the Pact of Paris became effective, that two of its signatories were violating its principles. China had seized the Chinese Eastern Railway and thus precipitated an attack by Soviet forces. The confounding of proclamations with policies, of procedures with politics, of form with function, and of promises with practice are errors Niebuhr has consistently struggled to set right.

He early declared war on the most fateful illusion of all, the liberal view of power, according to which power was an archaism, the last remnant of the barbaric, preindustrial, feudal age. Even an intellect as supremely endowed as President Woodrow Wilson looked to the disappearance of power from the international stage. Not so Professor Niebuhr, who set himself to observe as the datum of politics the fact of power and conflict, its sources and modes of expression, and the methods by which they might be kept consistent with the requirements of order. He found in the fateful concession that ethics makes to politics that coercion is a necessary instrument of social cohesion, whether it be coercion in Gandhi's protests of nonviolence in his march to the sea (to distill salt

24

from the ocean in opposition to the injustices of the salt tax) or coercion in the violence of management and labor at war in the first decades of this century. Moreover he found that power is never checked merely by the voluntary action of those possessing it, but only by raising a countervailing power against it. The realm of politics is the twilight zone where ethics and power meet, and it is in this troubled zone that Niebuhr has made his deepest thrust. No one can write on these problems without acknowledging an immense debt to this great mind. It happens that the most baffling issues he and his successors confront arise in international politics.

As a theologian, Reinhold Niebuhr has taken the moral problem as his major point of focus. As an historian and political scientist, E. H. Carr has chosen the analysis of foreign policy and national purposes. Although an English scholar, his influence has been greatest on American thought. Before World War II, Carr was lamenting the fact that no other field of knowledge was more encumbered by prejudice, half-truth, and ignorance. In 1939, in the preface to the *Ambassadors at Large Series* he edited, he noted: "In international politics, few of us have got beyond the stage of the small child which says, 'You are naughty,' to anyone who does something it doesn't like; for the temptation to impute moral turpitude to policies which do not suit our interests is almost irresistible."[9] One cure for this simple, black-and-white view is a critical examination of the realities of a nation's foreign policy, a task Carr set for himself in his monumental *History of the Bolshevik Revolution,* and in smaller works like *The Soviet Impact on the Western World.* Another antidote is an analysis and exposure of the faults of contemporary political thought as applied to foreign relations. Carr's *The Twenty Years' Crisis*, completed in the summer of 1939 and dedicated "to the makers of the coming peace," was written "with the

[9] Wladmir d'Ormesson, *France (Ambassadors at Large Series,* ed. E. H. Carr; London: Longmans, Green and Co., 1939), p. iv.

deliberate aim of counteracting the glaring and dangerous defect of nearly all thinking, both academic and popular, about international politics in English-speaking countries from 1919 to 1939—the almost total neglect of the factor of power."[10] In casting about for the causes of this neglect, Carr found serious thought on international politics in its infancy.

Until 1914 the conduct of international relations was the business of the professionals, and few people gave it heed. This state of affairs ended with World War I, when a powerful campaign was initiated to popularize international politics and thereby rid the world of strife. War was attributed to the wickedness of governments and, more specifically, to the nefarious role of secret treaties. This gave the impulse to an attack on war and hence to the organized study of international affairs.

It is often forgotten that in any field a felt need, a burning human goal, or a social purpose is the first step along the pathway to science. In the physical sciences the demands for better health led to the creation of medical science just as the need for roads and bridges brought about the science of engineering. More than one writer has argued that a social or technical need is a greater spur to the progress of mankind than are ten universities. Research for the sake of amassing data or thinking for thinking's sake is more often barren than not. The observer confronted by a basic problem is challenged to order his questions and direct his answers to some crucial point. According to the German philosopher Kant, reason approaches nature "not in the character of a pupil, who listens to all that his master chooses to tell him, but in that of a judge, who compels the witness to reply to those questions which he himself thinks fit to propose." International relations illustrates the rule rather than the exception for, as with all sciences during the interwar period, it passed through a

[10] E. H. Carr, *The Twenty Years' Crisis* (London: Macmillan Co., 1949), p. vii.

utopian stage "in which the element of wish or purpose [was]
. . . overwhelmingly strong, and the inclination to analyze
facts and means weak or nonexistent."[11]

However, this link between purpose and analysis, which is
inevitable in all of science, takes on a unique character in
the social realm. The laboratory scientist may have the
same emotions toward the eradication of cancer as the political scientist toward the elimination of war. But for the
laboratory scientist the emotions are strictly irrelevant to and
separable from the investigation, since in the physical world
the facts exist independently of what anyone may think about
them. For the social investigator, however, the facts may be
changed by the desire that they be changed, for their existence
is never wholly independent of his attitude or of the attitudes
of those he seeks to influence. The purpose of the social
observer is in itself one of the very facts, inasmuch as every
political or social judgment modifies or rearranges the facts
on which that judgment is based. The aim of present-day
observers of capitalism—including many socialists—is the
preservation and defense of capitalism. While Marx claimed
he was scientific, his approach to the analysis of capitalism was
inseparably joined to and interrelated with his goal of de-
stroying capitalism. The laboratory scientist may dedicate
himself to eliminating cancer, but this does not alter the facts
of his experiment. The purpose and position of the social observer inevitably shape and affect his research. The observer
of capitalism must have some kind of moral and intellectual
position concerning his subject, and it is this position which
intermingles with his analysis and indeed gives it meaning
and purpose.

The close connection between purpose and analysis in social
relations is not the end of the story. While those who bring
about an awareness of a vital social need and of the necessity
for solving a problem make a valuable contribution, rarely

[11] *Ibid.*, p. 5.

does the solution they propound have any connection with the underlying sources of the problem. They are like the utopian socialists whom Engels criticized for believing that "socialism is the expression of absolute truth, reason and justice, and needs only be discovered in order to conquer all the world in virtue of its own power."

The passionate desire to eliminate war determined the initial direction of international studies, and this desire so overshadowed all else that any analysis or criticism of the means proposed to achieve it was branded mischievous or destructive or worse. When President Wilson was on his way to the Paris Peace Conference, he was asked by some of his advisers whether he felt the design for a League of Nations would work. He replied: "If it won't work, it must be made to work." Carr has noted: "The advocate of a scheme for an international police force or for 'collective security,' or for some other project for an international order, generally replied to the critic not by an argument designed to show how and why he thought his plan will work, but either by a statement that it must be made to work because the consequences of its failure to work would be so disastrous, or by a demand for some alternative nostrum."[12] Carr's principal contribution has been his argument that this initial stage of wishful thinking must be succeeded by one of ruthless analysis in which existing forces and tendencies are taken into account and purpose brought into line with reality. I would agree with some of Carr's critics that he is sometimes blind to the opposite truth that there are occasions where reality must be brought into line with purpose.

Nicholas J. Spykman, late Professor of International Relations at Yale University, did as much as any scholar of his generation to ground international thought in political realities. He called his approach geopolitics, and wrote: "The fact that certain writers have distorted the meaning of the

[12] *Ibid.*, p. 8.

term geopolitics is no valid reason for condemning its method and material. It is, actually, an appropriate name for a type of analysis and a body of data which are indispensable to the process of reaching intelligent decisions on certain aspects of foreign policy."[13] He was constrained to dissociate himself from Haushofer and his adherents since the advocacy of policy is not a scientific endeavor, and it was on this point that the German school was led astray.

Spykman looked to geography as the prime conditioning factor in foreign policy, but warned that not everything from the fourth symphony to the fourth dimension could be explained in geographic terms. The position a state occupied in the world and its relationship to other centers of power defined its problem of security, and to assure its position a nation had to make "the preservation and improvement of . . . [its] power position a primary objective. . . ." For his candor Spykman was attacked as having an "excess of cynicism" and an obsession with Realpolitik. He replied: ". . . power has a bad name and the use of power is often condemned . . ." and added, ". . . there is a tendency, especially among certain liberals and many who call themselves idealists, to believe that the subject of power in the international world should not be spoken of except in terms of moral disapproval." However, he concluded: "Political ideals and visions unsupported by force appear to have little survival value."[14]

Spykman's major work was *America's Strategy in World Politics*, published in 1942. Perhaps nowhere in the literature of international politics are the arguments about isolationism and internationalism traced more systematically. Spykman perceived that the ingredients of these two policies were more profound and persistent than had been generally assumed, especially by those who maintained that the American people

[13] Nicholas J. Spykman, *The Geography of the Peace*, ed. Helen R. Nicholl (New York: Harcourt, Brace & Co., 1944), p. 7.
[14] *Ibid.*, p. 3.

could rather easily be educated to an internationalist point of view. For example, he showed that isolationism had both emotional as well as strategic aspects. Emotionally, it appealed to people and their families who as immigrants had turned their backs on Europe and wanted to forget the Old World. Now that the wars and conflicts of the rest of the world had reached their new homeland they sought refuge in the comforting doctrine that they need not bother about Europe. They were also, moreover, the inheritors of the course that for nearly two centuries had been asserted as the one viable American foreign policy. When in the early part of the nineteenth century England asked the New World to intervene to redress the balance of power in Europe, again when America was asked to participate in the two Moroccan and in the Berlin Conferences, and once more during the debate over the League of Nations, the controversy was whether the order and equilibrium of Europe and Asia constituted a vital American interest. Isolationists were prepared to expand their concept of an adequate zone of defense from the national domain to the Caribbean littoral or even to the whole Western Hemisphere. But even today, as reflected in certain attitudes to the European crisis, the vestigial remains of the psychology of Fortress America linger on.

The virtue and the balance of Spykman's approach resides in his understanding that the intellectual foundations on which a large bloc of internationalist thought was based were no more adequate than was isolationist thought. He argued that in successive crises the staunchest internationalists "have been those who were inspired by idealistic considerations. Some asked participation [in successive world crises] because they were pro-British; others because they believed that, in a period of ideological warfare, we had a moral obligation to support the people whose social and political structure most closely resembled our own."[15] But few made explicit the point that

[15] Nicholas J. Spykman, *America's Strategy in World Politics* (New York: Harcourt, Brace & Co., 1942), pp. 3-4.

the first line of defense for the United States lies in preserving a balance of power in Europe and Asia, albeit our second line falls in the Western Hemisphere.

Spykman moved with rapier thrusts against a whole host of popular doctrines. In 1942 he maintained: "Basically, the new order will not differ from the old, and international society will continue to operate with the same fundamental power patterns. It will be a world of power politics." To a nation seeking escape from the anguish of foreign policy, he gave this warning: "An equilibrium of forces inherently unstable, always shifting, always changing, is certainly not an ideal power pattern for international society. But while we can deplore its shortcomings, we shall do well to remember that it is an indispensable element for an international order based on independent states." In discussing collective security, where normally points like the definition of aggression, a world police force, and perhaps world government are touched, he stated a more fundamental principle, that "whenever . . . pressures become unequal, boundaries will move. The problem of collective security is the problem of equalizing these pressures; and as long as that problem remains unsolved, the phenomenon of expansion as such will continue to appear." In the face of all the talk of a brave new world, he warned: "History testifies to the constant reappearance of these expansion forms and the ever-recurring conflict patterns that result, and there seems to be no reason to assume or expect that these behavior patterns of states will suddenly change or disappear." This hardly meant, however, that American foreign policy should be enslaved by the past. "Not conformity with the past but workability in the present is the criterion of a sound policy. Not specially selected instances in the history of the United States, but the general experience of states should be made the guide for a program of action."[16]

All this is worth mentioning for at least two reasons. First, the new approach to international relations, based on the

[16] *Ibid.*, p. 7.

general experiences of states, is today rather widely accepted in the study of international politics. More important, it appears that it was the foundations on which Spykman's thought was based that allowed him to anticipate the future. For example, in the era of good feeling toward the Russians, he wrote: "A Russian state from the Urals to the North Sea can be no great improvement over a German state from the North Sea to the Urals." Even more daring, perhaps, was his statement during the Second World War: "Twice in one generation we have come to the aid of Great Britain in order that the small offshore island might not have to face a single gigantic state in control of the opposite coast of the mainland. If the balance of power in the Far East is to be preserved in the future . . . the United States will have to adopt a similar protective policy toward Japan." During an era of friendly Sino-American relations, he saw in a modern, vitalized, and militarized China of 450 million people "a threat, not only to Japan, but also to the position of the Western Powers. . . ." Nor to those who desired the total destruction of German power—a desire we have come to regret—did he give any comfort. In a statement labeled by one critic the most astonishing conclusion that could be imagined, Spykman insisted: "The present war effort is undoubtedly directed against the destruction of Hitler and the National Socialist Party, but this does not necessarily imply that it is directed at the destruction of Germany as a military power."[17] He places these predictions in a kind of rational context by adding that the charm of power politics is that one never need grow weary of one's friends. Thus there is in Spykman at least a touch of that quality of political prophecy associated with others in Western civilization who saw the future in the light of a more general conception of man and politics.

Finally, we shall consider the fourth scholar who, in the broadest intellectual sense, helped to lay the foundation for

[17] *Ibid.*, p. 460.

international politics—Hans J. Morgenthau, Director of the Center for the Study of American Foreign Policy at the University of Chicago. Because he belongs to a later generation than the others mentioned, his contribution is more difficult to assess; we are still too close to his work to do it justice. Few, if any, of his contemporaries have elaborated their philosophies with the same force, directness, and clarity. Morgenthau is keenly aware of the moral dilemma facing the student of social affairs—who at the same time stands in judgment and is a part of the social scene. In facing this dilemma he has displayed unrivalled moral courage. He has eschewed the popular trend, the simple solution, the painless banality. To quote Dean McGeorge Bundy of Harvard, Morgenthau "has taken on all comers" in a running debate on the nature of man and politics and the principles of foreign policy. By virtue of the courage and clarity that distinguished his work, those contesting his views have been enabled to recognize the points at which they chose to take issue with him. Indeed in recent years much of the literature of international politics is a dialogue, explicit or not, between "Morgenthau and his critics"—the title of a panel discussion at the 1955 annual meeting of the American Political Science Association.

It may be useful to review cursorily the broad outlines of his philosophy. The leading constitutional document first stating his philosophy is *Scientific Man versus Power Politics* (1946). Other studies have been written on the theme "science cannot save us," but few if any have grappled so successfully with this important problem of man's social existence. On the one hand, Morgenthau contests the prevailing view that political behavior can be studied by simply transferring the methods used in natural science. He reexamines the scientific method and shows that the conception of science which social science seeks to imitate is one that present-day scientists themselves reject. Modern science, as reflected in men like Eddington and Jeans, is a science of indeterminism that takes into account the contingencies and accidents of the natural world. Therefore, to believe that a rational and predictable world can readily be imposed on the uncertainties of politics is as questionable in the social realm as the parallel premise would be in the physical.

On the one hand, Morgenthau postulates a sociology of politics in which moral absolutes and sweeping solutions are challenged and dismissed. Men in politics seek power and they come into conflict with others engaged in the same quest. They use moral justifications to cover their aspirations and thus heighten and intensify the struggle. On the domestic or national level, conflicts are kept within bounds by constitutional institutions and generally accepted rules of the game; there is a minimum consensus on the goals that can appropriately be pursued, and those thwarted today have some expectation of success tomorrow. International society is marked by far more uncertainty, disorder, and unrestrained conflict. In the days before World War II, nations like Czechoslovakia or Ethiopia or France had little assurance that their interests would be safeguarded and preserved. Countries like Egypt and Israel and even Britain and France face the same problem today. Consequently, the brutalities and rivalries of egotistic nations, selfish because their survival is at stake, confound the rationalists and reformers striving to do away with power rivalries among states through universal free trade, international sanctions, and world disarmament.

If *Scientific Man* provided a blueprint for the building of a systematic theory of world politics, then *Politics among Nations* (1948) gave us the completed edifice. *Politics among Nations* was the product of twenty years of reflection and study; in the words of the author, it launched a frontal attack "on the way by which a false conception of foreign policy, put into practice by the western democracies, led inevitably to the threat and the actuality of totalitarianism and war."[18] The book sought to propound, especially as elaborated in 1954 in the second edition, a realist theory of international politics. It attempted to give the political scientist a focal point that would distinguish his inquiries from those of the economist, the lawyer, or the moral philosopher. Interest and power were put forth as the ordering concepts for students of international politics. As an example of the peculiar focus of this approach, Morgenthau offered the following historical event:

"In 1939 the Soviet Union attacked Finland. This action confronted France and Great Britain with two issues, one legal, the other political. Did the action violate the Covenant of the League of Nations and, if it did, what countermeasures should France and Great Britain take? The legal question could easily be answered in the affirmative, for obviously the Soviet Union had done what was prohibited by the Covenant. The answer to the political question depended, first, upon the manner in which the Russian action affected the interests of France and Great Britain; second, upon the existing distribution of power between France and Great Britain on the one hand, and the Soviet Union and other potentially hostile nations, especially Germany, on the other; and, third, upon the influence that the countermeasures were likely to have upon the interests of France and Great Britain and the future distribution of power. France and Great Britain, as the leading members of the League of Nations, saw to it that the Soviet Union was expelled from the League, and they were prevented from joining Finland in the war against the Soviet Union only by Sweden's refusal to allow their troops to pass through Swedish territory on their way to Finland. If this refusal by Sweden had not saved them, France and Great Britain would shortly have found themselves at war with the Soviet Union and Germany at the same time."[19]

[18] Hans J. Morgenthau, *Politics among Nations* (2nd ed.; New York: Alfred A. Knopf, 1954), p. 7.
[19] *Ibid.*, p. 11.

The legalist looking at such a problem subordinates other considerations to the law. The political scientist, concerned with another order of action, must subordinate all aspects to interest and power. Neither the lawyer nor the political scientist assumes that his is the only reality, but each seeks to understand a subject by ordering it in terms he judges most relevant. The example noted above goes a long way toward providing a basis for discovering the most relevant standard of thought for approaching the half-anarchic international order.

It is this general conception of international relations that Morgenthau seeks to apply to American foreign policy. *In Defense of the National Interest* (1950) is an attempt to show that any successful foreign policy must be founded on a rational conception of the national interest. The focal point in the debate over Morgenthau's theory has centered on his conception of the national interest. If I understand him correctly, he postulates that every nation by virtue of its geographic position, historic objectives, and relationship to other power centers possesses a clustering of strategic interests each more or less vital to its security. At any point in time, a rational foreign policy must attend to the safeguarding of these claims. The national interest stands above and absorbs the limited and parochial claims of sub-national groups, even though such groups seek to interpret the national interest in their own terms. Interests are the permanent part of the political landscape, whether in the county, the state, or in the rivalries of labor and management. It so happens that the present era in international relations compels statesmen to put first the interests of the territorial nation-state. Nowhere does Morgenthau maintain that the nation-state is immutable. In the past, the Roman Empire and its counterparts in non-Western civilizations commanded loyalties that exceeded the nation. In the present, world politics gives evidence that in certain critical respects the nation-state is already objectively obsolescent. Yet any responsible contemporary statesman, whether Khrushchev in the world communist empire, a British Prime Minister in associations with Europe and the Commonwealth, or an American President in the United Nations, must put first the security of his own people. To do otherwise would be treasonable, for by oath of office he owes them first allegiance; he acts and speaks for the generation who have chosen him and generations yet unborn.

Morgenthau has no illusions, particularly in a democracy, that public debates will rage over the content or the implementation of the national interest or that individual leaders from time to time will conceive it in conflicting and contradictory terms. In essence, the national interest is a broad intellectual category or a way of approaching foreign policy. He insists that rational statesmen measuring the forces and factors on the world scene must achieve some rough approximation to the demands of national security. Otherwise, historians could not possibly account for the remarkable continuity of policies from one administration to the next as in the postwar programs of Democrats and Republicans or, in Britain, the Socialists and the Conservatives. If a nation's territorial integrity is to be preserved, there can never be a wholly distinct policy based on political ideology or party creed even though they shape and influence the contours of this interest.

The pages of history are littered with the failures of foreign policies that ignored vital interests. Three examples are Nazi Germany's catastrophic program of fighting a war on two fronts, the West's failure before two World Wars to prepare early enough an effective resistance against expansionist Germany, and the tragic policies that led to the presence of Russian troops in East Germany. In each case, the countries concerned pursued a course of action heedless of the national interest that imperiled or destroyed the safety of its people. Looking back on these events, the historian can point to the forks in the road where policy-makers forsook the national interest. Looking ahead, the statesman has the obligation of choosing policies more attuned to the imperatives of security in his day. If there were no objective national interest, we could not judge either past or present policies as in fact they must always be judged. Morgenthau's writings on foreign policy are scattered in the journals of recent decades, and anyone wishing to see how he has applied his theory in practice must consult a wide range of sources.

II. THE COLUMNISTS

Scholars were not alone in transforming American thinking on foreign policy. Columnists and journalists must be given at least an equal share of the credit or responsibility. Scholars analyze, synthesize, and systematize the practices and ideas of their trade into coherent systems, whether these are called laws of political economy or principles of politics. Journalists, with a few exceptions, are far too busy to formulate their beliefs, but they occasionally possess what Lord Bryce called "the skill of sizing up," or the knack of profiting "by small indications, as an old seaman discerns, sooner than the landsman, the signs of coming storm."[20] An extraordinary individual may fit these searching impressions into a more general picture.

Foremost, of course, among contemporary observers is Walter Lippmann, who for the better part of the first half of the twentieth century has been the intellectual conscience of American policy-makers, calling them to task whenever they departed from first principles of foreign policy. Assistant to Secretary of War Newton D. Baker, and himself Secretary of the Inquiry that drafted and interpreted Wilson's Fourteen Points, frequent adviser to Presidents and diplomats, Lippmann has had a long, rich, and varied intellectual career.

[20] James Bryce, *Modern Democracies*, Vol. I (New York: Macmillan Co., 1931), p. 156.

During World War I he wrote in protest against the naïveté of the peace programs in England and America. He found them born of desperation and anguish, and suffering from the illusion that the answers to Europe's problems could be found merely by postulating the opposites of the tragic forces that were rending Western society. Liberal emotions flowed into causes that were noble and commendable but unhappily, for the most part, irrelevant. "Europe was fighting; fighting is monstrous. Europe was armed; let us work for disarmament. Europe was undemocratic; let us insist on democracy. . . . One nation refused to arbitrate; arbitration should be made compulsory." Against this Lippmann maintained: "We shall end war by dealing effectively with our problems, not by reiterating that war is horrible." As World War I was drawing to a close and America was entering an era reminiscent in many ways of that during and immediately after World War II, he noted a breakdown of confidence in the creativity of free ideas. Lippmann wrote: "There is more intolerance abroad than we have been used to, and the humane capacity for playing with ideas and speculating freely has almost disappeared. . . . For the life which ideas are intended to control is tumbled and varied and flowing, alive with curiosity, and exhaustingly subtle."[21] However, the public and its leaders took refuge in such abstractions as the outlawry of war, arbitration treaties, and referendums on war. During certain periods these abstractions have become the substance of policy; at other times they are the means by which the complexities of foreign policy are made intelligible and acceptable to the people. Lippmann believed that in the interwar period the former was the case, even though policy-makers were unconscious of the extent to which their thinking was dominated by such illusions.

[21] Walter Lippmann, *The Stakes of Diplomacy* (New York: Macmillan Co., 1915), pp. 8-9. The preceding quotations from Lippmann are drawn at random.

The world Lippmann wrote about in his first major treatise on foreign policy bears little resemblance to the present international society. There were, according to him, then only eight powers that counted: Great Britain, France, Russia, Italy, Germany, Austria-Hungary, Japan, and the United States.[22] Thirty years later the number had shrunk to two. During and after World War I, the most pressing problem was the weak state, whether Turkey or China or Manchuria, or the states of the Balkans or Latin America or Africa. Corruption, inefficiency, and weakness in such areas invited imperial expansion and created arenas of friction. Before Indian independence, a Hindu declared, "I'd rather be in hell than in the British Empire." His American friend asked, "How about being in the Russian or German Empires?" "I've thought of it," replied the Hindu, "that's why I am a loyal subject of the British Crown."

It was not the developed nations that constituted a *casus belli*, but rather the underdeveloped areas, which, because of their instability and uncertainty, became political vacuums into which more powerful forces surged. So long as these areas were "stakes of diplomacy," they were fair game for any predatory claimant, and there was always a distinct possibility of conflict that would deteriorate into warfare. Lippmann proposed a series of international commissions to deal with each crisis on the spot: in Morocco, the Congo, the Balkans, Manchuria. Perhaps he was protesting too much when he argued: "The idea is not overambitious. . . . What makes it especially plausible is that it grasps the real problems of diplomacy, that it provides not a panacea but a method and the beginnings of a technique. It is internationalism, not spread thin as a Parliament of Man, but sharply limited to those areas of friction where internationalism is most obviously needed."[23] Beyond this he insisted that the humane and

---

[22] *Ibid.*, p. 82. "When I say count I mean that the effective force of the world is in their hands, and that the decision in world affairs is for them."
[23] *Ibid.*, p. 135.

sympathetic peoples of the world must not leave the organization of the half-developed parts of the world to the illiberal powers. They must overcome their natural resistance to exerting influence and balance their power against the expanding powers, recognizing the corrupting perils of power but acting to transcend them.

In his earlier writings particularly, Lippmann was more hesitant about generalizing about human nature than some of the philosophers mentioned. He noted that in wartime the soldier is asked to sacrifice everything, perhaps even his life, and he is paid a dollar a day. No one imagines he would become a better soldier through economic incentives. Here the economic motive disappears as a factor in human nature. But there is also the businessman who takes a wartime contract and receives a handsome profit over and above costs. Few would maintain that his production of munitions would be as great with the economic incentive taken away. The patriotic code assumes one kind of human nature, the commercial code quite another. In Lippmann's own words, "This is one reason why it is so dangerous to generalize about human nature. A loving father can be a sour boss, an earnest municipal reformer, and a rapacious jingo abroad. His family life, his business career, his politics, his foreign policy rest on totally different versions of what others are like and of how he should act."[24] It remained for Lippmann to show in his later writings that for all the immense variety of codes of behavior and conduct these actions evoked, there were, after all, a few common impulses like desire for power and recognition that brought them into a meaningful pattern.

However, his insights into human nature, while suggestive, remain inconclusive, since this broad area is more properly the domain of the political philosopher. Lippmann has not developed a systematic and comprehensive system of thought.

[24] Walter Lippmann, *Public Opinion* (New York: Penguin Books, Inc., 1946), p. 93.

He has ploughed no more than a few important furrows, but these he has cut deep and wide. One is in the area of diplomacy, its nature, requirements, rules, and problems. Some critics have ascribed to Lippmann a too extravagant conception of the function and possibilities of diplomacy. He is said to be biased in favor of negotiations as the one alternative to war. In a culture that is endlessly tempted to substitute almost any other device for negotiations, however, Lippmann's critics would doubtless acknowledge that negotiations have in large measure stood the test of time. Americans more than other national groups have looked with a jaundiced eye on the diplomatic tradition. Lippmann perhaps more than any philosopher or pundit has opposed this prevailing trend. Ideas on diplomacy saturated with experience and weathered by time have flowed continuously from his pen. As early as 1915, he wrote: "The whole business of jockeying for position is at first glance so incredibly silly that many liberals regard diplomacy as a cross between sinister conspiracy and a meaningless etiquette." However, liberals forget that the stakes of diplomacy are real, whether they are strategic bases, dependable allies, or influence in emergent areas. What turns a territory into a diplomatic problem is the combination of natural resources, cheap labor, markets, defenselessness, and corrupt and inefficient government. Other nations will then struggle over it and seek to organize it for the future. By 1945 the problem had shifted from the struggle for domination of underdeveloped areas to the quest for partnership with the emerging nations. When one reviews the problems that have plagued a beleaguered postwar world, one is struck by the incidence of them in underdeveloped areas: Korea, Indochina, Syria, Egypt, Indonesia, and Iran.

Lippmann believes that negotiation is the essence of diplomacy and that the tragedy of our era is the conspiracy of a host of forces that make negotiation infinitely more difficult. Today every document or diplomatic exchange must be prepared with an eye to its publication, and the negotiator is bound to consider not only what he means but what the people will think he means and how they will feel about what they think he means. Delegates and plenipotentiaries are limited by uncertainty over the support they enjoy. American diplomats have, in addition, been limited in their negotiating by public harassment. Thus democratic representatives are distinctly handicapped when negotiating with representatives enjoying the full authority of a totalitarian state.

The problem is further aggravated when a democracy deliberately places crippling restrictions on its leaders and especially on its chief executive. "Our historic experience in times of crisis should have demonstrated that we expect a Lincoln raising an army or a Wilson or F.D.R. preparing us for a world struggle to do for us what we wanted done, better than we could tell them. We preferred to 'trust the President' rather than summon the Congress in the *Lusitania* crisis and so it has been whenever the intricate task of waging war or peace has plainly demonstrated that the flexibility of one mind was superior to the inertia of many." Americans never intended to give any one man such importance; they have always believed they possess that democratic control of foreign policy for which Europeans are constantly agitating. The United States makes no secret treaties; the treaties it does make have to be ratified by the people's representatives; and war cannot be declared without the approval of Congress. Yet the real power, as former President Harry S. Truman periodically reminds us, lies with the President, who guides and directs the broad course of foreign relations, and whose actions makes it difficult to retrace our steps. Wilson at Vera Cruz, McKinley in the Philippines, Eisenhower in the Middle East—all may have sought congressional approval for their actions, but when Presidents declare that vital interests are at stake the people's representatives have really but two alternatives: they may declare that the President already enjoys

43

the powers he seeks, or they may support the President in spite of their misgivings, on the ground that politics cease at the water's edge. In the case of the Eisenhower Doctrine, the Democratic opposition embraced both these positions. Our trust of the President may stem from the hidden and partial truth underlying the strong words of one genial cynic: "It is easier to summon Congress than to adjourn it; it is easier to lower the floodgates of heroic patriotism than to close them."[25]

The contrast between the young and the seasoned Lippmann lies precisely in his grasp of the problem of democratic diplomacy. In his earlier writings he saw this as a problem to be mastered if not quickly then at least decisively through the assertion of strong executive leadership. The claims that the moral influence of public opinions could lead the world to peace made him uneasy and restless from the first. All through the twenties and thirties, people were exhorted from political platforms, academic rostrums, and religious pulpits to exercise their international responsibilities. Policies were justified and inertia excused in terms of public opinion. Against this Lippmann inveighed: "It would be sheer hypocrisy to pretend . . . that any large section of the American people is informed, or interested, or thoughtful about international relations." Most people had conventional ways of thinking and reacting, and they had a number of vague and fixed loyalties which could easily be aroused. Opinions about foreign affairs tend to harden into molds—support for the United Nations, the Open Door, the Monroe Doctrine, anticolonialism, and Western solidarity. Since alternatives are provided, the President can direct the flow of patriotism and by his actions, proclamations, or selection of issues rally the nation to support one pattern or the other. The interplay between the President and the public gives a clue to the nature of democratic foreign policy.

Yet something profound and far-reaching has transpired

[25] Walter Lippmann, *Stakes*, p. 17.

since Lippmann began his inquiry. In 1915 he wrote confidentially: "The reason why we trust one man, rather than many, is because one man can negotiate and many men can't. Two masses of people have no way of dealing directly with each other."[26] "One diplomat may see what is in the other diplomat's mind, and time his utterance accordingly; a whole people cannot see quickly into another people's mind and its utterance is inevitably crude. The very qualities which are needed for negotiation—quickness of mind, direct contact, adaptiveness, invention, the right proportion of give and take—are the very qualities which masses of people do not possess."[27] Therefore Lippmann applauded the willingness of a democracy to recognize that the nation must be represented in mediation by an individual to the point of granting one man plenary power over war and peace.

By 1955 he was not so confident that this principle had been accepted. He spoke of the malady of democratic states and warned of the paralysis of governments. He found that one source of the mounting disorder in Western society was the gradual usurpation by legislatures of the powers of executives. Democracies without leaders react to events without governing them, and it will not do "to think poorly of the politicians and to talk with bated breath about the voters. No more than the kings before them should the people be hedged with divinity."[28] The twentieth century has witnessed a functional derangement of the relationship between the people and the government. "The people have acquired power which they are incapable of exercising, and the governments they elect have lost powers which they must recover if they are to govern."[29] This is our historic catastrophe, and it may lie at the heart of the alarming failure of liberal democracies to cope with the harsh realities of this century and of their decline in

[26] *Ibid.*, p. 26. [27] *Ibid.*, p. 29.
[28] Walter Lippmann, *The Public Philosophy* (New York: Macmillan Co., 1956), p. 14.
[29] *Ibid.*, p. 11.

influence and self-confidence. Lippmann seems far less sanguine in recent years that this trend can be reversed. Popular government had been heralded as the bearer of good tidings of peace. Instead, half the world today appears to be denying or despairing of democracy. The people's assemblies, whether national or international, run the gamut from apathy to bellicose passions. Indeed at times Hobbes's words in *Leviathan* seem prophetic: "For the passions of men, which asunder are moderate, as the heat of one brand, in an assembly are like many brands, that inflame one another, especially when they blow one another with orations." Lippmann has pondered these events as he has propounded his philosophy in more than twenty volumes. He sees but one answer, admittedly tentative, based on Jefferson's dictum that the people are not "qualified to exercise themselves the Executive Department, but they are qualified to name the person who shall exercise it." Taking this as a rough beginning, Lippmann finds the true boundaries of the people's power in their ability to give and withhold consent—"their consent to what the government asks of them, proposes to them, and has done in the conduct of their affairs. They can elect the government. They can remove it. They can approve or disapprove its performance. But they cannot administer the government"[30]—especially its foreign affairs.

In the post-World War II period, Lippmann more consistently than any other writer on international politics has sounded a recurrent theme now familiar to all his readers. He differs from other political realists in maintaining throughout a greater awareness of the actual limits of American power. Throughout the "cold war" era, he has suggested—very cautiously, it is true—that American policy-makers run the risk of setting their goals too high, politically, militarily, and ideologically. The United States is no longer the paramount power. In many important respects, the Soviet Union to all

[30] *Ibid.*, p. 14.

practical purposes has become an equal. Moreover, both super-powers are more limited than is sometimes appreciated in imposing their wills on smaller, less powerful nations around the globe. In the early stages of the struggle between East and West, it was fashionable to point to the bipolarity of postwar international politics. However, increasingly in recent years, Lippmann has argued that whereas militarily constellations of power continued bipolar in character, politically in certain important respects the world was tending to move toward a multipower pattern. In Korea, Formosa, Yugoslavia, Poland, and China, the super-powers are no longer able consistently to call the tune. National leaders like Syngman Rhee, Mao Tse-Tung, and Tito have stood up to the great powers and temporarily at least refused to accept their dictates on matters of vital interest. In this sense, politically at least, we are witnessing a limited diffusion of power partly because of the ambiguous character of thermonuclear weapons which have at best problematic influence in the vast continents of Asia and Africa. Not every crucial decision has been made in Moscow and Washington. The locus of decision has shifted to farflung capitals of the world, whether in Cairo, Baghdad, Warsaw, or East Berlin.

This trend, which runs counter to the dominant postwar trend, has encouraged Lippmann to call for more modest estimates of what the West can do and for greater imagination in shaping foreign policies. He has urged political and economic initiatives more in accord with these realities. He has warned that many of our policies and commitments exceed national power. He has been more willing to explore "fertile compromises" in Germany, the Middle East, and in Asia than most of his contemporaries. Especially in light of the West's failure to bring power in line with commitments, his injunctions have impressed serious students of foreign policy.

I do not know whether other outstanding writers or commentators like James Reston, the Alsops, Eric Sevareid, or Edward R. Murrow would accept this interpretation of the world distribution of political power or of the American constitutional system. I suspect they would lay greater stress on the powers of Congress. In a more general way, however, they, as Lippmann, have exerted a not inconsiderable influence in shaping thinking about international politics. Reston, without attempting to erect a fully elaborated theory, has done more to assess the domestic and international forces that mold foreign policy. Behind the dispatches appearing under Reston's by-line lies the skeletal framework of a broader view of the nature of world politics. He displays the same apprehension as Lippmann, Spykman, or Morgenthau over public declarations as a substitute for concrete policies, over propaganda debates for negotiations, over the disregard of vital national interests. Whether or not he considers himself an exponent of the international politics point of view, he surely has done much to move American thinking toward the realities of foreign policy as we find them today.

This is the more remarkable because Reston and his colleagues view foreign policy in day-to-day terms and describe emergent problems as part of a continuous flow of events. All of them have criticized the failure of American policy, particularly in recent days, to rally the nation's resources—intellectual, economic, political, and military—in response to a succession of challenges. They find that leadership is too often conceived of as a popularity contest. The slogan, "I would rather be right than be President" (or "Senator" or "Congressman") tends to be inverted. Not one of these writers is content with the present "state of the union" in what the people expect and receive of their chosen representatives.

This critique runs the gamut of the American political scene. Each columnist or commentator would have the American people lodge greater confidence and authority in our diplomats abroad. They have polemicized over the years against the dramatic shrinking of power of ambassadors and envoys abroad. Many of the strictures go to the issues of democratic diplomacy. Free societies are prone to view the diplomatic corps as a threat to popular sovereignty. They shrink from the subtle and complicated maneuvers of ministers and representatives continually probing the intentions and policies of allies and adversaries. The public requires that both strategy and tactics of Americans in foreign capitals be held under constant scrutiny. In consequence, Soviet diplomats enjoy a temporary advantage inherent in a controlled system where freedom of maneuver remains essentially unrestricted. They can seize the initiative and try out or set aside policies and "trial balloons." Not one of the writers would have us abandon the precious heritage of responsiveness gained through sacrifice and many decades of political experience. If I read their dispatches correctly, they are calling for new and more hopeful combinations of public and private actions by men in whom society reposes sufficient hope and respect to stand by them alike in good and bad days.

Such a doctrine of statesmanship applies to chief executives, secretaries, and other officials who hold a public mandate for their deeds. Obviously, government conceived in this image places heavier burdens on its leaders than "government by Gallup polls." Those who govern must be prepared to face public condemnation; they can never content themselves merely with registering or reflecting powerful waves of passion and sentiment. They hold in their hands, however, a weapon that strong and scrupulous men have not hesitated to exercise. They can educate the people in the fundamental lessons of politics. They can expose the truth as they have been given to see the truth—boldly, fairly, but in outlines which the public, caught up in the business of work-a-day living, cannot possibly know. Our columnist group believes that the people will act wisely if the salient facts are put before them. In this sense, they are the authentic democrats, for democracy at its center involves a faith in political intelligence.

In almost every period of American history, the function of leadership is crucial. The present crisis imposes a sense of urgency that is unparalleled in its requirements and opportunities. The pace of events is so great, the need of prompt and rational decisions so overwhelming, that a doctrine of effective and popular leadership becomes a sheer necessity. The common thread in the writings of this group is the weight they give to this basic principle.

III. THE POLICY-PLANNERS

Finally, in tracing the evolution of American thinking on foreign policy no one can afford to overlook the role played by that remarkable body of men who made up the Policy Planning Staff during its earlier more active years. Created in 1947 by General Marshall as the first regular office of the Department of State to be charged with considering problems from the standpoint of the totality of American national interest, it has bequeathed a corpus of thought that both reinforces the main stream of scholarly thinking on world politics and adds a new dimension of its own. While individual planners differ in the emphasis of their approach, they confront problems of foreign policy from a common philosophic base.

The writings of George F. Kennan, Paul H. Nitze, Louis J. Halle, C. B. Marshall, and Dorothy Fosdick carry the prestige and authority of the practitioner who cannot be easily dismissed as a spinner of theories within the sanctuary of some academic cloister. They are written by men who have been on the firing line. From the beginning this group felt the need of "an applicable body of theory," and sought to evolve an adequately stated "theoretical foundation to underpin the conduct of our external relations." Against the background of these principles, they sought to appraise current events and evaluate the governing concepts by which statesmen have been guided in recent decades. In the process a Policy Planning Staff approach to the baffling and stubborn complexities of foreign policy emerged. This approach is founded on certain common elements that run like red thread through the individual viewpoints of this talented group, whatever their individual differences. In my reading I discover at least five that call for attention.

The first common element is essentially negative in character. It rests on the proposition that there are few if any absolutes in international politics. Lord Acton counseled: "An absolute principle is as absurd as absolute power," and advised: "When you perceive a truth, look for the balancing truth." His philosophy is singularly appropriate to foreign policy, for when our diplomats and statesmen are dealing with a foreign country their role is at best a marginal one. They can help or encourage existing or latent tendencies on foreign soil, but it is for those more intimately responsible for another country's affairs to realize them. Needless to say, this runs counter to certain basic American emotions. It is tempting to proclaim that this troubled world could be free of all conflict if only peoples everywhere would adopt the political institutions that have been forged in the fire of our national experiences. "The Wilsonian thesis was . . . that, since the world was no longer safe for the American democracy, the American people were called upon to conduct a crusade to make the world safe for American democracy. In order to do this the principles of the American democracy would have to be made universal throughout the world."[31]

However, there is no absolutely best state for all peoples. We are reminded of de Tocqueville's words on the United States written in 1831: "The more I see of this country the more I admit myself penetrated with this truth: that there is nothing absolute in the theoretical value of political institu-

[31] Walter Lippmann, *Isolation and Alliances: An American Speaks to the British* (Boston: Little, Brown & Co., 1952), p. 22.

tions, and that their efficiency depends almost always on the original circumstances and the social conditions of people to whom they are applied." The ways in which peoples move toward more enlightened forms of government constitute the most profound of the processes of national life. They stem from the bedrock of national character and existence; they have an organic growth. For example, Kennan, writing on "When the Russians Rose against the Czar," concluded by saying that if changes were to take place in the Soviet Union, Americans would do well "not to impede or embarrass the process by claiming it for our own and by attempting to see in it the repetition and vindication, in universal terms, of our own history. It is her own laws of development, not ours, that Russia must follow. The sooner we learn that there are many mansions in this house of nations, and many paths to the enrichment of human experience, the easier we will make it for other people to solve their problems, and for ourselves to understand our own."[32] It is barely possible that in stressing this point Mr. Kennan and his colleagues have neglected the corollary that notwithstanding endless variations there are minimum standards of justice and order that any polity must observe lest the fabric of mankind be threatened. It may be that some of the classical writers were more attuned to this problem than the children of the present relativist age, for they were ever in search of the attributes of the best state, however transcendent these might be.

The present school of policy-planners has resisted as well a too absolute conception of the possible goals and accomplishments of foreign policy. It is well to be ever aware of the limits as well as the purposes of foreign policy, the boundaries as well as the magnitudes. The statesman confronting the world is constrained, more often than not, to act within narrow limits. His choices are severely restricted and events pass swiftly beyond the realm of conscious choice. The Cambridge

[32] *New York Times Magazine*, March 10, 1957, p. 40.

historian Herbert Butterfield has observed: "Behind the great conflicts of mankind is a terrible human predicament which lies at the heart of the story. . . . Contemporaries fail to see the predicament or refuse to recognize its genuineness so that our knowledge of it comes from later analysis. It is only with the progress of historical science on a particular subject that men come really to recognize that there was a terrible knot almost beyond the ingenuity of man to untie."

Such a predicament seems to be presented by World War II, for its roots are embedded fatefully and inextricably in the aftermath of World War I. France and England had been weakened far more deeply than they knew. Austria-Hungary had disappeared as a restraint on Germany. Russia was no longer a predictable and constructive force, for it had been seized by violent men who were implacably hostile to those capitalist societies to which political necessity might have united them as natural allies. Into this setting marched the one great united people in Central Europe, the Germans— "frustrated, impoverished, stung with defeat, uncertain in the breakdown of their traditional institutions." In the light of these facts it is all too easy to absolve Western statesmen of any responsibility and to regard them as "actors in a tragedy beyond their making of repair."[38]

The choices of Western statesmen were significantly and tragically narrowed by this tangled web of events. Yet in this crisis if nothing approaching a complete solution was to be found, neither was the possibility of making wiser and more effectual choices entirely eliminated. For example, it might have been possible to lend greater encouragement, support, and understanding to certain moderate forces within the Weimar Republic. A different attitude toward the defeated German people, one less dominated by distaste, suspicion, and social snobbery, might have strengthened the more liberal

[38] George F. Kennan, *American Diplomacy: 1900-1950* (Chicago: University of Chicago Press, 1951), p. 78.

forces which were not totally lacking in Germany at that time. Once the struggle seemed inevitable the West might have deterred it—especially in 1936 at the time of the occupation of the Rhineland—by a firm show of strength, or later by a resolute military build-up that even tyrannies would have had to respect. Finally, when war came, the allies could have made a decisive stand not for total victory but for those more limited military and political objectives sometimes possible in war.

Thus even in the historical eras when the statesman is most sharply restricted, choices exist for better and worse courses of action. However, the margins of power to effect actions outside a nation's jurisdiction are infinitely more limited than within its own borders. Great powers are never as omnipotent as they imagine. Power for Tolstoy was "merely the relation between the expression of someone's will and the execution of that will by others," but in foreign relations the use of power is never this direct. When the wills involved are outside one's own political society there is often little that can be done. Obviously the psychology that "Americans can do anything" ignores *The Limits of Foreign Policy*—the significant title of C. B. Marshall's book—and it can lead to the most painful disillusionment. Referring to the charge that the State Department lost China, "a land never ours to lose," C. B. Marshall sagely observes: "From the tone of the discussion one might never guess that indigenous impulses and predispositions counted for anything in China's course: for the native army's want of military zeal someone here must be held to account; for an oriental regime's loss of grip on itself blame must be fixed in Washington."[34] The belief that America is omnipotent is only one example of the grievous tendency of many Americans to deal in absolutes. In Marshall's words: "We forget that other nations are not boxcars to be shunted

[34] Charles Burton Marshall, *The Limits of Foreign Policy* (New York: Henry Holt & Co., Inc., 1954), p. 18.

around by an American locomotive; we forget that legislation, in and of itself, gives no certainty of achievement; we forget that victory is not peace in our time but only a prevention of defeat; and most of all we tend to forget that the only certainty in human affairs is uncertainty, and that plans and policies must be contingent and flexible." The various members of the group join in protesting these errors, and admonish, in Mr. Kennan's words: "We must be gardeners and not mechanics in our approach to world affairs."

A second element common to the policy-planners is a general dissatisfaction with the governing ideas of the twenties and thirties and the practices of still more recent days. The prevailing dogmas of the earlier years conceived of power politics and the balance of power as the simple evils from which wars emerged. Basing their actions on the concepts of scholars in the thirties, the victors in World War II sought to replace the balance of power with solemn pledges and imposing political machinery. The conclusion was drawn that states were divisible into aggressor and peace-loving states, as more recently the distinction between law-abiding and law-breaking states has been attempted. Mr. Halle has trenchantly observed: "It seems strange to us now, though the logic will escape no one, that Germany, Italy and Japan were named the aggressor states while the Soviet Union was associated with China and ourselves as one of the peace-loving powers. On the basis of this continuing refusal to see a balance of power as either good or necessary, we cooperated with the Soviet Union in creating the German and Japanese 'power vacuums' on either side of her into which, while we confidently demobilized our forces, she proceeded to expand her power. We saw our error again at the eleventh hour and ever since have led western civilization in a desperate effort to restore that Balance of Power which it has been our custom to decry."

There were, to be sure, a few bold spirits like Mahan and Spykman who were charting new paths toward a profounder analysis of the sources of American security. But they comprised but a tiny coterie and their efforts remained suspended in the midair of history—"an isolated spurt of intellectual activity against a background of general torpor and smugness in American thinking about foreign affairs."[35] The illusion was nursed that other people were as Americans, or more precisely, Americans who happened to wear beards; that others shared our values and might soon adopt our institutions; that a few clear-cut blueprints on universal disarmament or the outlawry of war would do for the world what our basic laws had done for us; and that others would recognize as we did that they could obtain most of their objectives without force and that, therefore, they would accept a freezing of the status quo. We assumed that the Anglo-Saxon concept of law could quite readily be made as applicable to states as to individuals at home.

American concepts and institutions were partly the largess of history, and this is one reason Americans are peculiarly susceptible to believe that they are so readily transportable. We did not invent them. "The American," as de Tocqueville points out, "was born free without having to become so." The nation was spared many of the struggles that come with new ideas, for most of our first principles had been hammered out in the hard conflicts of the Old World. Moreover, in the beginning the colonists were left to their own resources, and by the time the British homeland attempted to reestablish the lead, the habits of freedom and independence had been staunchly implanted. Few if any of the one-time colonial areas are today so richly blessed by tradition, nor can they point to a system of law and politics based on the writings of men like Locke, Rousseau, and Montesquieu. Is it any wonder that some Americans misjudged the problems and difficulties of installing a freely chosen, responsible, and limited government?

[35] Kennan, *American Diplomacy*, p. 6.

A third bond uniting members of the original Policy Planning Staff is their attitude toward progress. Their viewpoint is a distinct counterbeat to the resounding conviction of most Americans. Woodrow Wilson spoke for the times when he proclaimed that selfish national purposes were being supplanted by universal principles of mankind. He heralded the "slow, painful struggle forward, forward, up, up, a little at a time, along the entire incline, the interminable way." Some of his heirs, less forthright or less fastidious about the truth, have cast aside the encumbering notion that progress need be painful or slow. The glaring failure of recent events to accord with this sanguine and tidy theory would seem to invite, at the very least, a sober stocktaking. In any event, when history departs too radically from any theory, it is customary to reformulate the theory. Not so in this case! If history has stubbornly refused to conform to the straight-line pattern of progress, the trouble must lie in the errors of a traitorous statesman, or in the deceit of Yalta, Munich, or Versailles. Were it not for one evil man or nation the upward march would continue. But for a single aberration, the pathway would be free from thorns, "the tax burden light, the budget in balance and the future secure." The unending frustrations of daily life prompt men to grasp more tenaciously than ever the vision of progress, for they try to project their unfulfilled hopes onto their nation or the world.

"Man would fain be great and sees that he is little; would fain be happy and sees that he is miserable; would fain be perfect and sees that he is full of imperfections." This diagnosis is no less telling now than it was when Blaise Pascal set it forth. We continue to pin our hopes to a prospect as towering as inevitable progress in order to shield ourselves from the pathos and meaninglessness of our individual attainments. In the Soviet Union, human history is conceived of as a relentless unfolding, stage by stage, toward a plateau of perfection embodied in the classless society. In our own country the goal has been a world made up of free and democratic regimes.

To the "planners," any and all these concepts of progress and human perfectibility rest on shaky foundations, engender fanaticism and self-righteousness, and fall far short of reality. Mr. Kennan warns against looking to the diplomatist or the policy-planner "for any belief in human perfectibility, for any optimistic philosophy of public affairs." He is, instead, like the physician who has "a shabby and irritating group of patients: violent, headstrong, frivolous, unreasonable. He will go on treating them as long as he is permitted to, saving them from such follies as he can. . . . But do not ask him to enthuse about them, to idealize them or to expect them to change. . . . He has seen them too much. He knows them too well. He loves them too deeply."

A fourth unifying feature shared by the little band of theoretical practitioners is their passion for history. Part of their constraint to be historians lies in an uneasiness with earlier interpretations. Students and statesmen in the period between the wars assumed that the history of Talleyrand's world and Bismarck's was venerable lore. When history was used at all it tended to serve as a marker for tracing the upward curve of international institutions and behavior, a use of history "which squints and overlooks half the facts and half the difficulties," inviting others to set the record straight. History is the best teacher but its lessons are not on the surface. Thus, eminently useful, for example, are the soundings made by C. B. Marshall on the origins of isolationism, or by Kennan on the original national purposes of this country, or by Halle on the nation's civilization and its foreign policy. The West has a long historical experience and this calls for study and reflection; particular histories can be slighted only at grave peril to the future. I am impressed with the recurrence in the writings of these men of this kind of thought: "Here, in this

Soviet problem, we have the greatest possible need for the broad historical perspective."[36] But this is history not for history's sake but history derived from a preoccupation with the problems of foreign policy; for this reason it has its own individual, peculiar focus. For example, an advocate of this approach in writing about a statesman would not feel compelled to tell all about the statesman—his good intentions, his breeding, his social life, his descendants and heirs, in addition to the implications of his policies or proposals. His tendencies and states of mind would be considered appropriate objects of study, but only as they relate to the conduct of foreign policy. This may disturb the professional historian who might wish, say, that all the personal and institutional details surrounding the Pact of Paris be set forth; whereas Mr. Kennan believes that it is the broad tendency of American statesmen to meet concrete international problems with legal formulas that sets the guidelines for research.

The fifth link that joins these men—men of whom former Secretary of State Dean Acheson has said: "Any foreign office in the world would be incomparably richer through their presence"—is their common effort to understand themselves, their nation, and the outside world. They see foreign policy as a realistic business addressed to the nature of man and politics and to the world as we find it. In Mr. Halle's words: "We must have as shrewd an understanding of ourselves as of our environment. These requirements are not met by showing the outside world in its sordid reality, with all its wrinkles, scars and warts, while rendering ourselves in unblemished marble."[37] "Inconsistencies . . . are inherent in the nature of man, that moral centaur, half beast and half god, within whose being the struggle between good and evil remains unresolved."

[36] George F. Kennan, *Realities of American Foreign Policy* (Princeton: Princeton University Press, 1954), p. 92.
[37] Louis J. Halle, *Civilization and Foreign Policy* (New York: Harper & Brothers, 1955), p. 27.

The members of the Policy Planning Staff, unlike many social scientists, hold to a more or less explicit conception of human nature. According to Halle, it is "the concept of man on which our civilization is based . . . of a beast with a soul, a creature nine parts animal and one part divine whose mission it is to overcome the animal element and realize his possibilities of divinity."[38] In the Christian tradition, the good in men is a spark of light in the darkness, and the mission of mankind is to make the spark grow. The awareness that this concept is under fire runs through this discussion; but it is striking that a group with a clear vision of the true nature of politics and diplomacy should start with this historic view of man which is so squarely at odds with the Enlightenment, Darwinism, Freudianism, and Marxism. Perhaps this anti-modern view is one of the reasons they all return unashamedly to what Kennan has called "the forgotten art of diplomacy from which we have spent fifty years trying to escape." If we look for a single statement that best summarizes their collective view of the way a powerful nation can relate itself to its international politics with the outside world, we discover it in this summary paragraph by Mr. Kennan:

"This task [world peace] will be best approached not through the establishment of rigid legal norms but rather by the traditional devices of political expediency. The sources of international tension are always specific, never general. They are always devoid of exact precedents or exact parallels. They are always in part unpredictable. If the resulting conflicts are to be effectively isolated and composed, they must be handled partly as matter of historical equity but partly, also, with an eye to the given relationships of power. Such conflicts, let us remember, usually touch people at the neuralgic points of their most violent political emotions. Few people are ever going to have an abstract devotion to the principles of international legality capable of competing with

[38] *Ibid.*, p. 164.

the impulses from which wars are apt to arise. This is particularly true of democratic peoples, beholden as they are at times to the most imperious seizures of political emotionalism."[39]

Is it any wonder that the spokesmen of the older, legalistic approach have made Kennan and his colleagues their special target? Aside from enjoying the easy conscience of men who have not hesitated to speak the truth, perhaps their other consolation may come from knowing that the philosophers, columnists, and policy-planners, often without knowledge of one another, stand on common ground in arriving at the same conclusion.

IV. UNITY AND DIVERSITY WITHIN AN AMERICAN APPROACH

The philosophers, columnists, and policy-planners were selected as prototypes of one important approach to international politics. While they share common assumptions about the nature of reality, they have, of course, differed widely in their prescriptions and judgments of courses of action, because in every event there is a multitude of contingencies calling for assessment and prediction. The scholars and journalists and planners would not always see in the same light great issues like Summit talks, Suez, or Communist China. Yet in reviewing their writings, it is truly remarkable how often their opinions and conclusions have been similar. They approach problems not with one mind but within a common framework, and the fact that their judgments have not always proved wrong would seem to indicate that a unifying approach is valuable. Full precision in political prediction eludes them, but their estimates serve nonetheless to illuminate the future. Perhaps one cannot hope for more.

[39] Kennan, *Realities*, p. 36.

CHAPTER 2

LIBERALISM AND CONSERVATISM
IN AMERICAN STATECRAFT

That exercise of force is often necessary in the pursuit of worthy objectives is regretfully accepted, but that power should become an objective in itself, a goal for individual, social, or state action, is considered both undesirable and wicked, a condemnation which is unfortunate because it hampers a sound understanding of one of the basic aspects of all social life.—NICHOLAS SPYKMAN

If our account of the unfolding of American thinking on world politics is even approximately true, there remains outstanding another crucial and basic problem. The ideas and philosophies we have been considering are for the most part those of theorists or political thinkers. Yet a perennial problem for Western civilization has always been the relationship between theory and practice. For their part, scholars and writers are inclined to believe that history consists largely in the application to practice of theoretical truths churned up in the thinking or inner consciousness of wise and farseeing people. We recall the statement by John Maynard Keynes that ". . . the ideas of economists and political philosophers, both when they are right and when they are wrong, are more powerful than is commonly understood. Indeed the world is ruled by little else. Practical men, who believe themselves to be quite exempt from any intellectual influences, are usually the slaves of some defunct economist. Madmen in authority, who hear voices in the air, are distilling their frenzy from some academic scribbler of a few years back. I am sure that the power of vested interests is vastly exaggerated compared with the gradual encroachment of ideas. Not, indeed, immediately, but after a certain interval; for in the field of economic and political philosophy there are not many who are influenced by new theories after they are twenty-five or thirty years of age, so that the ideas which civil servants and politicians and even agitators apply to current events are not likely to be the newest. But soon or late, it is ideas, not vested interests, which are dangerous for good or evil."[1]

On their side, those who pride themselves on "muddling through" are profoundly suspicious that oftentimes the word is not flesh, that it tends to be futile, irrelevant, and dissociated from events. Frequently a policy appears to be based on shaky if not false foundations, yet in spite of its deficiencies may "blunder through." The New Deal was an example of a moderately progressive, pragmatic political movement that at some point or another offended the sensibilities of every intellectual and theorist but enjoyed vast success that escapes the imagination of the intellectual and his programs. Woodrow Wilson, the perfect modern example of the theorist in politics, "excelled in the exposition of fundamentals. . . . His political method was to base his appeal upon broad and simple principles, avoiding commitment upon specific measures." He thought mainly along a priori lines. For this reason the purity and nobility of his thinking and writing were rarely tarnished by the dross of political practice. Perhaps for this reason he seemed to stand out as the symbol of hope for Europe and America. John Maynard Keynes could write: "When President Wilson left Washington [for the Paris Peace Conference] he enjoyed a prestige and a moral influence throughout the world unequalled in history. His bold and measured words carried to the peoples of Eu-

---

[1] John Maynard Keynes, *The General Theory of Employment, Interest and Money* (New York: Harcourt, Brace & Co., 1936), pp. 383-84.

rope above and beyond the voices of their own politicians."[2] Mr. Keynes observed: "The President's programme for the World, as set forth in his speeches and his notes, had displayed a spirit and a purpose so admirable that the last desire of his sympathizers was to criticize details—the details, they felt, were quite rightly not filled in at present, but would be in due course. It was commonly believed at the commencement of the Paris Conference that the President had thought out, with the aid of a large body of advisers, a comprehensive scheme not only for the League of Nations, but for the embodiment of the Fourteen Points in an actual Treaty of Peace."[3]

But in fact, according to Keynes, the President had thought out nothing; when it came to *practice* his ideas were nebulous and incomplete. Except in the most general way, he had no notion of what he or America wanted and he was ill-informed on the conditions and history of Europe. In consequence he was easy prey for someone like Clemenceau of France, who had a policy, knew which details were vital and what interests were essential, and felt about France what Pericles felt about Athens—that nothing else mattered. Clemenceau had one illusion, France, and one disillusion, mankind, including his colleagues at the peace conference not least. Present-day historians of the Paris Peace Conference record that it was Clemenceau, the cynical actor, not Wilson, the idealist and theorist, who was the architect of the peace, ill-fated and tragic as it was.

It is entirely possible that this sweeping criticism of the great American President by a British intellectual goes too far; subsequent historians like Professors Edward Buehrig and Arthur Link have doubtless endeavored to right the balance. However, to many critics President Wilson seems to epitomize the characteristic weakness of the political intel-

[2] John Maynard Keynes, *The Economic Consequences of the Peace* (London: Macmillan Co., 1920), p. 34.
[3] *Ibid.*, p. 39.

lectual—failure to grasp the distance that lies between the proclamation of an ideal and its realization in the face of persistent, deep-rooted obstacles. Writing of intellectuals in German political life, Meinecke observed: "They could give to their political aspirations a spirit of purity and independence, of philosophical idealism and of elevation above the concrete play of interests . . . but through their defective feeling for the realistic interests of actual state life they quickly descended from the sublime to the extravagant and eccentric." The root cause of the divorce between intellectuals and practitioners may be a sense of alienation and a result of the nearly unbridgeable gulf growing out of the painfully separate and unique tasks in which each is engaged and expects the other to engage. The intellectual is asked to supply a ready-made and well-tested doctrine or philosophy of international society to which the statesman can confidently turn. The practitioner is expected to behave according to the tidy and rational plan the intellectual has of the universe. These demands which require of intellectuals and statesmen more than lies within their power have again and again through history set the one against the other or invited the one to rationalize his failures in terms of the other's shortcomings.

The examples of this clash are legion. One has only to mention trade unionists and intellectuals in the British Labor Party. Unionists denounce intellectuals for their visionary points of view, said to be out of touch with the practical problems bedeviling movement leaders. Intellectuals in turn condemn what they describe as narrow and uninspired bureaucratic thinking. The history of the Bolshevik Party in the Soviet Union offers another example of the struggle between party intelligentsia who included Bukharin, Kamenev, Radek, and Trotsky, and practical politicians such as Lenin and Stalin. In American politics the party intellectuals and grass roots leaders often find themselves at odds, and in two recent Presidential campaigns the Democrats suffered from such a clash.

In international politics examples of the allegedly inherent differences between scientists and diplomats are not difficult to come by. For President Wilson, peace would have been attainable if conflicts among states were settled "not by diplomats or politicians each eager to serve his own interests but by dispassionate scientists—geographers, ethnologists, economists—who had made studies of the problems involved."[4] This same philosophy or viewpoint hovered over the creation of the League and the United Nations. The difficulties of attaining worthwhile goals were almost inevitably attributed to deviousness or obstruction by the practitioners. In presenting the draft covenant of the League to the Paris Peace Conference, President Wilson warned that "if the deliberating body of the League of Nations was merely to be a body of officials representing the various governments, the peoples of the world would not be sure that some of the mistakes which preoccupied officials had admittedly made might not be repeated."[5] Somewhat later Lord Cecil charged in the House of Commons that Prussians were not confined to Germany, that officials and practical men in Britain who clung to things as they were comprised the chief hindrance to progress. Only the pressure of public opinion could set them right. Some of us recall a similar argument put forward in connection with the establishment of world government. Most of the difficulties confronting these and other bold international experiments were due to the expert or professional who, it was said, somehow had a personal stake in keeping things as they were.

I. REFORMISTS AND REALISTS

You will have noted by now that the group of intellectuals whose approaches have occupied our attention as philosophers, columnists, and policy-planners fit rather poorly this picture

---

[4] Ray Stannard Baker, *Woodrow Wilson and World Settlement* (New York: Doubleday & Co., 1922), Vol. I, p. 112.

[5] H. Temperley, ed., *History of the Peace Conference of Paris* (London: Oxford University Press, 1920-24), Vol. III, p. 62.

of the typical theorist continually at war with practitioners. These men who together have laid the cornerstone for a more coherent and systematic approach to world politics are all of them self-conscious political realists. They have been in the forefront of those who warn of the divorce of political thought from political action.

Furthermore, we have seen that one of the failures of the intellectual community in the aftermath of World War I was its reluctance to deal with politics in a world system neither ordered nor controlled by an all-powerful central authority. It chose to abjure the toils of power politics—a luxury that practitioners can rarely indulge themselves—since at most they were considered a passing phase of an international society that was about to disappear with the birth of a brave new world. According to this point of view, the end of power politics was to be accomplished in three ways. Ultimately, power politics would be eliminated through instituting a world government. Practically, power politics would be abolished when its main exemplars, the totalitarian states, had been erased. Provisionally, this evil system would be progressively and decisively undermined through the example of a moral and upright nation foreswearing relations with corrupted and power-seeking nations, pursuing policies of neutrality, and abstaining from the morally ambiguous exercise of influence or coercion in world politics.

The irony of this period in American foreign relations stems from the fateful influence that such a philosophy had on the conduct of foreign policy. If one reads the memoirs of men like President Franklin D. Roosevelt, Sumner Welles, or Joseph Grew, their profound embarrassment over the implications of this creed seems plainly apparent. However, the gap separating their thinking and that of intellectuals who fathered such views tended to be swallowed up in the spirit of the times. It is not by accident that until the past decade the United States has vacillated in its policies between three courses of action. Before both World Wars, we tried to abstain or withdraw from the impure and corrupted politics of the European continent. We refused to give guarantees against German expansionism, especially to France, for to have done so would reduce the force of our moral example. Similarly, an intervention in the affairs of Europe in order to bolster and strengthen democratic forces in the Weimar Republic would have weakened our moral position. But neutrality and abstention from the unhappy rivalries of the world lost any justification when Germany and Japan threatened American security and attacked us at Pearl Harbor. We turned then from neutrality to a holy crusade against the evil incarnate in fascism. We engaged in the world struggle not selfishly or for political advantage but in order that conflict might cease once and for all and that the evil men who had been responsible might be destroyed. These wars were not ordinary struggles for territorial adjustments or specified political objectives. They were holy wars of "unconditional surrender" against solitary infidels and troublemakers who had caused the catastrophes and with whose demise rivalry and aggrandizement would cease. After the Second World War, it was essential that what had been undertaken and achieved in war be sealed and perfected in peace. The agents of power politics lay mortally wounded; now the climate in which their nefarious policies had thrived must be cleansed and transformed and international organization substituted for politics. Secretary of State Hull and others proclaimed that in the new commonwealth of the United Nations, the problem of power would disappear. What this meant in concrete political terms was that the status quo with its prevailing lawfulness based on the relative satisfaction of the victorious powers must be made permanent through the regularized procedures of new international organizations. Thus through policies of neutrality, holy war, and the substitution of organization for world politics, the philosophy of the interwar period made itself felt.

By World War II, the barrenness of this theory made it imperative that there be a point of view that would explain the war and the preconditions of peace to Americans as Winston Churchill and certain British intellectuals had done for their people.

This was the legacy that the political realists were called upon to provide. For this group, beginning with Niebuhr and ending with Kennan, rivalry and some form of strife among nation-states came to be viewed as the rule and not a mere accident of the past. There are harmonies and disharmonies among states but the failure of every scheme for world peace in the past must be sought in the stubborn conditions out of which disharmonies emerged and not through holding up a blueprint of a commonwealth of perfect harmony. In all social groups—whether the state or in smaller, more intimate communities—a contest for influence and power goes on. On the international scene, rivalries among states remain largely uncontrolled by effective law or government. The business of statesmanship and diplomacy under these conditions is to limit the struggles and restrict their scope. The means available are a mixture of military power and diplomacy employed in the unceasing pursuit of new balances of power and rough equilibriums among contending parties. The aims include adjustment and accommodation on the basis of mutual recognition that an equilibrium does not exist. The realist strives to mitigate the rivalries among nations, through checks and balances and by compromise and bargaining. Abstract moral principles may be the ultimate object and purpose of the bargain or agreement, but an abstract principle is not an essential part of the bargain itself. In President Wilson's words: "There is indeed an element of morality in the very fact of compromise in social undertakings." Realism would prepare men for the tragic and stubborn discrepancy of means and ends in international politics. It accepts for the guide and premise of its thought the permanence and ubiquity of the struggle for power. But it strives unceasingly through every means at its disposal to contain and limit concentrations of power and to compose and relieve tensions that could lead to a situation of war.

II. LIBERALISM AND CONSERVATISM

The political and philosophical molds in which popular approaches to domestic and international politics are cast in most Western countries are neither reform nor realism but liberalism and conservatism. One reason for this is doubtless the instrumental and procedural nature of the former. Realism or reform give appraisals of the nature and dynamics of the political process, its requirements, limits, and laws. Liberalism and conservatism by contrast partake of the character of political ideologies. Quite commonly they provide moral justification for the claims of interest groups and they may also in more general terms constitute a philosophy. In Acton's phrase "Liberalism is not only a principle of government but a philosophy of history." One of the difficulties about liberalism and conservatism results from their alternating meaning as philosophy, political ideology, or public mood. In addition, they plainly lack fixed meanings; consider, for example, that liberalism has meant at various stages Manchester laissez-faire, moderate state-interventionism to safeguard liberty and equality (e.g., the liberalism of the New Deal), and utopianism in world affairs. Nevertheless, public policy, including foreign policy, has been influenced by these living political doctrines and, while recognizing with Erasmus that every definition is dangerous, we may usefully explore their place in Western civilization. Their political currency from the Founding Fathers to the incumbent President who defines his program as "liberal conservatism" suggests they are perhaps the prevailing Western political creeds. If this be true, a discussion of America's foreign relations should give heed to the meaning of these philosophies. We recall Coleridge's

words in *Essays on His Own Times*: "However . . . it may
be the fashion to talk of speculation and theory, as opposed . . .
to practice, it would not be difficult to prove, that such as is
the existing spirit of speculation, during any given period,
such will be the spirit and tone of the religion, legislation, and
morals, nay, even of the fine arts, the manners and the fash-
ions. Nor is this the less true, because the great majority of
men live like bats, but in twilight, and know and feel the
philosophy of their age only by its reflections and refractions."
If manners, art, and legislation are influenced by prevailing
Weltanschauungs or world views, foreign policy must also
be subject to their sway.

Liberalism and conservatism as they have been used in
political debate appear at first glance to be simple and straightforward terms. "What is conservatism?" Abraham Lincoln
asked. "Is it not adherence to the old and tried, against the
new and untried?" Others tell us that conservatism seeks to
defend the status quo while liberalism aspires to leave it
behind. Conservatism finds its treasures in tradition, custom,
prejudice, and prescription. According to Chesterfield "the
bulk of mankind have neither leisure nor knowledge sufficient
to reason right; why should they be taught to reason at all?
Will not honest instinct prompt, and wholesome prejudices
guide them, much better than half reasoning?" The English
constitution is for the conservative an arch-example of custom
and prescription for "its sole authority is that it has existed
time out of mind." Conservatism with its abiding veneration
of the past need not be aligned irrevocably against change as
such although this is its besetting danger. In Denis Healey's
apt phrase, "The Conservatives have a congenital grasp of
the rules of thumb for protecting British interests as defined
in the Victorian heyday. But they are slow to recognize
changes in those interests and even slower to understand
changes in the world within which their rules of thumb must

71

be applied."[6] Conservatives oppose too rapid social change because of its consequences. Burke assayed to distinguish profound and natural alterations and the radical infatuations of the day. He preferred a gradual course in order to prevent "unfixing old interests at once: a thing which is apt to breed a black and sullen discontent in those who are at once dispossessed of all their influence and consideration [and at the same time] . . . prevent men, long under depression, from being intoxicated with a large draught of new power. . . ."[7] Insights such as these into issues of interest and power have given conservatism an historic relevance sufficient to evoke Harold Laski's remark: "Burke has endured as the permanent manual of political wisdom without which statesmen are as sailors on an uncharted sea."

Nevertheless, this wisdom has been judged and found wanting in the face of rapidly changing conditions in industrial societies. For conservative movements, the exercise of power easily becomes an end in itself and the exclusive aim of political activity. In Karl Mannheim's words "The Conservative type of knowledge originally is the sort of knowledge giving practical control. It consists of habitual orientations towards those factors which are imminent in the present situation."[8] Thus it makes obsolescent administrative techniques serve as a substitute for policy in a world that is ever changing. The demands of a technical society for new institutions, status and power for rising social groups, and far-reaching national programs have led the most progressive peoples to by-pass the conservative point of view. In modern societies, liberalism, being less disposed uncritically to defend every status quo has enjoyed certain a priori advantages. Moreover, liberalism in its various stages has been linked with industrialization

[6] Richard Crossman, et al., *The New Fabian Essays* (New York: Frederick A. Praeger, 1952), p. 162.

[7] Quoted in Clinton Rossiter, *Conservatism in America* (New York: Alfred A. Knopf, 1955), p. 41.

[8] Quoted in Crossman, *New Fabian Essays*, p. 162.

and with democracy. Initially, it rallied its followers, especially in Britain and France, to the goal of overturning feudal aristocratic authority, including the authority of the mercantilist state. As the political ideology of a rising middle class, in Reinhold Niebuhr's words, it sought "to free the individual from the traditional restraints of an organic society, to endow the governed with the power of the franchise, to establish the principle of the 'consent of the governed' as the basis of political society; to challenge all hereditary privileges and traditional restraints upon human initiative, particularly in the economic sphere and to create the mobility and flexibility which are the virtues and achievements of every 'liberal society' as distinguished from feudal ones."[9]

In the same way, however, that conservatism ran afoul of the bewildering pace of events that transformed a feudal order into sprawling industrial societies, liberalism became the victim of its own origins. On the one hand, both liberalism and socialism "tend to imagine that changes are morally or practically desirable simply because they are changes. Man reared in the doctrine of automatic progress cannot help feeling that everything that will be will be right. But most historical changes are morally neutral. It is difficult to maintain that the brotherhood of men is better realised in Eastern Europe than it was under the Austro-Hungarian Empire."[10] On the other hand, liberalism was identified too narrowly with the claims and interests of the middle class, first as a fighting creed but subsequently as the justification of a new status quo that was threatened by too much government interference. Liberalism in its historical development takes on a dual meaning. In the beginning, while it came into being as a defense of individual freedom, it was freedom interpreted in behalf of industrial and commercial groups. Consequently,

[9] Reinhold Niebuhr, "Liberalism: Illusions and Realities," *The New Republic*, Vol. 133, No. 27, July 4, 1955, p. 11.
[10] Crossman, *New Fabian Essays*, p. 169.

in our own day the original libertarian point of view has become the main bulwark for conserving the power of large enterprises and corporate groups. On the other side, the middle classes, once having unleashed in the world the enduring truth of liberalism that justice depends upon freedom from outside restraint, have witnessed its application by others. As liberalism in the beginning served to justify protests by entrepreneurs against the restraints of government, newly emergent classes like labor seeking security and freedom themselves have called upon the state to redress the balance of power. The source and origin of restraints upon freedom for one segment of American life is the overwhelmingly powerful enterprise, while for the other it continues to be the state. Thus liberalism having had its birth in the demands of society for freedom from restraint by the state now in at least one of its versions witnesses the appeals of society—or at least a part of society—that the state become the protector of liberty, equality, and security against the overwhelming power of large industrial groups. To quote Niebuhr again: "Thus in every modern industrial nation the word 'liberalism' achieved two contradictory definitions. It was on the one hand the philosophy which insisted that economic life was to be free of any restraints. In this form it was identical with the only conservatism which nations, such as our own, who had no feudal past, could understand. . . . On the other hand the word was also used to describe the political strategy of those classes which preferred security to absolute liberty and which sought to bring economic enterprise under political control for the sake of establishing minimal standards of security and welfare."[11]

Perhaps we should not be too surprised that terms like liberalism take on different meanings. We recall the felicitous phrase of Justice Holmes: "A word is not a crystal, transparent and unchanged; it is the skin of a living thought and

[11] Niebuhr, "Liberalism," p. 11.

may vary greatly in color and content according to the circumstances and time in which it is used." In any case, the
semantic problems of liberalism arising from its dual meaning
and use—simultaneously to justify the free play of the market
in an uncontrolled economy and the centralization of power
in the state as a means of arresting the concentration of power
in the hands of a too powerful industrial class—are not its
most serious difficulty. Liberalism is steeped in the principles
of the French Enlightenment and in faith in man's essential
goodness and his capacity to subdue nature. The articles of
faith of the Enlightenment creed include the beliefs that civilization is becoming more rational and moral, that injustice is
caused by ignorance and will yield to education and greater
intelligence, that war is stupid and can be overcome through
reason, that appeals to brotherhood are bound to be effective
in the end and if they fail for the moment we need only more
and better appeals, and that conflict is simply a matter of
misunderstanding. Liberalism as a total philosophy of life
accepted the Enlightenment view of human progress and
perfectibility. Democracy for such a creed is a simple rational
possibility. In Lord Bryce's words in the preface to Ostro-
gorski's *Democracy and the Organization of Political Parties*
(1902): "In the ideal democracy every citizen is intelligent,
patriotic, disinterested. His sole wish is to discover the right
side in each contested issue, and to fix upon the best man
among competing candidates. His common sense, aided by a
knowledge of the constitution of his country, enables him to
judge wisely between arguments submitted to him, while his
own zeal is sufficient to carry him to the polling-booth." One
can wonder why such a gross contrivance as a polling booth is
necessary at all in the face of this paragon of political virtue.
Such ideas were basic to all the political miscalculations of the
Enlightenment. It failed to take seriously the factors of
interest and power, the rudiments of political order, the
organic and historic character of political loyalties, and the

necessity of coercion in forming the solidarities of a community. Indeed the failures of liberalism have tended to inhere in precisely this blindness to the perennial difference between human actions and aspirations, the perennial source of conflict between life and life, the inevitable tragedy of human existence, the irreducible irrationality of human behavior, and the tortuous character of human history.

The corrective to these liberal illusions in Western civilization has been conservatism. Conservatism speaks for the skeptical and cautious side of human nature, which sees all about it too many examples of man's sinfulness, frailty, and caprice. It is full of grave doubts about the goodness and rationality of man, the sagacity of the majority, and the wisdom of reform. It seeks to put the calipers on the possibilities of human attainment. It tends toward pessimism and displays a natural preference for stability over change, continuity over experiment, the past over the future. Two momentous events sparked its emergence: the French Revolution and the Industrial Revolution. Conservatism appeared as a reaction against the extravagant radicalism and utopianism of the former and the dismayingly rapid pace of social change brought about by the latter.

Moreover, while the conservative tradition is a Western phenomenon, its impact has been greatest in particular countries like Great Britain. In France, the background of the Ancien Régime and an organic feudal order ought to have given conservatives an objective past to which to appeal. It would have done so but for one insoluble problem. French conservatives with their rationalism were never able to agree among themselves as to just what it was they wished to preserve. By contrast, Great Britain was able to absorb both the liberalism of John Locke and the conservatism of Edmund Burke. Its constitutional monarchy provides a fusion of the old and the new political philosophies. The conservative tradition grew up in reaction against the destructive forces released in the process of emancipation from aristocracy and feudalism. It was therefore reasonable that European and in particular British conservatives should sound the tocsin against Jacobinism and industrialization in behalf of the vestigial qualities worth preserving in a decaying feudal order.

For America, conservatism from the outset lacked a context in which it could raise its voice. The boundless opportunities of a new continent, the abundance of natural resources, the spirit of freedom, and the release from the shackles of an established order hardly provided fertile soil for its rapid growth and flowering. The industrialists who carved an empire out of this vast wilderness, such as the railway builders and traders, were scarcely conservatives in the European sense. Their very successes made them easy prey for the liberal illusions of progress and perfectibility. There have of course been conservative thinkers who were not without distinction. Especially in the field of foreign policy, the Federalists left us a legacy of precept and example that seems partly valid even today. It was not that American soil was rocky ground from which conservatism could take no nourishment. Rather, in the revealing words of Clinton Rossiter, it was "a lush jungle in which a more adaptable group of principles—democracy, egalitarianism, individualism—sprouted in easy abundance and choked off conservatism except in isolated spots, like the pre-Civil War south."[12]

You may respond that American business reflects the conservative tradition and perpetuates a mode of thinking going back to Edmund Burke. Perhaps if we hold the tenets of American capitalism, or more particularly of the present moderately conservative administration in Washington, up to the mirror of the historic model of conservatism, we can test this proposition at least in a rough and approximate way. The reader may keep score for the present-day conservative as the roll is called of conservatism's first principles. According

[12] Rossiter, *Conservatism*, p. 223.

to Clinton Rossiter, writing in *Conservatism in America*, "the traditional Conservative doesn't go around all the time mumbling epigrams about reverence and righteousness."[13] "The genuine Conservative is not a crusader; he goes about his mission not zealously but dutifully."[14] "Realism, common sense, adaptability, expediency, respect for unpleasant facts" are his trademark. "The Conservative is not an extreme individualist."[15] "Society, the total community, which is a great deal more than government, is historically, ethically and logically superior to the individual."[16] "In discussing the nature of government, he likes to point out to radicals that it is natural rather than artificial, to individualists that it is good rather than evil, and to collectivists that it is limited rather than unlimited in potentialities and scope."[17] "He continues to assert the beneficence of an aristocracy of talent and virtue, one that is trained for special service and thus entitled to special consideration."[18] "The preference for liberty over equality lies at the root of the Conservative tradition." "Man, says the Conservative, is a composite of good and evil, a blend of ennobling excellencies and degrading imperfections. He is . . . not perfectible. . . . Never, no matter how he is educated or situated or restrained, will he throw off completely his other innate qualities of irrationality, selfishness, laziness, depravity and corruptibility. . . . Although some Conservatives find support for their skeptical view of man in recent experiments in psychology, most continue to rely on religious teaching and the study of history [and] . . . prefer to call the motivation for iniquitous and irrational behavior by its proper name: Original Sin."[19]

The points at which the qualities and convictions of American "conservatives" from the Civil War to the present match up with those of traditional conservatism are not without consequence. They believed and believe in the superiority of

[13] *Ibid.*, p. 51. [14] *Ibid.*, p. 55. [15] *Ibid.*, p. 40.
[16] *Ibid.*, p. 36. [17] *Ibid.*, p. 31. [18] *Ibid.*, p. 24.
[19] *Ibid.*, p. 21.

liberty over equality, accepted as part of a concept of equal opportunity the fact of natural inequality, saw the necessity for some form of aristocracy albeit taking the form of an appeal for a businessman's government, were suspicious of most change except industrial expansion, and espoused laissez-faire. But the discrepancies are greater than the identities. For American "conservatives" there is a tendency to substitute morale for morality, economics for ethics and politics, and the mood if not the methods of the extreme Right for moderation. The Eisenhower moral crusade is not the first of its kind, the essential role of expediency and mere politics are frequently obscured or derided, rugged individualism is glorified at the expense of a proper regard for the supremacy of the community, instability rather than stability is fostered by harsh language, and radical anti-statism and a fatuous optimism prevail in the leading views of man and human progress. In a nutshell, American conservatism is more optimistic, materialistic, and individualistic than the conservative tradition. One historian notes that "they were the . . . only Right in Western history to push individualism so far as to assert that a man could never be helped, only harmed, by the assistance of the community."[20] Mr. Rossiter concludes: "The extra measure of moral indignation that George Kennan finds in our foreign policy; the worst excesses of tariff legislation, the moral blindness of those who insist on the identity of Socialism and Soviet Communism . . . all these are the major counts in the indictment of political conservatism."[21] By ignoring the capacity for evil in men and states, the American conservative has provided no adequate means for dealing with it. By dismissing society—its nature, needs, and problems—conservatism has left unanswered and even unasked the eternal questions regarding the good society, the class structure we have and we want, the relationship between leadership by our "best members" (who are not necessarily all lawyers and businessmen)

[20] *Ibid.*, pp. 162-63.   [21] *Ibid.*, p. 239.

and our democratic precepts, the proper and necessary purposes of government in modern society, the prospects for a
balanced individualism that is based on natural social and
moral allegiances and is not a sand-heap of separate particles
of humanity, the requirements of statecraft beyond the simple
proposition of "applying business methods to government,"
and the essentials of private and public morality. All these
and more are issues that cry for attention, reflection, and
exposition but on most of them latter-day conservatives have
chosen a posture of resounding silence.

How can one account for this silence and for the glaring
omissions of American conservatism seen in the light of an
historic Western tradition? Perhaps the answer can be sup-
plied in the form of a sweeping generalization. "American
conservatism is not the traditional conservatism of Western
political history. That conservatism was rooted in the aristocratic tradition; American conservatism is a decayed form of
nineteenth century liberalism." American conservatism is the
faith of the business community. At one point in Europe's
history it was a revolutionary creed. It opposed the traditional
restraints of a feudal society and sought to enlarge the liberties
of the middle classes. Its claims of liberty, however restricted,
were passionate, compelling, and urgent. But, as others have
argued, the odyssey of the original liberalism can be traced
in the movement from John Stuart Mill's *On Liberty* to
Herbert Hoover's *The Challenge to Liberty*. Conservatism
in recent decades has become less a rallying cry than an ideological façade. It has sought less to draw more men to its
cause than to protect the economic power of those already
under its shield. In domestic affairs its dynamic qualities have
disappeared; in world affairs it has retained the worst illusions of traditional liberalism. Indeed American conservatism,
which stands as the arch defender of nineteenth-century
liberalism, has proved itself particularly inept in the one

80

sphere where historically it enjoyed an unquestioned superiority: the realm of foreign policy.

III. LIBERALISM, CONSERVATISM, AND
FOREIGN POLICY

In the Western world this superiority had rested not on moral foundations but on conservatism's greater political realism. Conservatism recognized the complexities of power partly because of its experience in wresting it from feudal lords and partly because of an enlightened tradition of political reflection and writing. Not only had conservatives wielded power; they were more articulate about its use than the latter-day economic overlords, whose power was covert and non-political. Traditional liberalism by contrast was informed by higher ends of justice but, especially in the half-organized, half-lawless international society, it faltered in the realm of means. In Europe the contrast is seen at the time of the French Revolution in 1793 in the three-cornered duel in the House of Commons between Edmund Burke, Charles James Fox, and William Pitt. Fox was the leader of a faction of Whigs who opposed war with France on legalistic and rationalistic grounds. Looking to England's treaties with the Low Countries lying in the path of French expansionism, Fox found no legal rights and duties that would justify intervention. Moreover, England had stood aside when Poland was invaded. Hence Fox appealed to consistency in maintaining: "We had seen the entire conquest of Poland, and invasion of France, with such marked indifference, that it would be difficult now to take it up with the grace of sincerity."[22] For him there was no awareness of the bearing which French control of the Low Countries would have upon the traditional political, military, and economic interests of Great Britain. Against this argument Edmund Burke, the leader of a faction of

[22] Hans J. Morgenthau and Kenneth W. Thompson, *Principles and Problems of International Politics* (New York: Alfred A. Knopf, 1950), p. 338.

81

Whigs determined to support William Pitt, Prime Minister and Tory leader in war against France, rejected the view that a logically inconsistent foreign policy is necessarily a bad one. "Nations . . . were not to sit like judges, to act with perfect impartiality, to the exclusion of all ideas of self. Their first duty was to take care of themselves; and that of England particularly was to have a watchful and jealous care of the aggrandizement and encroaching movements of France. France was near; Prussia and Poland were distant; and unless there were apprehensions of the injury to Poland ultimately reaching England, there was nothing that rendered it expedient for her to interfere. England saw Sweden overturn the constitution of Poland: she afterwards saw the czar depose Stanislaus and put Augustus on the throne of that kingdom. In short, she saw various revolutions in Poland and ultimately a partition of it, and never stirred a hand."[23] What then was the ground for acting now. Pitt's answer is a timeless one: "The hon. gentleman defies me to state, in one sentence, what is the object of the war. In one word, I tell him that it is security."[24] Fox saw clearly the counterplay of ideas and the plane on which they were in conflict and the limits of every ideological crusade. "If it was maintained that opinions held in France must contaminate the minds of Englishmen, this would lead to a revival of every species of intolerance, and to a more rigorous scrutinizing of opinions than could be safe for states or individuals. . . ."[25] But conservatives like Burke and Pitt saw more clearly the hard choices which had to be made in a nation's survival.

More recently, when Britain was plunged into its deepest crisis, Winston Churchill came forward as the exponent of a conservative point of view. Significantly Britain's typical exponent of the business creed, Neville Chamberlain, displayed the same miscalculations in international politics that middle-class liberals showed in the United States. He assumed that

[23] *Ibid.*, p. 348.   [24] *Ibid.*, p. 349.   [25] *Ibid.*, pp. 344-45.

diplomacy was no more than a series of business transactions among peoples of different tongues, and he expected that dictators could be beguiled much as honest British businessmen. He thought that Hitler must have his price, a price which reasonable men should be prepared to pay. The demonic fury of the Nazi movement was beyond his ken because he had never plumbed the depth or height of human nature. The Western conservative tradition has dealt for generations with an endless succession of rivalries and combinations based on common fears, ancient sanctities, ethnic loyalties, and common goals. The conservative understands these forces because he has had to manipulate, persuade, coerce, resist, and accommodate them. However, because American conservatism has not been schooled in this tradition, it lacks an understanding of the complexities of power.

Therefore in foreign policy, it fluctuates between isolationism and imperialism, between underestimating our responsibilities and overestimating our power. In one moment it implies that our interests in Europe are of no consequence and prompts us to cut our losses (and save taxes). In the next moment it is ready to force European nations to adopt free enterprise systems, to throw up their interests in Asia and the Near East, or to unite at our behest. In Korea, conservatives vacillated between total victory and withdrawal and but for a popular President would probably have rebelled at the armistice. According to their likes, the United Nations ought to represent a law-making international body (Senator Taft in about 1944), or should be turned out of this country for jeopardizing our sovereignty and constitutional rights. In Asia and the Middle East, where the struggle with communism is ultimately economic and political, American conservatives are prepared to make vast and far-reaching military commitments but balk at more modest but not less essential economic programs. With a naïveté approaching Chamberlain's, they presume to appease and beguile Middle Eastern

83

nationalistic movements through proclamations and threats against our unhappy and sometimes imprudent European friends who happen to be more vulnerable than we are, but not greatly so, in certain areas of the world. They crudely assume that a calculating generosity must inevitably bring gratitude, that friendship and favor can be curried and bought without regard to long-standing enmities and hatreds.

Finally, American conservatives who have none of the sense for the organic growth of communities of which the European conservative tradition always has taken account assume that our moral authority can be strengthened anywhere in the world through simple declarations of goodwill or overt display of our power. They assume, for example, that the Eisenhower Doctrine can build a community no less vital than the Atlantic Community. They forget that the latter has become a political reality not solely through the pressures of contemporary history but primarily because it was founded upon the common traditions, mutual interests and shared values, hopes, and fears of Western civilization. These imponderables are the factors most difficult for American conservatives to grasp. If one reflects that European conservatives had been peculiarly at home in this realm, its character as *terra incognita* for American conservatism contributes a final ironic note. In the same way that society has been lost sight of within ordered national groupings, community is dismissed from the conservative's calculations on the international scene. The consequences for our policies are both appalling and frightening. Proposals for the most part advanced by conservative Senators to go it alone in Asia and the Middle East—a viewpoint Senator Mansfield recently described as "isolated internationalism"—are based on a reckless exaggeration of our moral resources in Asia in the same way that former President Hoover in his policy of "Fortress America" underestimated our community and spiritual affinity with allies and partners in Europe. Thus conservatism has moved from crisis to crisis, alternately overestimating and underestimating America's interests and power.

Nor has liberalism in the main been as sure of its ground in world as in national affairs. Prior to World War II, the Left in England and Scandinavia had urged collective action against the aggressors at the same time they were engaged in voting down appropriations for rearmament. The American labor movement has a history of isolationism and some of its present-day leaders speak with less than consummate wisdom. American liberals have tended consistently to exaggerate the influence of reason and moral force in the world. They have been endlessly tempted to espouse alternately an isolationist viewpoint that would shield liberal joys from the alien diseases of a decadent Old World or an international approach that endeavors to refashion the strange and ancient societies of Europe and Asia. Indeed among liberals, isolationism and internationalism tend to be cut from the same cloth. Both tend to underrate the resistance of external forces to the attainment of liberal goals and values. Liberal isolationists from Jefferson, who urged that we cancel all our treaties, through Bryan to those liberal revisionist historians who in the interwar period sought to show that America had only an insignificant stake in resisting the expansion of Imperial Germany by preserving some kind of equilibrium in Europe and Asia have all been the victims of one illusion. They have erred by believing that a liberal society could remain free to achieve its national purposes even though power was being concentrated in one nation or combination of nations bent on dominating Europe or, in Hitler's case, the world. They overlooked the fact that sooner or later the marriage of overwhelming power and unlimited ambition anywhere in the world causes the United States to rally all its forces to resist tyranny and take recourse to a form of national organization that Harold Lasswell has aptly described as the "garrison state." Put to this test, liberal goals like freedom are sacrificed to overriding demands of national security.

We have paid a high price for two recent expressions of this particular liberal illusion. The first is in part the responsibility of apologists for the political-military strategy which prevailed at the end of World War II. They defended the decision through which military strategy was divorced from political objectives providing for the withdrawal of American and British forces and the advance of Russian troops into the heart of Germany. It was argued that whether Soviet influence was extended a few hundred miles west of Prague was of little if any consequence for the shape of the postwar world. Without arguing the point whether this movement of Russian forces was inevitable, most competent observers today are agreed that these decisions by Allied leaders were among the most fateful of the war. Almost every policy for Europe since 1946 has been designed either to contain further Russian expansion or to roll back the Soviet Union from its advance position along a line extending from Stettin to Trieste. Another example of this illusion can be drawn from the events of more recent days. The Franco-British adventure of 1956 in Suez can be condemned on numerous counts. Liberals, however, have seen fit to go one step further and to join their unqualified moral indignation with political estimates of the most questionable character. They have implied that the reduction of British and French influence in the Middle East was a net gain for the world, oblivious to the fact that the subtraction of this component of Western power, however one views it, is a severe blow to our total influence in the region. The best proof of this lies in the desperate and inevitable attempt of the United States through the Eisenhower Doctrine to substitute our influence for that of our friends. The most urgent warning against this form of liberal thinking comes from Arab leaders like Charles Malik of Lebanon, who hastened to advise President Eisenhower that unless American influence were part of Western influence in the Middle East, it would prove ineffective in halting the spread of communist influence. Incidentally, liberal internationalism has helped to confound the problem by insisting that either an all-powerful United States or the United Nations would be able to shoulder all Europe's burdens and do so more capably in resisting the spread of communism anywhere in the world.

Thus the supreme tragedy of contemporary American thinking on foreign policy stems from the failure of either liberalism or conservatism to measure up to its task. Ironically, liberalism has been most successful when its spokesmen reflected some of the insights of the conservative tradition. President Franklin D. Roosevelt is perhaps the classic example of a liberal American President who was at home in the troubled world of international politics partly because he was a renegade Hudson Valley aristocrat. He wished to preserve the American system and to this undertaking he brought all the skill and ingenuity of conservatism whose exponents have seemed, as it were, to wield power by instinct and experience. Henry Steele Commager, in a review of Arthur Schlesinger's *The Crisis of the Old Order*, comments on Roosevelt's profoundly conservative character: "He was conservative personally—born to wealth and tradition and noblesse oblige; trained at Groton and Harvard; deeply rooted in the land; a devout churchman. He was deeply conservative in politics . . . and—as events were to reveal—in foreign policy."[26]

In the same way, American conservatives who have contributed most in foreign policy have been tainted with a measure of liberalism in their approach. We can only note in passing that President Eisenhower with his devotion to America's international responsibilities is no less a classic example than President Roosevelt. For Mr. Eisenhower has perceived both the limits of American power in the vast expanses of

---

[26] *New York Times Book Review*, March 3, 1957, p. 3.

Asia and the necessity of confronting Russian power with firm countervailing power in the face of its expansion into the power vacuums of the world. He has accepted compromises in Korea and Indo-China because he recognized that short of an endless struggle on the mainland of China there was no alternative to the acceptance of a balance of power in Asia. At the same time in Formosa and in the Middle East he has not hesitated to assert American influence and power, for he realized that to do otherwise might upset the world balance of power. His failures have been a strange blending of the pacifism and rationalism of liberalism and the conservative illusion that smiles and goodwill would turn even the most stubborn foe into a friendly American.

In short, liberalism and conservatism have proved adequate to their tasks only when two conditions have prevailed. First, liberal or conservative leaders whose foreign policies have been most successful can more accurately be termed realists. They have succeeded because their liberal or conservative policies were founded on a realistic estimate of the perennial factors in the historical and political situation. Secondly, the shortcomings and failings of a liberalism that is too much the child of the Enlightenment and of a conservatism that tends uncritically to embrace a crusading nationalist point of view require a blending of the deeper insights of the two. Liberalism alone cannot save us unless it is freed from its worst illusions about human nature and politics. Conservatism—especially American conservatism—is bedeviled by its passionate attachment to each successive status quo and its tendency to see the advance of mankind through the narrow squint of upper-middle-class American life. England's political advance must be reckoned at least partly due to the creative interplay between its traditions of Lockean liberalism and Burkean conservatism. The one has a keen sense of justice while the other is more aware of all the inescapable aspects of community life that are organic in character. Historic conservatism perceives that acknowledged rights and duties, acceptable standards of justice and mutual interests, are more often the result of slow and unconscious growth than of conscious political intervention. It likewise concedes that every political and social realm has its hierarchies of power and authority, not least on the international scene. Finally, it argues that it will not do to assume that peace and order and a more stable community can be had through an effacing of these arrangements. The source of all conflict in the world is never solely the great powers or political parties. As often as not, the weak tempt others to aggression; powerlessness is hardly an assurance of responsibility (a vivid example may be the conduct of certain smaller states in an international assembly such as the United Nations). One of the creative functions of conservatism is continually to remind liberals that whether in field or factory, school or church, congress or the international society, there are hierarchies of leadership and an almost endless number of organic processes that hold the community together, give it whatever cohesiveness it enjoys, and regulate and integrate its life.

However while conservatism in the West has seen the organic processes of each community in true perspective, American conservatism, which is chiefly the remnant of a once vital laissez-faire liberalism, has been blinded to these realities. On the one hand, it has clung to the errors and illusions of Enlightenment liberalism, which saw an easy harmony of interests emerging from every conflict of interests; on the other, to a narrow conception of the hierarchies of leadership in America's national and international life defending the special privileges of the parochial segments of the business community or internationally of the nation as a law unto itself. Because the wisdom of traditional conservatism has been so imperfectly appropriated by American conservatives, it becomes the common property of all those groups, including liberals, who seek for greater realism in world affairs. Indeed, liberalism stripped of its utopian errors appears at this point to offer the best hope, partly because liberal realists like George F. Kennan, Reinhold Niebuhr, and Hans J. Morgenthau have been the most diligent in seeking a coherent, relevant, and intelligible theory of international politics.

Yet liberals in public life continue to utter the old clichés, to prate about principle and decry pragmatism, and to act imprudently in the face of harsh realities, as in recent proposals for unilateral arms reduction or the abdication of responsibility for a sound American foreign policy by leaving the initiative to the United Nations. There is no apparent reason why the errors of the Enlightenment should continue to bedevil much of American liberalism, particularly if liberals were to accept the wise doctrines of a group like the Policy Planning Staff. However, the evidence that this has or is likely to take place is not convincing. Until the United States becomes the home of a realistic liberalism, especially in foreign affairs, the role of an enlightened conservatism and a responsible liberalism will continue to be essential. Whatever their limits, we have in their interplay and tension the best hope for America.

CHAPTER 3

STATESMEN AS PHILOSOPHERS: WRITTEN
AND LIVING THEORIES

There is no substitute for one man's mind grasping
the nation's interests, for one man's judgment deciding
how these interests can best be served, for one man's
will seeing the decision through, for one man's soul feeling the anguish and exhilaration of great deeds.—HANS
J. MORGENTHAU

THE PERIODS in American history when learned men and
public leaders effectively join hands to face current problems
are comparatively few and far between. This in spite of the
fact that theorists and practitioners frequently exhort one
another to cooperate and give aid that is sorely needed. The
nature of the demands they lay upon one another, however,
are often beyond reach. Theorists would like full blueprints
of the various elements in the process by which decisions have
been made. Practitioners complain that learned men find it
difficult to think and act within the limits prescribed by real
situations. Moreover, "the academic approach to policy problems is apt to exhibit two tendencies. The first is a tendency
toward abstraction and generalization; the second is a tendency
to emphasize historical analogies."[1] Decision-makers grow impatient with the judicious and painstaking habits of the scholar,
his quest for knowledge of both past and present, and the
luxury of reserving judgment in which he indulges.

Nothing is served by obscuring the deep gulf which separates the man of thought from the man of action. Both sides

[1] Paul H. Nitze, "The Role of the Learned Man in Government," in
The Review of Politics, Vol. 20, No. 3 (July 1958), p. 279.

inherit and come to defend a professional suspicion if not contempt of one another. In retirement, Dean Acheson can speak with deference and genuine respect of certain scholars in international relations. In his days as Secretary of State, however, he expressed doubt concerning help from any "academically or analytically minded men." It is reported that "Mr. Dulles says that he would welcome assistance from those who have more knowledge of and experience with the foreign policy problems which the world now faces than he has, but he asks where are such people."[2] The wide gulf between thinkers and doers is partly temperamental, partly professional, and oftentimes the product of a defensive attitude resulting from an awareness that each of us after all is mortal.

Statesmen in general take for granted the importance of theory and philosophy. Even the staunchest pragmatist who prides himself on playing by ear frequently ends by making a philosophy of expediency. Policy-makers speak of "theory in action" or "operating concepts" in international affairs. In 1946 Mr. Dulles observed: "No nation's foreign policy can be ascertained merely from what its officials say. More important are the philosophy of its leaders and the actual manifestations of that philosophy in what is done."[3] Sometimes a leader's philosophy remains inarticulated and implicit. It remains for the scholar to reconstruct from the leader's words and deeds the principles by which he charts his course. Such theories are rarely systematic, consistent, or fully coherent but because political actors lack fully elaborated doctrines is no reason for concluding that they move without direction or purpose. For example, Harry S. Truman's actions in foreign policy were rooted primarily in one dominant and overriding conviction. On the strength of the lessons of the interwar period he fervently believed that aggression must be

[2] *Ibid.*, p. 281.

[3] John Foster Dulles, "Thought on Soviet Foreign Policy and What To Do about It," *Life*, Vol. xx, June 3, 1946, p. 113.

met by collective action that was immediate and overwhelming in effect. The Truman Doctrine and the police action in Korea were squarely founded on this principle.

It is sometimes said that academic advisors continually hark back to the analogies of history. The warning is given: "Historical analogies have great utility in illuminating complex situations and in helping one to sort out the significant from the merely striking. But action based too closely on historical analogies is apt to be sterile and unimaginative."[4] If academic minds alone deserved this warning, the consequences for national policies would be less far-reaching. In actual fact, however, statesmen are more disposed than theorists to base their policies on some "grand simplification" drawn from a narrow segment of historical experience. Military leaders fight the last war and politicians with their penchant for casting things in simple and unambiguous terms are forever tempted to view each successive crisis in the context of the preceding one. The nature of the communist threat is colored by the West's fateful and tragic experience with the Nazi threat. "Parleys with Hitler were fruitless; talks with the Russians are doomed to fail." "Hitler did not keep his promises; neither will Soviet leaders." "The Nazi challenge was military in nature; the communist peril must also be fundamentally military in character." "Hitler's ambition for world domination was unlimited in scope. Communists will never rest before they rule the world." The point is not that such historical precedents are without truth or relevance. One tyranny carries many of the marks of others that have gone before. But history is too complex, variegated, and diverse to cast in a single mold. The precedents for communism beyond nazism may be Islam, the "Religious Wars," Napoleon, the Crusades, or other revolutionary movements. It is shortsighted to look no farther than a single political movement. Perhaps this is inevitable for practitioners who

---

[4] Nitze, "Role of the Learned Man," p. 280.

merely "dabble" in history and theory. "A wrong theory, an oversimplified theory, or a theory applied out of context can produce disastrous results."[5] Ironically, those who take pride in their skepticism over theory and who prefer to prick out a policy by the case method are not infrequently most vulnerable to error. The statesman's theories may be based on hidden assumptions and unexamined premises that become frozen over time into nearly absolute dogmas of "no entangling alliances," "collective security," or "support or opposition to the United Nations." Doctrines of this kind may initially be propounded to enhance public understanding, but sooner or later they evolve into guides to action and eventually substitutes for flexible foreign policies.

However, it would be unfair to stop with the suggestion that those who shoulder the heavy burdens of responsibility may sometimes be entrapped by their too simple theories. So, for that matter, are philosophers. Beyond that, the history of thought, including thought on international relations, testifies that those who face the harsh choices of international life often anticipate the insights of the theorists. The quality that distinguishes the great statesman from his run-of-the-mill contemporary is his capacity for viewing the concrete case in terms of the general. He may be compelled by the pressures of the moment to treat each problem on its merits, but when these demands recede he will have redress whether in aphorism or generalized statement to the underlying theory by which he proceeds. Thus, for example, if one wishes to appraise Dean Acheson's theory of international organization, his public statements under fire as he struggled to work out acceptable policies for the Korean Crisis or the Berlin Blockade are probably too fragmentary, contingent, and incomplete. It would also be necessary to examine his views as he drew on these experiences to erect a broader conception of the role

[5] Paul H. Nitze, "The Implications of Theory for Practice in the Conduct of Foreign Affairs," an unpublished paper, p. 2.

and limits of the United Nations. A man's writings are more likely to provide the schema of his philosophy than his actions in the midst of domestic and international political cross-currents. This is plainly an alternative that is open to a Churchill in greater measure than to many leaders who spend all their days in practical affairs.

I. INTERNATIONAL RELATIONS THEORY
AND PUBLIC OPINION

The real issue raised by statesmanship and theory stems from the problems of simultaneously choosing wise foreign policies and rallying a people in support of them. The crucial public may be the members of a political party, the Congress or Parliament, a wider national public, or members of a coalition. In each case the problem is one of enlisting consent. Sometimes the crisis or challenge is so inescapable, as in war, that the public has no alternative but to yield and give support. At other times choices are more uncertain. Then the task of the leader is to draw together the common interests that a majority of people may share. The great mass of people can hardly be privy to the narrow choices and careful distinctions embodied in policy-making. If they are to throw their weight behind particular programs, it must be on broader grounds. At some point complex decisions must be stated as simple choices, difficult issues reduced to a few basic propositions, and the questions asked in a way capable of arousing emotional responses. Both American and British experience provide examples of the bewildering and perplexing nature of democratic foreign policy; while the two systems have differing institutions and techniques, the problem they face is common.[6]

A debate in the House of Commons on February 28, 1945, is singularly revealing in this regard. Midway through the

[6] I choose the British example for discussion merely because the issue is articulated with exceptional clarity in a single parliamentary debate.

debate, a younger Conservative member rose to deliver a speech on the Polish settlement negotiated by Prime Minister Churchill, President Roosevelt, and Premier Stalin at the Crimean Conference and incorporated into the so-called Yalta agreements. The debate had ranged far and wide as some members denounced the Prime Minister for yielding too much to the Russians while others condemned him for claiming too much for Britain's postwar role. The member, Captain Peter Thorneycroft, who in 1951 was to become the youngest member of Prime Minister Churchill's Cabinet and in 1957 was named Chancellor of the Exchequer, chose the occasion to cast his specific comments on Yalta in the framework of a more general statement on foreign policy which raises the central questions with which we must be concerned:

"I believe the real difficulty in which my hon. Friends find themselves is not so much Poland at all. I believe it is in the apparent conflict between documents like the Atlantic Charter and the facts of the European situation. We talk to two different people in two different languages. In the East we are talking to the Russians. The Russians are nothing if not realists. . . . I believe that the Russian Foreign Office is perhaps more in tune with the advice which would be given to the Tsars than to the potentates of the twentieth century. In such circumstances we talk in language not far removed from power politics. In the West we are faced by the Americans. They are nothing if not idealists. To them we talk in the polite language of the Atlantic Charter. Somehow or other we have to marry those two schools of thought. If I could persuade the Americans, particularly in the Middle West, to have something of the Russian realism in international relations, and persuade the Russians to have the idealism that exists on the East Coast of America, we might get somewhere, but let us face the fact that the process will be a long and painful one. You do not move suddenly from a world in which there are international rivalries into a world where there is international cooperation. It is the world we are in that the Prime Minister has to deal with. We could not come back from Yalta with a blueprint for a new Utopia. . . . The rights of small nations are safeguarded by a mixture of diplomacy and military power."[7]

Neither Captain Thorneycroft's views on Poland nor his discourse on the Russian and American antagonists in the Cold War were acceptable to the "hon. Friends" that day. Indeed, we do well to remember that the debate over Yalta was not initiated by Republicans in the American political campaign in 1952. It was evident as early as 1945 that the moral and political ambiguities of the agreements were bound to inflame public opinion and supply ammunition to contending political groups. Then as now Yalta was a clear question of right or wrong, good or evil, black or white. Few were persuaded by what Captain Thorneycroft had to say. Realistic appraisals of the limits of action in foreign policy are poor competitors in the market-place of ideas. Whereas such appraisals are nearly always complicated, tentative, easily distorted, and uncertain, the recipes and formulas of demagogues and utopians are bold and militant, emotional and, for desperate souls, almost always satisfying. What is of course obvious should be added: namely, that all the failures and difficulties of foreign policy do not originate with the people. Bad foreign policy may as often result from bad driving as from backseat political driving. One is reminded of the cartoon with the caption that reads: "How often have I told you children not to bother daddy when he is passing on a turn."

How is the statesman to deal with this dilemma? He can offer his policies on their merits and trust that the people will support them, or he can lay bare the forces compelling him to follow a fateful course. More often, however, he is driven to couch his actions in more popular and palatable appeals.

[7] *Parliamentary Debates* (Hansard), House of Commons, Vol. 408, February 28, 1945, pp. 1458-59.

In coming to terms with a public that is resistant to every harsh and cynical claim, he oftentimes must have recourse to new modes of popular diplomacy which in earlier eras were largely unknown and unnecessary.

If anyone has been immune to the ravages and tyranny of majority rule, with its heavy demands for simple slogans and glittering solutions in foreign affairs, it should have been Mr. Winston S. Churchill. His approach to international relations is reflected in the statement we have noted of his disciple Peter Thorneycroft; in a sense, Churchill is the last and, as such, perhaps the noblest of the classical conservative statesmen. More frequently than one can count he has espoused unpopular causes or championed programs that were out of tune with public sentiments. He repeatedly warned a proud people that Britain would have to be subordinate to the United States in the postwar world. He challenged and criticized the diplomatic make-believe that sought for peace in pious sentiments about the Kellogg-Briand Pact outlawing war or the cozy and complacent idolatry of words and phrases embodied in the Covenant of the League of Nations or the United Nations Charter. In the conduct of war he promised only "blood, sweat, and tears."

However, when the acceptance of crucial policies for which he was responsible hinged on skill and tactics, he hesitated not a moment in appealing to the public and Parliament in terms best calculated to win their acclaim. There is no better example of this than the Yalta settlement. Here we can observe, stripped of all side issues or extraneous points, the simple and inescapable clash between the claims of political realism and public support. This crisis illustrates the dual nature of the problem of explaining a foreign policy based on an existing situation of fact, namely, the prevailing strength of the Soviet Union in Eastern Europe resulting from the Red Army's advance to the Elbe, and the insistent moral demands of a popular assembly. Mr. Churchill's justification of the concessions made to a Russian sphere of influence in this area provide a sample of a moralistic formulation of a policy whose sole rational defense was rooted in intractable political facts. On the other side, the parliamentary debate is richly furnished with the counter-arguments of utopian spokesmen who found his idealism too mild and fellow realists who were uneasy about his choice of tactics.

In his opening speech, the Prime Minister endeavored to show that Yalta was a settlement grounded in moral principles safeguarding the rights of all the parties. He began by pointing out that the Russian claim to the Curzon Line in the east had been unchanged. He said: "I have never concealed from the House that, personally, I think the Russian claim is just and right. If I champion this frontier for Russia, it is not because I bow to force. It is because I believe it is the fairest division of territory that can in all the circumstances be made between the two countries whose history has been so intermingled."[8] He added that the Curzon Line had been drawn in 1919 by an expert commission, on which one of Britain's most distinguished diplomats, Sir Eyre Crowe, had served, at a time when Russia had few friends among the allies. Finally, he examined the Russian seizure of Polish territory and propounded the view that: "under the world organization all nations great and small, victors and vanquished will be secured against aggression by indisputable law and by overwhelming international force. The published Crimea Agreement is not a ready-made plan imposed by the great Powers on the Polish people. It sets out the agreed views of the three major allies on the means whereby their common desire to see a strong, free, independent Poland may be fulfilled in cooperation with the Poles themselves, and whereby a Polish government which all the United Nations can recognize, may be set up in Poland."[9]

[8] *Ibid.*, Vol. 408, February 27, 1945, p. 1275.
[9] *Ibid.*, p. 1278.

If Mr. Churchill expected to satisfy the House of Commons that the Polish settlement was not only necessary but also just, he was disappointed. If he expected to allay what *The Times* (of London) has frequently called the hagridden fears of the problems of power that possess the more utopian members of Parliament, his hopes proved short-lived. Sir William Beveridge of Berwick upon Tweed, author of the Beveridge Plan, responded to the Prime Minister in words of haughty contempt: "We have to stick to principle. We have to stick to principle in international affairs, and if it happens that one cannot both stick to one's friends and stick to principle, one must stick to principle; because principles do not change, but friends, even if they appear for the moment to be unreasonable, may change and become reasonable. Opportunism, appeasement, self-regarding policies, power politics, all lead to the grave of all our hopes."[10]

There were other members who asserted that Britain had long been the trustee of Poland and therefore was not free to yield Poland's rights to Russian power. If Britain were to be guided by expediency, she would prove herself no better than Nazi Germany. If she yielded to this temptation, World War II would have been fought in vain. Commander Sir Archibald Southby sought to persuade his wayward colleagues to return to the path of virtue when he said: "With much of the Yalta Agreement I am in accord, but if our foreign policy is to be based upon expediency and not upon principles then it is bound to fail, and I cannot in honour express my confidence in it. . . . I hold that there is a greater loyalty than that which we owe to any one man, Government or party— the loyalty to those fundamental ideals of justice, liberty and honour to uphold which we have twice in our lifetime seen the British sword drawn."[11]

The Prime Minister's defense of Yalta came under attack from other directions and from other camps. He had been

[10] *Ibid.*, p. 1315.   [11] *Ibid.*, p. 1437.

challenged in behalf of high principles; now he was held to account for the gulf that seemed to separate his lofty pronouncements and the cruel, stark demands of the balance of power wrought by the conduct of the last stages of the war. Thorneycroft calmly but firmly reminded his colleagues: "I do not regard the Polish settlement as an act of justice. It may be right or wrong, it may be wise or foolish, but at any rate it is not justice as I understand the term. It is not the sort of situation . . . [before] a disinterested body . . . in which the strength and power of one of the parties is never allowed to weigh in the balance. The sooner we recognize that we are a long way from that sort of thing happening the better."[12]

One speaker after another, including those who supported the Prime Minister, conceded that Yalta was inevitable. The Russians could not be expected to recede from territory that they had seized in the last days of the war. But the hypocrisy of claiming that this was an act of justice compatible with the Atlantic Charter was more than they—or by implication, the people—could swallow. It may be useful to quote from a long but revealing statement by Lord Dunglass of Lanark:

"It would be comfortable to believe that relationships between different communities of men were always governed by reason, but the reality as history reveals it, is that the governing principle is that of power. Power has not been destroyed in this war; it has been redistributed. It is still used. . . . Any settlement at this time must take account of it.

"I think a valid criticism of the peace settlement of 1919 was that it allowed too much for the triumph of reason, and too little for the fact of power. While all that is true, yet it is also true to say that the world can never pass from the old order of the rule of force to the new order of the rule of law, except by way of a period during which the Great Powers themselves are willing, and are seen to be willing, to exercise restraint in the use of power. The position in post-war Europe

[12] *Ibid.*, pp. 1456-57.

will be a state of great power and great weakness side by side, and that does not lead to stability. One reason why there is world concern over the differences between Russia and Poland, is because it is the first case, a test case, in the relationship between a Great Power wielding great military might and her smaller and weaker neighbour."[13]

Lord Dunglass concluded: "When the Prime Minister says that he accepts this as an act of justice, I must take a fundamentally opposite view. We have dozens of times in our history accepted this kind of an arrangement as a fact of power."[14]

Then there was a summary statement by Mr. Raikes of Essex, South-East, which said of Thorneycroft's speech: "The most eloquent speech . . . did not base it on justice; with great honesty he said he thought it was an unjust settlement. . . . One thing is certain, however great the vote may be today, it will not be because they believe that the motion was just. Well may the Prime Minister say, like Canning, 'Save, oh save me, from my candid friends.' "[15]

The exchanges in this brilliantly instructive debate taken together epitomize the problem of foreign policy in a democratic state. Policies that are founded on the realities of the external world must be translated into terms that appear less harsh, strident, and offensive. In preparing the Fulton Speech in which he outlined for the West his conception of the Soviet threat, Mr. Churchill tells us that he tried to soften popular reactions by formulating his propositions in mild, mellifluous, guarded, and carefully shaped statements. Yet we know how these words, seen now to be true, were received at the time. In Britain, Mr. Ernest Bevin, himself a shrewd realist but an aspiring politician as well, declared: ". . . as atomic energy evolves . . . the necessity of its use as a weapon will have disappeared by reason of the new world organiza-

---

[13] *Ibid.*, pp. 1304-05. [14] *Ibid.*, p. 1306.
[15] *Ibid.*, p. 1491.

tion."[16] Churchill was a kind of Cassandra warning of dangers that had been rendered obsolete. In the Soviet Union, *Pravda* assailed him in this way: "He openly proclaims power politics, which must be realized by an Anglo-American military alliance. To whom is it not clear that all of this, as a matter of fact, means nothing else than the liquidation of the United Nations Organization."[17] In the United Nations, the *Christian Century* reported: "No one doubts . . . his magnificent courage . . . but the situation into which the world is now passing so swiftly demands more than courage. It requires a contemporary mind and . . . principles which place people above politics, humanity above the vanishing glories of Empire."[18] No one ought to be surprised, therefore, that Churchill as political leader confronted with these attacks at home and abroad should wring from the total character of a policy or action its moral component. His popular appeals, based more on moralisms than realism, have been frequent, as when he said: "The British race is not actuated mainly by the hope of material gain. . . . It is stirred on almost all occasions by sentiment and instinct rather than by a program or world calculation." Or again: "We seek no territory; we covet no oil fields; we demand no bases for the forces of the air or of the seas. . . . We do not set ourselves up in rivalry or bigness or might with any country in the world."[19] In all these phrases, there is more about moral principle and less about political necessity, more about ultimate ends and less about proximate means. This is the background and the reality that underlies the conduct of democratic foreign policy. Practical actions must appear more felicitous than they are; prudence must be englobed in virtue. It is vulgar and debasing for any

16 *The New York Times*, October 6, 1946, p. 1.
17 *Pravda*, March 11, 1948, quoted in *The New York Times*, March 12, 1946, p. 4.
18 "A Future without Churchill," *The Christian Century*, Vol. LXII, January 31, 1945, p. 134.
19 *Parliamentary Debates*, Vol. 407, January 18, 1945, pp. 397-98.

Western statesman to concede that foreign policy is a commodity that must be marketed and sold, yet the stories even of great leaders like Winston Churchill appear to substantiate this truth.

Now let me say a word on institutions and foreign policy. While both Britain and America face this problem, they appear to deal with it through varied institutions and in different ways. At one level, there is substantial agreement in the diagnosis and the remedy proposed. The theorists and some practitioners in Britain stand shoulder to shoulder with American writers in singling out as a besetting problem the complexities and uncertainties of public diplomacy. None of them is prepared to accept the substitution of public relations for diplomacy, whether for domestic or international consumption. Nor, I should hasten to add, do they for one moment feel that the price paid for popular influence on foreign policy is too great. However, they share a conviction that diplomacy in a democracy is a sensitive instrument which must be mastered and comprehended before it can serve the interests of peace.

Lord Strang, Permanent Undersecretary of State in the Foreign Office from 1949-1953, in a series of two talks for the British Home Service, discussed precisely this topic of "Foreign Policy in a Democracy."[20] A country's foreign policy, he defines, as "the purposes or objectives pursued by its government in its relations with the governments of other states, and the methods adopted by it in order to achieve those purposes."[21] He goes on to note that every foreign policy is the result of a decision by the government concerned. Its machinery and procedures shape the character of the decisions. In Britain the linchpin in the decision-making apparatus is the Foreign Secretary, dependent on the Foreign Office, responsible to the Parliament, and limited by existing

[20] *The Listener*, Vol. LVII, No. 1450, January 10, 1957, pp. 47ff.; Vol. LVII, No. 1451, January 17, 1957, pp. 92-93.
[21] *Ibid.*, No. 1450, p. 47.

facts. The limiting facts include habit, custom, and permanent interests. "No British Foreign Secretary, for example, can get away from the fact that Great Britain is a small, densely populated island with wide overseas interests, inescapably dependent upon foreign trade for the maintenance of its relatively luxurious standard of living. So there will be, in its main lines, a persisting element of sameness in the shaping of foreign policy."[22] When there are changes, they usually come about gradually in response to a changing environment. This environment is a combination of the external and internal worlds in which democratic statesmen live and make their choices.

The external world for England has changed since 1900. Then and now her first interest has been to deny to any one power domination on the European continent. In the nineteenth century Britain pursued this national interest through a policy described as "splendid isolation," withholding her power to throw it to one side or the other of the scales of the balance of power in order to maintain equilibrium. Beginning in 1904, when Lord Lansdowne made his famous agreement with France to reduce tensions in the disputed colonial areas of Egypt, Morocco, and Newfoundland, Britain has moved toward increased commitments on the continent. She supported France in Morocco in 1912, working out joint naval arrangements. By 1914 she was morally and politically, if not legally, committed to come to the aid of France. Following World War II, the objective threat of a Russia poised on the borders of a weak and enfeebled Germany led to the Dunkirk Treaty with France and the Low Countries, to NATO, to European economic cooperation, and most recently to negotiations for a common European market. None of these steps was deliberately planned; they were brought about progressively under the steady whiplash of events, with each step requiring the gravest kind of heart-searching. Britain's fundamental objec-

[22] *Ibid.*

tives are essentially unchanged but external developments have called for a shift in the means and policies for achieving them.

Similarly, at every step, the interplay between external and internal pressures has been decisive. The Foreign Secretary must seek and respond both to professional and political advice. As a politician there are additional considerations he must weigh. Increasingly the ordinary men and women, no less than their elected representatives, are constrained to influence foreign policy. The Foreign Secretary is subject to appeals from pressure groups, political and industrial groups such as trade unions, party organizations whether central or local, the whole gamut of opinion represented by the press and the general sentiments of the public which are continually being gauged and evaluated, sometimes with questionable accuracy, by public opinion polls. The Secretary is a member of the government and under the general direction of the Prime Minister must conform his policies to government policy. At least once a week, he lays before his colleagues in the Cabinet matters for their decision and must carry them through the force of his argument, the strength of his position, or the support of the Prime Minister. If he is weak, has strong rivals in the Cabinet, or if Ministers are divided on policy, his policies may be amended or sometimes even rejected for better or for worse. The most fateful relation of all imposed by the machinery of government is that between the Foreign Secretary and the Prime Minister. Occasionally Prime Ministers have taken foreign affairs into their own hands or sought the counsel of advisers outside the Foreign Office. Sometimes the Prime Minister may be wiser than his colleagues in the Foreign Office, as may have been true with Winston Churchill. Nevertheless, the Prime Minister, isolated from the daily intelligence that flows into the Foreign Office from outposts abroad, cannot have an intimate knowledge of every shift and turn in the external world. Lloyd George and Neville Cham-

berlain as Prime Ministers seized the prerogatives of their
Foreign Secretaries both times without notably happy results.
The ideal relation is perhaps that which existed between
Churchill and Eden about which Sir Llewellyn Woodward
has written: "Mr. Churchill's collaboration with Mr. Eden
was so frank and sagacious, and his own temperament so little
inclined to backstairs methods, that there was never any
question about what might be called a 'double' foreign
policy."[23]

Thus in Britain the formation and shaping of foreign
policy is part of the democratic process. Myriad factors bear
on the Foreign Secretary and "he must make up his mind
how far they should be permitted to affect the course he
thinks would be the best, whether judged professionally, or
from a cool assessment of the public interest broadly conceived."[24] Whatever these limitations, the authority of the
executive in Parliament for the formation of foreign policy
is not seriously questioned. This authority is if anything more
deeply entrenched with the growth of party discipline, the
maturity of the British electorate, and the knowledge that
the overthrowing of the government means general elections
for all the members. This may suggest one possible source of
tension between Britain and America, for if in the one executive power stands unchallenged and in the other is under
attack, this can occasion misunderstanding and affect the
national outlook.

If it is true that more and more people in the democracies—
including the United Kingdom—are involved in the actual
process of making foreign policy, their influence is even
greater in the control of foreign policy. In Britain there are
at least three ways in which popular or parliamentary control
is exerted on foreign policy. The first relates to treaties. In
contrast to the American system, where Congress has the

[23] *Ibid.*, p. 69.
[24] *Ibid.*, No. 1451, p. 92.

power to ratify treaties, parliamentary approval of treaties is required only where legislation is needed. The negotiation and ratification of treaties is the responsibility of the Crown, but it is customary when treaties are signed to lay them on the table in the House of Commons for twenty-one days. If, but only if a debate is called for, the sense of the House can be taken. A second control stems from a more general type of debate either on foreign policy as a whole or on some aspect that has attracted unusual public interest. The opposition may demand the debate or the government can take the initiative. Whether such a debate causes the government to modify the substance or adjust the formulation of its policies, it can have a restraining influence. Woodrow Wilson caught the sense of these debates when he observed: "You dare not lay a bad case before mankind." A third point of contact between the government and Parliament comes in question periods. Kenneth Younger, former Minister of State for Foreign Affairs, characterized this process in the following words: "At each stage the policy is open to attack, and Ministers are subjected to every kind of comment and criticism. From the Minister's point of view, ill-informed or even stupid questions may be quite as informative as those of the experts, and the murmurs of approval or protest evoked from different sectors of opinion in the House can be as significant as anything that is said."[25]

Through possible discussions of treaties, general debates, and parliamentary questions, to say nothing of its control of the purse, Parliament exerts restraints and controls upon a foreign policy that has already evolved and developed—this despite its lack of a specific constitutional function comparable to the U.S. Senate. Even though a government cannot as readily be overthrown as, say, in France, the prospect of eventual defeat in an election makes it sensitive to public reactions, although not as sensitive as in France or the United

[25] *Ibid.*

States. In recent years, the governments of Prime Ministers Clement Attlee, Winston Churchill, and Anthony Eden have all clung to unpopular policies in the face of substantial opposition, in the hope that history would prove them right. It has been suggested that: "A government may fairly claim that it can be in a better position to judge the national interest than the public itself . . . it can hope that public doubts will respond in time to repeated and authoritative expositions of the government's case; or, best of all, that events themselves will vindicate the policy."[26]

The American approach to this problem is as many-sided as most American reactions to the problems that trouble and haunt us. Underlying popular thinking, however, is a native and deep-seated suspicion of diplomacy. A leading study of Anglo-American relations begins: "Clemenceau once said that war is too important an activity to be left to the soldier. Peace, surely, is too vital to be entrusted solely to the diplomat."[27] It is generally assumed that foreign policy is as much the responsibility of the people or the Congress as it is of the President and the Department of State. We read in a responsible study: "The makers of [foreign] policy are rather the legislators . . . , civil servants, newspaper editors and columnists who devote more or less continuous study to these matters. . . ."[28] Some Americans are even disposed to take umbrage when the suggestion is made that democratic diplomacy has its difficulties. They reply, What about the nazis or the communists. Would you prefer their systems of diplomacy? This misses the point rather badly, for it is as if one would ask a marriage counselor if he is against marriage or a minister discussing human frailties if he is in favor of sin. Nor will it do to dismiss anyone who grapples with these

[26] *Ibid.*, p. 93.
[27] Henry L. Roberts and Paul A. Wilson, *Britain and the United States: Problems in Cooperation* (New York: Harper & Brothers, 1953), p. vi.
[28] *Ibid.*, p. xi.

issues as a pessimist who is defeatist and faint of heart about the future of democracy.

Nonetheless, both apologists and critics are frequently wide of the mark in their views of the American system. Despite the complexity of our constitutional arrangements for the conduct of foreign relations, with its division of powers between the Congress and the President, it is noteworthy that a good deal of flexibility and more continuity than might be expected has resulted. When the major foreign policy decisions of the last decade pass in review, the degree of consensus between the two branches of government is little short of astounding. The United Nations Charter, which repudiated the broad lines of policy of several generations of American policy-makers, was approved overwhelmingly, the North Atlantic Treaty Organization was ratified by a vote of 82 to 13, and the agreement with the federal government of Germany was accepted by the Senate 77 to 5. Even policies affecting troubled and unsettled regions like the Far East and Middle East, where nothing approaching a really promising solution was possible, have ultimately been accepted with less rancorous political debate than political parties might have indulged themselves.

It would serve no purpose, however, to conceal the fact that one source of tension between Britain and America inheres in constitutional and procedural differences. British leaders complain that consultation is difficult if not impossible with this country. The process of rallying a consensus in our vast sprawling continent requires us to say things that we understand but that mislead and confound outsiders. Whereas British foreign policy generally speaks with one voice, the cacophony of American statements is more like a symphony orchestra playing in discordance as often as in harmony. It is never quite clear to what extent American negotiators can commit their government. No one can say how greatly arrangements entered into with American executives may be whittled down in practice. It is puzzling for the outsider at any one time to know where a policy decision rests in the American system. The crucial difference between America and Britain resides in the power of a British sovereign on advice of ministers, to declare war and make treaties while in the United States the war power theoretically falls to Congress and treaties must be concluded by the President with the advice and consent of two-thirds of the Senate present and voting. In practice, the consequences of these differences are less than might be assumed, for the Senate can no longer with fairness be called the "graveyard of treaties." Executive agreements to an ever-increasing degree provide an alternative to the extended process of seeing an agreement through the Senate. Legislative action requiring simple majorities is another practical device for speeding decision, say, on the Marshall Plan and mutual security assistance. The two-thirds requirement with all its difficulties rarely impedes necessary action in foreign policy. It has, however, caused negotiators to proceed with care in making commitments in areas that failed to command broad public agreement.

The nub of the problem in our present discussion has more to do with appearances than with performance. For foreign observers our vast and sprawling governmental arrangements remain a continual source of bewilderment and dismay, of nagging fears and doubts. They note that within a fortnight the President, Secretary of State, and Secretary of Defense may define national policies for vital problems in conflicting and contradictory terms. In the absence of party discipline, prominent congressional leaders—indeed the government's principal leader in Congress—may speak in opposition to the President's announced policy, and in some cases, as with the threat of sanctions against Israel for its so-called aggression against Egypt in the autumn of 1956, apparently succeed in overturning it. An administration must find its support in ever-changing coalitions and the task of its spokesman in

Congress is less that of leader than sheepdog tirelessly round-
ing up wayward and uncertain followers. The Secretary of
State appears before the Congress not as the Foreign Secretary
with the full weight of the Cabinet and the government
behind him but more as a servant, if not a suppliant, of the
most representative branch of the government. Administrative
spokesmen appear before congressional committees not to
debate with the opposition, as in Parliament, but as witnesses
to be examined and cross-examined. Sometimes this relation
may be reasonable and moderate, depending on the temper
and influence of the committee chairman or the skill of the
Assistant Secretary for Congressional Liaison, but again the
principal architect of American foreign policy may be required
to come hat in hand for day after day of relentless and
rancorous questioning. We are told that Secretary Dulles
resolved at all costs to avoid the error of his predecessor
Dean Acheson. He was determined that his congressional
relations not deteriorate, for he believed that this had caused
Mr. Acheson's undoing. Thus he early sought to protect his
flanks in Congress through agreements and concessions to
conservative Republicans. Yet his early successes were to prove
a pyrrhic victory, and they reveal the true nature of an almost
impossible task, for these gestures and pronouncements con-
trived to placate the Right served only to alienate allies abroad
and more liberal supporters at home. Finally, the Secretary
is not master even in his own house. Postwar foreign relations
have resulted in a whole network of important executive
agencies, largely independent of the Department of State.
Most of them have their own missions in foreign capitals
alongside but separate from traditional diplomatic missions.
The Economic Cooperation Administration and the Mutual
Security Agency speak in the name of American foreign policy
but without strong leading strings from the seat of authority,
the State Department. There has even been a separate agency
responsible to the President and not the Secretary for dealing
with disarmament under Harold Stassen.

Thus the American system, while it has worked surprisingly well in practice, continues to confuse and confound those for whom it must ever remain an alien system. Before dismissing their reactions as merely perverse and wrong-headed, we are perhaps well-advised to recall our own uncertainties about those institutions with which we are really quite familiar, including the British parliamentary system.

II. THE BRITISH AND AMERICAN PHILOSOPHIES ON FOREIGN POLICY AND THE PUBLIC

The tensions that result from differences between American and British institutions are less pervasive, intractable, and significant than the conflicts of philosophy. America and Britain, which share a common heritage of legal and political ideas, are at odds in their approach to foreign relations. Their troubles arise partly because the principles on which they act are not clear to one another. Oliver Franks, after completing his years as Ambassador to the United States, wrote: "If I had to state what I thought the most prevalent single cause of misunderstanding and suspicion between the United States and Britain, I should name the failure to communicate the assumptions of a proposal."[29] From socialists like Ernest Bevin or Denis Healey on the Left to conservatives like Captain Thorneycroft and Winston Churchill on the Right, one notes a more or less consistent outlook on the limits and possibilities of foreign policy. Indeed it is possible, and I hope to show that representatives of other British Commonwealth countries follow in substantial measure the broad outlines of this approach. What are the component elements in the British way of thinking about foreign policy? Can we describe it in general terms, recognizing the many exceptions? I believe the chances are good enough to warrant a try and I should like to suggest

[29] Oliver S. Franks, *Britain and the Tide of World Affairs: The BBC Reith Lectures, 1954* (London: Oxford University Press, 1955), pp. 34-35.

that there are four pillars that undergird the British outlook and that are fundamental to understanding this approach.

First, the British outlook is more disposed than the American one, perhaps because of the greater continuity of British experience, to seek the objective historical roots of a problem and to see foreign policies as the means of coping with problems that are never entirely novel or unique. Lester B. Pearson, Nobel laureate, former Secretary of State for External Affairs of Canada and former President of the United Nations Assembly, has warned that "if current opinions and popular prejudices are not to impose themselves with relentless force on our minds, we must judge them in the light of historical knowledge and historical experience, and of the truths that have been tested by such experience."[30] The chief reason for viewing our problems in their historical setting is that they are in one sense the same problems with which men have grappled before. Insecurity, ambition, expansion, and the search for peace and order are timeless issues that loom up again and again. "Though the scale of our political problems has increased, and the stakes have mounted so high that they may involve survival for the human race, the essential character of those problems is not new."[31] Men and states have confronted one another in the past across geography that does not change, embracing values and interests that sometimes persist for generations.

The consequence of such an approach for foreign policy has been to put stress on the inevitability and necessity of continuity in a nation's course of action in world affairs. Moreover, continuity is something more than a thing of the spirit. It takes root in objective material facts. One group in British life has seen continuity in the doctrines of a political party and has maintained that the British socialist movement

---

[30] Lester B. Pearson, *Democracy in World Politics* (Princeton University Press, 1955), p. v.

[31] *Ibid.*, pp. 3-4.

had an unbroken record on foreign policy from its formation at the beginning of the century midway through the century. Party intellectuals like Harold Laski and Leonard Woolf trumpeted the existence of a distinctively socialist approach to foreign policy whose only continuity would be with historic socialist doctrines, not with British experience. Today most objective historians, looking at the actual policies of the socialist government from July 1945 through the end of 1951 as distinct from the echoes of party pronouncements, find striking continuities with the programs of Winston Churchill and his predecessors. Under Ernest Bevin in particular, "the continuity of British foreign policy prevailed because British interests remained the same and the suspicion of state for state survived."[32] The diplomatic performance of the labor government was completely at odds with party proclamations about a distinctively socialist foreign policy. In place of its earlier pious commitments to a new world order free of balance of power politics, militarism, and imperialism in which Left would speak to Left in Britain and Russia, the labor government, once in office, abandoned this naïvely benevolent way of thinking for a firm and realistic postwar policy that took account of the threats to historic British interests. Ernest Bevin and Clement Attlee, who had shared responsibility in wartime for the decisions of the coalition government, rallied the Labour Party to a policy that ran counter to much of the party's ideology and tradition. Bevin in particular was tireless in his efforts to instruct labor members that "revolutions do not change geography, and revolutions do not change geographical needs."[33] More recently it is striking that laborite intellectuals like Denis Healey have sought to reformulate socialist theories to make them accord with the experiences of this period. He declares: "Because the

[32] M. A. Fitzsimons, *The Foreign Policy of the British Labour Government, 1945-51* (Notre Dame, Indiana: University of Notre Dame Press, 1953), p. 179.
[33] *Ibid.*, p. 26.

Party as a whole lacks any systematic theory of world affairs, it has too often fallen victim to the besetting sin of all progressive movements—utopianism. In particular it tends to discount the power element in politics, seeing it as a specific evil of the existing system rather than a generic characteristic of politics as such."[34] Its shortcomings, Healey insists, arise largely because it "has always been more alive to change in world affairs than to continuity."[35] "Though war is at least 3,000 years older than capitalism, many socialists believe that capitalism is the only cause of war, and that therefore the Soviet Union could not commit aggression because it has a 'socialist' economy. Others maintain that the only serious danger of war springs from disparities between the living standards of the peoples; yet it is difficult to find a single war in modern times which was caused primarily by such disparities."[36] Healey's criticism of the Labor Party is primarily for its lack of a sense of history. If politics and interests are permanent rather than transient, any party will have to accept Britain's historic responsibilities, their true configuration, and their continuity with important changes in the present.

This commitment to a historical perspective also affects the estimates that are made of other states. For example, the British outlook has tended to assume that traditional Russian aims have remained broadly the same for several centuries. As a great land-locked empire, Russia has pushed out in a multi-pronged expansionist drive for "windows to the West." Toward the southwest its thrust has been into the Balkans, reaching out especially for control of the Bosphorus and the Dardanelles. Another drive has aimed at filling the void left by the contracting remains of the Ottoman Empire. To the southeast it has sought influence in Persia and Afghanistan and, to the east, control in Outer Mongolia and the Maritime

---

[34] R. H. S. Crossman, et al., *The New Fabian Essays* (New York: Frederick A. Praeger, 1952), pp. 161-62.

[35] *Ibid.*, p. 162.   [36] *Ibid.*, p. 163.

Provinces. The Baltic States have been of concern both to czars and bolsheviks and the denial of Poland to the antagonist has been "a matter of life and death."

Recognition of historic Russian objectives—or, for that matter, the goals of any state—shapes the approach of statesmen and diplomats to concrete problems. Mr. Churchill, for example, maintained both privately and publicly that Soviet interests would have to be recognized. In wartime associations with Premier Stalin, the British Prime Minister repeatedly gave assurances that the West would not tolerate a Polish government unfriendly to the Soviet Union. Following the joint Anglo-Soviet declaration at Yalta, Churchill explained: "The Poles will have their future in their own hands, with the single limitation that they must honestly follow, in harmony with their allies, a policy friendly to Russia. This is surely reasonable."[37] China's conduct in the postwar world was interpreted in its historical context by another British statesman, Woodrow Wyatt, who declared in 1950: "I think that the Chinese are acting, in part, on the basis of their traditional expansionist attitude toward surrounding countries. It has long been a policy of China to expand into other countries in the South and Southeast. . . ."[38] This devotion to history as the informing basis for an understanding of international politics has prompted the British to be keenly sensitive to any encroachment by a great power into an area in which its historic ambitions have long been kept in check. The most recent example is the Middle Eastern crisis and, with its own decline of national power, British promptings of the United States to resist expansion.

Second, Britain and the Commonwealth have had more than their share of policy-makers who justify actions in foreign affairs on grounds of the realities more than as noble ideals or aspirations. Quite obviously there are many statesmen and

[37] *Parliamentary Debates*, Vol. 408, February 27, 1945, p. 1280.
[38] *Ibid.*, Vol. 481, November 30, 1950, p. 1339.

countless situations that offer the adverse case. Mr. Healey has said of the Labor Party, "at worst it is so little conscious of Britain's national interests that its attention can be attracted to world affairs only by high-flown formulas which quickly lose their relevance."[39] We have also the conservative example with which we began this discourse and we think of the promises of Chamberlain, Baldwin, and Gladstone. However, in a speech at Dacca on December 9, 1956, that stamped him as one of Asia's most perceptive leaders, the then Prime Minister of Pakistan, Mr. H. S. Suhrawardy, warned: "Certainly the foreign policy of every country has got to be extremely practical and realistic. It cannot be based on sentiment." The current realities for Pakistan in the case of Egypt are rather instructive. On the one hand, Pakistan with the rest of Asia condemned the Franco-British-Israeli attack on Egypt, although Suhrawardy was unwilling to call it aggression. On the other side he noted: "I find, judging from all the sentiments of the people here, that certain things which unfortunately Egypt has done have rather shaken our faith and made us pause a little and become a little more wise in the precipitancy of our actions." It is fair to suggest that Egypt's support of India on Kashmir and its indifference to the need of Pakistan representation in Cairo were among the realities that prompted this reaction and along with Commonwealth ties tempered Pakistan's moral condemnation of the West. This speech carries realism into other areas and problems and its candor would be remarkable in any free country. On democracy and foreign policy, Suhrawardy observed: "It is not usual . . . to speak on foreign policy at a public gathering and as a matter of fact I shall be very discreet on many points and will have to gloss over many things and also to keep back from you many matters which obviously influence your government in arriving at a certain policy regarding foreign affairs." On the question of total as against limited war:

[39] Crossman, *New Fabian Essays*, p. 162.

"There can be local wars with conventional weapons and we have seen that there have been local wars in which the two blocs have been indirectly drawn in but have refrained from directly attacking each other." And on neutrality: "Now we know that, so far as neutrality in peace is concerned, our country has very little chance of remaining neutral, if it is to the advantage of a big country to overrun it for tactical and strategic reasons. As I have already pointed out, on more than one occasion, that when Germany wanted to attack France it did not consider at all whether Holland or Belgium was neutral. It chose to overrun them in order to attack France and turn the Maginot Line. Hence, by remaining neutral you do not escape the chance of being attacked."

We began our discussion with the example of Winston Churchill's defense of the Yalta agreements, but I would mislead you by leaving an impression that Churchill was prone to justify foreign policy solely in moralistic terms. We recall his statement that: "Foreign policy is not a game, nor is it an academic question, and . . . not an ideological question. . . . Foreign policy is in fact a method of protecting our own interests and saving our own people from the threat of another war, and it is against that criterion that the foreign policy of any government has to be measured."[40] The problems that face a nation that would preserve its national security call for flexibility in the choice of alternatives. It may be said of foreign policy as of war: "The best plan of acquiring flexibility is to have three or four plans for all the probable contingencies, all worked out with the utmost detail. Then it is much easier to switch from one to the other as and where the cat jumps."[41] These alternatives are never wholly satisfying, and they conflict with one another in various ways. One day Britain opposes Spain, say, for membership in the United

[40] *Parliamentary Debates*, Vol. 427, October 23, 1946, p. 1706.
[41] Winston S. Churchill, *The Second World War: Closing the Ring*, Vol. v (Boston, Houghton Mifflin Co., 1951), p. 162.

Nations; later it seeks for itself and others diplomatic relations with the same country. In one context, the Soviet Union is the threat, but, with the rise of the Nazis, Churchill said bluntly he would make a pact with the devil himself to stop Germany's expansion. Policies like these must be justified not in absolute but practical terms, as when Churchill on October 18, 1951, defended Britain's program in the Middle East by saying: "Our own self-interest demands that we take cognizance of the Muslim world, its legitimate aspirations, and try to help out."[42]

A third quality of Britain's approach is a characteristic conception of the function and scope of international institutions. For the overwhelming majority of British statesmen the United Nations has been a forum for discussion and negotiation. It has rarely been conceived of as a law-making or law-enforcing body. By claiming too much for its authority, the United Nations risks discrediting the very idea of international order. Its possibilities for private or quiet diplomacy are as great as its role for parliamentary or public diplomacy. According to this conception, the time is not yet ripe for genuine legislation or the application of sanctions to compel action by this international body, but there are numerous activities in which it can fruitfully and effectively engage. The corollary of this view is the recognition that a multitude of diplomatic activities can be carried on outside the United Nations and indeed the charter urges members to seek first an adjustment of their conflicts before bringing them into United Nations. "The development of common interests or the establishment of a stable power pattern must precede and not follow the creation of rigid legal or institutional forms."[43]

Moreover, there is less disposition among British statesmen to equate the moral law and United Nations resolutions. Rather than conceiving the United Nations as somehow the

---

[42] *The Times* (London), October 19, 1951, p. 5.
[43] Crossman, *New Fabian Essays*, p. 170.

embodiment of moral virtues, thus confusing positive and natural law, the British prefer to see it as a piece of political machinery whose decisions are an outcome of the cut and thrust among national delegations interacting with one another.

Additionally, other international institutions carry on their world programs and the international system so-called is a pyramid with the United Nations at the top. Denis Healey suggests that nations might "create regional institutions linking countries which are likely to have a continuing common interest however the major changes in the world develop."[44] If world politics calls for anything, it is for restraints on power and the host of international institutions that have a purpose to serve is striking. In the future one Britisher predicts: ". . . the adjustment of national differences by negotiation and compromise will become more urgent than the construction of international institutions or the execution of moral blueprints."[45] In Europe, particularly, Britain will have a more important role to play.

Fourth, the hallmark of Britain's foreign policy is its self-conscious pragmatism, its acknowledged acceptance of palliatives when fundamental solutions appear beyond reach, and its emphasis on compromise and trial and error. How often does one read the injunction, "We should look round in our empirical fashion for ways of meeting our problem." British pragmatism has run counter to the American disposition to declare its intentions by drawing a line and making it clear to friend and foe alike that aggression across this line will be resisted, if necessary by war. We say this prevents a miscalculation such as brought on World War I. A British diplomatist has commented: This "does not come so naturally to us. We prefer to deal with events as they arise and not be committed by answering hypothetical questions."[46] Some of the techniques

---

[44] *Ibid.*, p. 173.   [45] *Ibid.*, p. 179.
[46] Franks, *Britain and the Tide of World Affairs*, p. 33.

of policy promise limited successes at best. "There are such things as the neutralized zone or buffer, which has been tried by land in Korea, and might perhaps usefully be attempted elsewhere on land or water. There are cease-fire, truce and stand-still arrangements, and agreements not to use force in a given situation."[47] In Lester Pearson's view, "Wise men should not scorn devices or expedients of this kind which can gain time for more fundamental solutions to mature. . . ."[48] Probably this outlook has its origins in the limits of Britain's or Canada's power, itself encouraging prudence, patience, and accommodation. Not by accident Pearson and others in this tradition have been untiring in urging this approach in and outside the United Nations. They have been opposed to proclamations that were founded on absolutes, including absolute force. Massive retaliation is hardly a congenial doctrine for this school of thought. "There is something very frightening about the idea of playing 'all or nothing' with any kind of weapon." "Except in the event of a reciprocal spasm of mutual annihilation, the free world's force should be used only for limited political objectives, of which the chief will be to deter aggression; or if it breaks out, to localize it, defeat it and prepare the way for a peace settlement. This is something different from the doctrine of massive retaliation. It is less a matter of punishing the aggressor than of defending the area of freedom and preventing another conflict."[49] This is pragmatism in foreign affairs, pragmatism which in recent years has had to take for granted accommodation, retreat, the severe limits of British power.

The American outlook, like the British, is a product of national character and tradition. Denis W. Brogan, comparing the present-day American scene to the America he encountered in 1925 for the first time, writes: "Compared with the European, the American is still optimistic, cheerful, energetic—convinced that if not all is for the best in the best of all pos-

[47] Pearson, *Democracy*, p. 19. [48] *Ibid.*, p. 19. [49] *Ibid.*, pp. 33-34.

sible countries, it is on the way to becoming so."[50] This has colored the American attitude toward international institutions and toward prospects of a brave new world. If we seek for the roots of this viewpoint, we are likely to find them in the confluence of two profound intellectual forces: the French enlightenment and sectarian Christian perfectionism. These attitudes fed on successive milestones in American history that seemed to confirm, embody, and establish their truth. The American Revolution became the national epic which vindicated the heroic properties of reason and virtue. It established God's American Israel. These heroic origins of the American Republic signified more than the birth of a new state; they made possible a new way of life in which freedom and truth reigned supreme. The American Revolution is the background against which the future of all colonial peoples are judged. The tension that grew up between Churchill and Roosevelt at the end of World War II on the question of colonialism and empire had its roots in the influence that the Revolution exerted on their respective world-views. In this country we have been prone to feel that enslaved peoples everywhere can and should take the course we chose in 1776, while the British see the evolution of freedom more in the image of members of the British Commonwealth. Another milestone, incidentally, is the American intervention in 1917, which tipped the scales in favor of the allied powers. The British viewed this action in the light of the eighteenth or nineteenth century as a measure to restore equilibrium to Europe. The American conception preferred to view it as the action of the self-conscious saviour of mankind.

Down to the present day, rationalism and perfectionism are the well-spring from which our proclamations on foreign policy take their strength. We are offended to think that the aims of a foreign policy are limited, that the object of war is not victory but specified political objectives, that a balance of

[50] *Harper's Magazine*, Vol. 214, No. 1281, February 1957, p. 27.

power and balance of terror have become the deterrents of warfare, that if conflict breaks out our first interest should be in localizing and containing it, that we should think less about punishing an aggressor and more about preventing new conflicts, and that Communist strategy when it seeks to exploit our "contradictions" may, though uttering another Marxist cliché, point to the hidden source of our problems with other parts of the world. Foreign policy is only rarely justified in terms of the imperatives of national existence, even when its foundations are consciously and deliberately based on them. "It is a very perilous thing," President Wilson declared in an address at Mobile on October 27, 1913, "to determine the foreign policy of a nation in the terms of material interest. . . . We dare not turn from the principle that morality and not expediency is the thing that must guide us, and that we will never condone iniquity because it is most convenient to do so."[51] It would be degrading to our own people and to peoples in other lands to confess the ambiguities of our actions. Thus the Truman Doctrine of March 12, 1957, which was a rational and expedient act designed to replace British with American power in central Europe, was presented as the defense of free democratic nations everywhere in the world against "direct or indirect aggression." It translated a concrete American interest for a limited area of the world into a general principle of worldwide validity, to be applied regardless of the limits of American interests and powers. It is said that this general doctrine, which in its universalistic terms provided so little guidance to action, had to be cast in this mold. Congressional support required for popular support was possible only in the framework of an anti-communist crusade. Later on, however, it was necessary for Secretary of State Dean Acheson to reformulate the Truman Doctrine in a speech before the National Press Club on January 12, 1950: "I hear almost every day someone say that the real interest of the United

[51] Quoted in Hans J. Morgenthau and Kenneth W. Thompson, *Principles and Problems of International Politics* (New York: Alfred A. Knopf, 1950), p. 24.

States is to stop the spread of Communism. Nothing seems to me to put the cart before the horse more completely than that." The thing to oppose, he noted, is Russian imperialism of which communism is but "the most subtle instrument . . . the spearhead." The Marshall Plan was represented as a means of guaranteeing that Europe would be immune to communist infiltration and make further aid unnecessary. In recent days the debate on the Eisenhower Doctrine has once more revived this same issue. What is it we oppose in the Middle East? Is it nationalism, communism, or Soviet penetration? The answers to this are symptomatic of the confusion we feel, partly because such questions are alien to the American penchant for justifying policies in terms of universal claims. Perhaps some of our British friends are right when they observe: "By temperament most Americans are men of action. Faced with a situation they feel frustrated unless they are doing something about it. Time for them is an enemy to be overcome, not, as we British tend to think, an ally to work with. They find release in action, in getting over and done with."[52] Perhaps this is why we prefer to see something total and all-inclusive like communism as the enemy we oppose and whom we are to overcome.

It is also broadly true that the historical roots of problems occupy us less immediately than they do the British. It is said that "the American judges persons and nations more by their present than their past and more by his estimate of their future than their present."[53] This is perhaps not surprising. Within a brief decade Americans have been torn from the privacy of domestic pursuits and thrust into a position of world leadership. The past half-century has witnessed the discovery that the world was our proper concern. Is it any wonder that, compared to a nation with several centuries of world leadership, we should be less disposed to look to the ancient and forgotten sources of a problem? Nazism and

[52] Franks, *Britain and the Tide of World Affairs*, p. 32.
[53] *Ibid.*, p. 35.

communism have been treated as forces that were entirely unique but with their weakening or disappearance old problems return to plague us.

The wonder is that, despite its uncertainties and its lack of a period of apprenticeship, American foreign policy has evolved a relatively consistent course of action. It has met and for the most part checked Russian expansion. It has accepted its international responsibilities around the globe. However, these actions are not always clear outside our own borders. A leading British diplomatist has explained: "There are many . . . who have based their judgment of America on what Washington says, instead of what Washington does. And it is a dangerous procedure."[54] Its deeds have been better than its words and when new events have called for new directions it has proved itself worthy of the task. Leaders who have not themselves been particularly distinguished have seemed in responsible positions to rise to their responsibilities. Moreover, the sense of moral mission has been the fuel that empowered Americans to go beyond any narrow sense of duty and interest. In summary, the tension between the American and British philosophies of international relations stems less from any conflict of thought-in-action and more from the gap between American words and deeds. Taken as a whole, postwar American foreign policy has been moderately prudent and realistic. Its justification has been less in the framework of concepts of political realism and more in the tradition of the rationalism and legalism which prevailed in the 1920's and 1930's. Ironically enough, the philosophy of international politics of the philosophers, columnists, and planners which we examined earlier is closer to the British than the American approach. This leaves American foreign policy with foundations for action that are misleading, misconceived, and likely to produce sharp reactions. American policy-makers have continued to talk in the slogans that intellectuals espoused before World War II. There has been what amounts to a cultural lag be-

[54] *Ibid.*, p. 30.

tween the best theories of international politics and the ones expressed by policy-makers. Thus Mr. Dulles maintained that moral force is a motive power in forcing states like Britain or France or Russia to behave in certain ways. This notion of an autonomous moral force was characteristic of earlier thinking, but scholars today relate moral force to coercive power whenever they seek to trace the impact of an all-powerful idea. Policy-makers cling to a doctrine of aggression that is vaguely reminiscent of the Pact of Paris concept that aggression must and would be outlawed once and for all. Modern thinkers are more inclined to see aggression as but one of many crimes that this tragic and unhappy world fosters, and they are less sanguine about proscribing it especially by legal fiat. Yet modern American leaders continue to think and speak in the discourse of an earlier age.

There is a kind of final irony in the tension existing in the realm of philosophy that exacerbates Anglo-American relations. American policy, which in certain respects has been more realistic than British policy, clings to doctrines and justifications that are at least partly obsolete. When British decision-makers take America at its word, they run the risk of denouncing words that obscure realistic decisions or of confounding claims with intentions and results. In the final analysis this problem is probably the chief cause of tension between the two philosophies and in a deeper sense it is the chief problem that Britain and America share in common. "There is a risk of too wide a gap developing between those who govern us and us who are governed."[55] If the hiatus grows too wide between the leaders who speak in one language to one another and in a different way to those who are led, foreign policy or democracy or both must perish, victims of a challenge that proved greater than human resources. The future of the West may hang on our ability to meet this profound issue.

[55] *Ibid.*, p. 63.

III. THE UNSOLVED PROBLEMS IN STATESMANSHIP
AND THEORY

The tension between Britain and the United States need
not obscure the unities between us. It is appropriate to call
attention to the indissoluble bond that joins English-speaking
peoples. We share a common cultural heritage and social and
political accomplishments that lead even writers as judicious
as Walter Lippmann to speak of us as one people. The issue
that is raised by recent events is whether this community can
withstand the burdens of three major unsolved problems. The
first arises from the frightening loss of prestige and power by
Britain and by other European powers, accompanied by an
equally frightening accretion of power by the United States.
Britain's loss of prestige is frightening because its foreign
policy was enhanced by its reputation for success. Can it survive the gnawing awareness, both in Britain and abroad, that
it can no longer be master of its fate? America's growth in
strength is frightening because we are inexperienced in shoul-
dering the vast responsibilities in world affairs, having moved
to the center of the stage only a short decade ago. We shall
be endlessly tempted to conceive the impotence of our friends
as a sign of our own omnipotence, their loss of prestige as
proof of our increase in moral stature, and their retreat as a
token of our advance. Most perilous of all, we are bound to
compare our success and their failures and interpret it as a
ratification of a moralistic over a pragmatic approach. Much
as the Puritans saw wealth as a proof of virtue, some of our
leaders point with pride to the triumph of moral force. The
shift of power from Europe and Britain to the United States
makes for frustration, and, in the extreme, acts of desperation, for those who have lost their power. On the other side
of the Atlantic it can also make for pride, vainglory, and a
tendency to obscure the vestigial prestige that Britain enjoys
in areas like India, where curiously enough British policy was

the result of declining British power and the plausibility of freedom as a moral principle. It is worth considering that the United States, as it inherits Britain's world responsibilities, also takes on the moral burden that falls to those who wield influence over others. Hence Britain's predicament is our problem and we would do well to be as diligent in searching for points of concurrence between our mutual interests as we are in proclaiming our superior power and virtue. Writing of the recent catastrophe in the Middle East, an Indian commentator, the editor of *The Eastern Economist*, observed: "The U.S.A. had no consistent policy in the area. Mr. Dulles seemed unaware that innumerable countries friendly to the U.S.A. had any stake in the use of the Suez Canal or Arabian oil, or in keeping the U.S.S.R. out. He was thus breaking the first rule of a foreign policy: Find out who your friends are and help their interests along. If you don't you must not be surprised if they ultimately, in desperation, decide to act without you. Equally, the natural friends of France and Britain in Asia were conscious of the evils of colonialism to the point of failing to see who their friends were and where their interests lay."[56]

A second unsolved problem results from our conflicting views over the nature of the diplomatic process. We have been more inclined to see negotiations as activities which were successful and honorable only when carried on in the spotlight of public opinion. From President Wilson's slogan of "open covenants openly arrived at" to President Eisenhower's yearning to turn over the negotiation of a Middle Eastern settlement to the United Nations, this trend of thought has been dominant, though lately more among statesmen than philosophers. Yet the progress of recent weeks in the mitigation of these conflicts has resulted almost entirely from the efforts at private or "quiet diplomacy" of men like Lester

[56] Odysseus "Foreign Policies Without Power," *The Eastern Economist*, Vol. XXVIII, No. 6, February 8, 1957, p. 189.

Pearson, Dag Hammarskjöld, and Secretary Dulles. The difference between their approach lies in the willingness of only one to explain what experience had taught him. Mr. Pearson characterizes the Wilsonian slogan as "of very doubtful validity."[57] He warns that we flatter ourselves if we think that "face" is an Oriental monopoly or that Western diplomats can afford to take stands for public consumption and then abandon them at will. On the contrary, "few things seem harder to abandon than the bold black headline which at the beginning of the conference has announced your policy to the world: few things harder to face than the wrath of the radio or news pundit who, after having already proclaimed that policy to be superlatively wise and one which he has been advocating all along, then finds that it has been changed."[58] The purpose of negotiation is the reconciliation of interests; this is made more difficult when compromise becomes equivalent to capitulation if not treason. "In serious negotiations, if you succeed in finding a satisfactory and honourable compromise you have not surrendered, you have succeeded."[59] Yet the public, if it has been told, say, that any relations with China or Yugoslavia or Poland are immoral, cannot but view renewed contracts with them, whatever the benefits, as rootless surrender of principle.

A third unsolved problem is, of course, the one with which we opened our discussion: the dilemma of conducting foreign policy in a democracy. With all of its troublesome problems, we would have reason for optimism if certain things were true. If one could say that American statesmen were as forthright in pointing out the nature of the problem as are Pearson, Suhrawardy, or Churchill, we could be hopeful. If our theorists and our political leaders spoke with one voice, we could be hopeful. If public opinion periodically became impatient with slogans and simple formulas, we could be hopeful. If the American President saw it as his duty to take the people

[57] Pearson, *Democracy*, p. 56. [58] *Ibid.*, pp. 56-57. [59] *Ibid.*, p. 58.

into his confidence, to guide and instruct them in the harsh realities with which he is daily confronted, we could be hopeful. If our allies were as tolerant of the outbursts of public emotion on this side of the Atlantic as they are of their own, we could be hopeful. Until this bright and happy day, however, the most we can hope is that our leaders may come to reflect an underlying realism and wisdom that can come only as we improve our instincts and philosophy if not our comprehensive knowledge of foreign relations. One slight ground for hope rests in the fact that another democratic people developed these instincts at least to a limited degree. If statesmen can summon the moral courage for dealing with real issues, for narrowing the gap between foreign policy for the public and foreign policy for the diplomats, and for using the powers they have, then these unsolved problems may yield. The challenge is very great. In the words of Lord Strang, it is nothing less than the dilemma of democratic diplomacy. If we quote his somber words in conclusion, it is not to contribute despair but to indicate the order of the challenge. He notes:

"It cannot be denied that this public ventilation and discussion of the issues of foreign policy, often at awkward moments, has a hampering effect upon the flexibility, resourcefulness, and imagination with which diplomatic operations might otherwise be more fruitfully conducted. The publicity has in large measure, and rightly, done away with the secret treaty; but it has also impaired the secrecy of negotiation and the secrecy of negotiation is the essence of diplomacy. It may be questioned, too, whether the impact of public opinion upon the action of governments will always make for peace and international understanding. Even with the most responsible public opinion and the best kind of government, it might on the contrary make for worse rather than better international relations. 'Parliaments,' it has been said, 'are usually more nationalistic and belligerent than executives, and people than parliaments.' But, on the other hand, there are times, which we have known in our own experience, when peoples will go to the other extreme and neglect their future security. . . . In the home field, one symptom of this lack of resolve is the drift to inflation: in the foreign field it can lead all to easily to policies of appeasement."[60]

It will not help to hide our heads in the sand or to make soothing statements to bolster morale. These are real and genuine problems to be faced bravely and well.

IV. ONE WORD OF HOPE

The importance of the American trend of thought described in earlier pages rests precisely in its capacity for supplying partial answers to some of the problems. Recognition of difficulties need not lead to an impasse. The political realism associated with Lippmann, Spykman, and Niebuhr embraces intellectual resources sufficient to fill the gap in an American outlook that appears inadequate. Executive leadership, honesty as to goals and limitations, and the replacing of a fatuous moralism that misleads the people, confuses our allies, and deceives our foes—all lie within reach. They await only a more courageous acceptance by leaders who aspire to statesmanship worthy of the name.

[60] *The Listener*, No. 1451, p. 93.

PART TWO

THE CENTRAL PROBLEMS OF
FOREIGN POLICY

CHAPTER 4

THE LIMITS OF PRINCIPLE IN
INTERNATIONAL POLITICS: NECESSITY AND
THE NEW BALANCE OF POWER

[If the moralist] is to deserve a hearing among his
fellows, he must set himself this task which is so much
humbler than to command and so much more difficult
than to exhort: he must seek to anticipate and to supple-
ment the insight of his fellow men into the problems of
their adjustment to reality.—WALTER LIPPMANN

No PROBLEM on the agenda of America's relations with the
rest of the world is more bewildering, compelling, and ultimately decisive than the moral evaluation of foreign policy.
It must be apparent in the second decade of the Cold War
that we judge ourselves and in turn are judged by the principles we affirm and those we realize. National morale and
international prestige are casualties of moral outlooks that
are either too egocentric or too pretentious. A country's moral
stock in the world rises and falls as its moral claims are
plausible and convincing and its policies in line with its
declarations. Yet intellectuals and policy-makers alike are
alternately tempted to exaggerate or underestimate the influence of moral principles and fall prey either to moralism or
cynicism. Perhaps this is more true of the United States than
the rest of the English-speaking world, where questions of
political morality are decided in specific cases as required by
contemporary events, oftentimes with the conscious avoidance
of generalized propositions. In any event, most Americans
are offended to know that principle and necessity are fre-

quently in conflict when man acts politically. They are distressed to learn that it is the essence of politics that man chooses goals and objectives which are limited both in application and scope and therefore fully satisfying only for particular groups and nations. For example, in practice those measures which are for the good of labor often work an injustice upon management. Only in pure thought can actions and policies remain uncorrupted and undefiled by at least some margin of injustice, even though philosophers from Adam Smith to Kenneth Arrow would dispose of this tragic dimension of social choice through one artifact or another. This universal aspect of the corruption of absolute justice within the realm of politics finds its outstanding expression in international politics. There my nation's justice can mean your nation's injustice, my nation's security and its requirements can appear as the cause of your nation's insecurity. Armaments, defense preparations, and alliances essential to a nation's safety are simultaneously a threat to security as viewed through other eyes.

Faced with such conflicts, the moralist maintains that at present men pursue a double standard of conduct in their private and public lives. Privately, man is honest and ethical; publicly, he covers his acts with a tissue of lies and deception. His virtue in private affairs is seen as the conquest of culture over barbarism, of a rational age over an irrational one. In an earlier stage in man's evolution, his private conduct was marred by brutality and violence, but education, a legal order, and free institutions transformed him. In a similar way the cultural lag from which nations have suffered in international relations is perceptibly being erased. The forward march of history is carrying nations from a retarded condition into a new and enlightened era when private standards will become public international rules. Those who doubt are denounced as foes of progress and men of little faith.

The shattering effects of two World Wars have thrown a

dash of political realism on the sanguine expectations of this moralistic viewpoint. Its hopes and predictions bear little resemblance to the recent conduct of states. The melancholy unfolding of the past four decades has left the most ardent believers shaken and uncertain; in practice, simple moralistic viewpoints have tended to induce their opposite, namely, a bleak and hopeless cynicism. The cynic, diametrically opposed to the moralist, tends to argue that politics and ethics diverge only because they are unlike quantities. Politics are means and ethics are ends. Means may be evil, but good ends, to which means are subordinated, can endow means with good ethical content. The dictum that the end justifies the means seems in the realm of politics to furnish a simple clue to the problem. Yet for men and for nations, the universal practice is to justify every evil measure by claiming it serves an ethical goal. For Stalin the gross brutality of liquidating the kulaks found justification as an inevitable step in the history-fulfilling communist design; for Hitler the cremation of so-called inferior races was excused as a necessary hygienic measure if Teutonic superiority were to continue unimpaired. Since nations in the present anarchic world society tend to be repositories of their own morality, the ends-means formula has prevailed as an answer to the moral dilemma, for undeniably it is a concealed but essential truth that nations tend to create their own morality. In its extreme form, however, this development has found nations accepting as ethical whatever redounded to their own material advantage and judging whatever was detrimental to their purposes as immoral and evil. Yet it inheres in the nature of man and politics that statesmen and nations never wholly escape the judgment of elementary ethical standards. The history of politics discloses that no people have completely divorced politics from ethics; that, however grudgingly, they have come to see that men were required to conform to standards more objective than those of success. Neither moralism nor cynicism has the intellectual resources for illuminating these vital issues. Fortunately we are free to turn to other contemporary alternatives.

I. FOUR CONTEMPORARY APPROACHES TO PRINCIPLE AND NECESSITY

One source of hope is the intellectual ferment that results as outstanding minds turn to reflect on these problems. It has been said that first-class problems attract first-class minds; by this test the moral problem has in recent years proved one of our most challenging and persistent concerns. Four writers in particular have probed more deeply than many of their contemporaries: one a historian, another a legal philosopher and international jurist, a third a political theorist and a fourth a theologian. Quite obviously others have made significant contributions, but this group is noteworthy—to paraphrase William James—for making an unusually stubborn attempt to think clearly. Moreover, the conclusions they draw, while complementary, are not identical; from their differences as well as agreements certain guiding principles emerge.

Herbert Butterfield, the Cambridge historian and Master of Peterhouse, has analyzed international morality and the historical process in a series of important writings. The most characteristic statement of his viewpoint appears in books like *Christianity, War and Diplomacy; Christianity and History* and *Christianity and European History*. Morality, in his view, is not one thing for the statesman and another thing for the rest of mankind. There is no such thing as a separate political ethic. Philosophers and poets, no less than decision-makers, must daily choose not between good and evil but between lesser evils or partial goods. The quality of the decision fundamentally at least is no different in politics or business, education or family life. Therefore Butterfield has argued: "I don't see why in politics the virtues which I associate with the Christian religion should be suspended: humility, charity, self-judgment, and acceptance of the problem Providence sets

138

before one; also a disposition not to direct affairs as a sovereign will in the world but to make one's action a form of cooperation with Providence."[1]

Professor Butterfield grounds his conception of international morality in three general propositions. First, morality as he conceives it derives ultimately from a "higher law" espoused alike by "lapsed Christians" and religious thinkers, according to which nothing but human beings exist or matter. Second, morality must be sharply distinguished from every form of moralistic program and creed that, embodied in a crusade, would claim for its partial insights a more ultimate standing than they deserve. Third, an international order exists as the ultimately relevant objective standard against which national interests must be measured.

The first proposition prompts Professor Butterfield to insist that the social order requires men who would preserve themselves and their values to have "respect for the other man's personality, the other man's end. . . ."[2] In a word, men in the final analysis live in a moral order, however ambiguous its particular forms and expressions may be. Present-day thought has difficulty with this conception, for, on the one hand, liberal philosophies that accept as their sole premise the "rights of man" run the risk of encouraging an unbridled egotism according to which man need obey the law only if he agrees with it. On the other hand, thinking that starts with the "duties of man" is likely to end by making him the slave of the state. That is why both man and the state must be subject to a transcendent moral and political order that prompts them to treat one another as more than means to an end. In this connection "if in the Anglo-Saxon world there has been the necessary amount of the spirit of give-and-take,

[1] Herbert Butterfield, "Morality and Historical Process in International Affairs," unpublished manuscript for June 12, 1956, meeting of Columbia University Seminar on Theory of International Politics, p. 1.
[2] *Ibid.*, p. 2.

the disposition to compromise, respect for the other man's opinion and the reluctance to resort to desperation-policies,"[3] this may be due to our greater security, longer political experience, or state of urbanity free from violence, but it may also be due to the survival of religious influences. We are members of a single Western civilization or cultural community that embraces the moral criteria of the Judaeo-Christian tradition. In some communities, the absence of "a higher law" or regulative principle makes for doctrinaire politics and "those who have no religion are particularly liable to bring a religious fanaticism to problems of mundane organization which ought to be matters for transaction and negotiation. Lord Acton was probably right when he said that liberty is impossible except amongst people who have a sense that the whole political game is being played in a realm over which there rules a higher law."[4]

If the beginning of wisdom is the recognition that men live finally in some kind of a moral order, the next step is an awareness that the moral is not the merely moralistic. Moral judgments can sometimes be used as a screen to conceal practical responsibilities to society and to oneself. "A careless librarian, who establishes no regular system for the checking of his books may be satisfied just to heap blame on the people whose delinquencies have resulted in gaps in his shelves."[5] His pious preachments against dishonesty and in favor of virtue can hardly excuse his lack of responsibility. Moreover, moral judgments may also spill over into Pharisaism exemplified by the priggish moralizers Christ condemned in the Gospels. If there are obscurities in the Gospels, this text is not among them. Nothing is clearer than the distinction between those who claim to be and those who are righteous. We recall the parable of the Pharisee and the publican in the eighteenth chapter of the Gospel according to St. Luke: "Two men went

[3] *Ibid.*   [4] *Ibid.*   [5] *Ibid.*, p. 3.

up to the temple to pray; the one a Pharisee, and the other a publican. The Pharisee stood and prayed thus with himself, God, I thank thee, that I am not as other men are, extortioners, unjust, adulterers, or even as this publican. . . . And the publican standing afar off, would not lift up so much as his eyes unto heaven, but smote upon his breast, saying, God be merciful to me a sinner. I tell you, this man went down to his house justified rather than the other: for every one that exalteth himself shall be abased, and he that humbleth himself shall be exalted." The moral lesson to be drawn is not that some states are pharisaic and others publicans but rather that all nations are strongly disposed to endow their particular national ethical systems with universal validity. Nations find themselves today in a situation not too dissimilar from that obtaining domestically within the United States prior to the Civil War. The sanctities of religion and science are invoked to show that one course of action, one nation's program, will execute a divine mandate. Nations go to war not in dispute over territorial boundaries but to make the world safe for democracy or to destroy human wickedness incarnated in evil men like Hitler and Mussolini. Wars of righteousness in which compromise and limited objectives are looked on as treason are today's counterpart of earlier historical wars of religion.

Professor Butterfield's diagnosis of the present crisis brings him to offer some practical alternatives. He finds that "once the aggressor is held in check, and once a balance of forces is achieved, the healing processes of time, and these alone, can solve our problem. . . ."[6] The core of his prescription for peace and morality, therefore, is time and the absence of war and revolution. Any conflict that time and reason cannot solve will not be solved by war. He is persuaded that it is possible to live with ideological deadlocks and to discover a modus

[6] *Ibid.*

141

vivendi, as in the struggle between Catholicism and Protes-
tantism, and Islam and Christianity. With patience and good
luck, justice can eventually emerge. His critics ask whether
this is not a counsel of perfection. How would this precept
have applied to Hitler? Apparently Butterfield believes that
a balance of forces against Hitler sometime prior to 1939
might have prevented the conflict and allowed time to work
its healing effect.

A more general alternative to wars of righteousness is a
restoration of the international order. "On moral grounds, as
well as on prudential calculations, national egotism requires
to be checked, superseded and transcended."[7] Partly this
demands "every possible variation and extension of the art of
putting oneself—and actually feeling oneself—in the other
person's [or nation's] place."[8] It requires states to recognize
themselves as imperfect parts of an imperfectly ethical world
and to show somewhat greater awareness of the moral complexities and disparities in the objective environment underlying the state behavior of others. Beyond this, statesmen
must ask the question whether their policies are likely to
produce the kind of international order in which their own
values can survive. In this sense they transcend national self-
interest at the point of the query, "Everything considered,
what is best for the world?" Indeed "a state may fairly ac-
quire virtue from the very fact that it contrives to make its
self-interest harmonize with something that is good for the
world in general."[9] A case in point may be the liquidation of
large segments of the British Empire when morality and the
necessity of reducing its overseas commitments converged in
a common policy. In this same connection, the intrinsic logic

[7] *Ibid.*, p. 10.
[8] Professor Butterfield distinguishes between the moralist and the statesman
in this way: "The moralist and the teacher, the prophet and the preacher,
address themselves to the improvement of human nature itself. . . . The
statesman is concerned to improve human conduct rather by the process of
rectifying conditions." *Ibid.*, pp. 8-9.
[9] *Ibid.*, p. 10.

of the Marshall Plan comes naturally to mind. In Mr. Butterfield's words: "Whether we are practising diplomacy, or conducting a war, or negotiating a peace treaty, our ultimate objective is the maintenance and the development of an international order. This is the purpose which transcends national egotism and puts the boundary to self-interest—the purpose to which all our more immediate aims in foreign policy have reference."[10]

It is striking that another tiny European country has given us the second writer of note on international morality. Judge Charles de Visscher of Belgium is a philosopher and international jurist, formerly a member of the International Court of Justice and now Professor at the University of Louvain. An English translation of his classic treatise, *Theory and Reality in Public International Law* has recently been published by the Princeton University Press. In importance it has already been compared by some to the writings of Grotius and Vattel. Whatever its place in the annals may be, however, its doctrines for present-day international law are profoundly significant. In the first place, Judge de Visscher's writings strike a distinct counterbeat to the overly sanguine propositions of many Western international lawyers and moralists who, he implies, have sought to build upon a heedless sacrifice of reality. He finds few basic solidarities in the international order; he looks for but cannot find a genuine world community. By contrast, the modern state owes its historical cohesion to external pressures and resulting national loyalties. In contact with the world outside, the state, like any social group, becomes conscious of itself and its solidarities. International society, lacking in these incentives to greater solidarity, substitutes for them an appeal to sacrifice and to a common supranational good, but this perception is closed to the great majority of mankind. In the state vital interests and the most highly political experiences evoke supreme solidarities. In

[10] *Ibid.*, p. 11.

the international realm, the opposite is true, for minor solidarities of an economic or technical order can be found, but the nearer one approaches vital questions, such as the preservation of peace and the prevention of war, the less influence the community has on its members. "If the international community, or more accurately the sense of such a community, finds so little echo in individual consciences, this is less because power obstructs it than because of the immense majority of men are still infinitely less accessible to the doubtless real but certainly remote solidarities that it evokes than to the immediate and tangible solidarities that impose themselves upon them in the framework of national life."[11]

Moreover, Judge de Visscher believes that "neither politics nor law will ensure equilibrium and peace in the world without the 'moral infrastructure.'" This structure is essential to understanding contemporary world politics. At present, in matters political, men are disposed to transfer their most important moral impulses to the state. "The morality that peoples practice in their mutual relations is in large measure the product of their historical partitioning. They are refractory to a higher morality only because their sentiments like their interests continue to gravitate exclusively about the units which are today the Nation-States. These, though theoretically subordinate to the higher unity are in fact real and almost absolute centers of moral cohesion."[12] "Sacred egoism," the fascist formula, was only the most blustering expression of collective morality, which makes the national good the supreme good and civil duty the absolute duty. "Merely to invoke the idea of an international community, as the habit is, is immediately to move into a vicious circle, for it is to postulate in men, shut in their national compartments, something they still largely lack, namely the community spirit, the

[11] Charles de Visscher, *Theory and Reality in Public International Law*, tr. by Percy Corbett (Princeton: Princeton University Press, 1956), p. 92.
[12] *Ibid.*, p. 94.

deliberate adherence to supranational values."[13] Judge de Visscher is sharply critical of much of earlier international law and bases his indictment largely on grounds that "it exaggerated the specificity of international law, separating it off from the moral, social and political data which form its sphere of application and condition its effectiveness."[14] Every legal or social reform that would be successful must take account of the moral infrastructure. The failures of collective security, of the outlawry of war, and of the belief that states would be swayed by appeals to world public opinion are all examples of thinking that suffers from the illusion that moral foundations are unimportant. Political community has its roots in moral factors unhappily sometimes missing in many of the areas that have taken on recent importance in American foreign relations.

It is a fair question, then, to ask how Judge de Visscher seeks to meet these seemingly overwhelming and impossible problems. If we can give a much too abbreviated response, he calls for a drastic change in the modern conception of the state and its power: "These [concepts] pulled down from their present eminence as the supreme goals of political organ- ization, must be subordinated to the ends of the human person."[15] The human ends of politics and the obstacles to their attainment are the common problems of contemporary law and politics, whether in the national or international sphere. The human end of politics from a purely formal point of view "may be defined as the pursuit of the common good, understood as that which in a community should ensure the good of each in the good of the collectivity."[16] Whenever the notion of the common good is no longer harnessed to human ends, a fatal deterioration in the ends of power sets in. These human ends have been dealt with somewhat naïvely and impatiently in some of the declarations by the United

[13] *Ibid.*, p. 98.   [14] *Ibid.*, p. xi.
[15] *Ibid.*, p. ix.   [16] *Ibid.*, p. 71.

Nations in the proposed Covenant on Human Rights. But de Visscher concludes: "It is the fate of any idea of a highly spiritual character to be exposed to some distortion when it is introduced into a new environment. . . . [Yet] the bond that is being established beyond any shadow of doubt between the rights of man on the one hand, and the maintenance of peace and respect for law on the other hand, constitutes the first assertion by the international organization of a great moral and civilizing principle. . . . A functional conception of power here joins hands with Christian doctrine, making human values—the only values that can command universal acceptance—the ultimate point of convergence of peace and law. We must neither count upon its immediate efficacy, nor reject the hopes that it awakens."[17]

The third scholar whose writings should be mentioned is Hans J. Morgenthau, a political theorist who looks with the realist's discerning eye at moral claims in world politics. He submits impressive evidence that most protestations of selfless and humanitarian behavior by states are not matched by their conduct in practice. For instance, the keeping of promises, the protection of minorities, and the repudiation of war as an instrument of national policy are honored as often in the breach as in the keeping, especially when vital interests are at stake.

Yet Professor Morgenthau's analysis of the influence of moral principles is by no means as negative as sometimes assumed. In one broad area he has called attention more clearly than any of his peers to the far-reaching consequences of practical morality. This area comprises the moral restraints on the use of national power. A state pursuing its objectives in a world of unmitigated power politics would seem to be justified in employing any means that would strengthen its power and weaken that of an antagonist. Indeed in an earlier era court poisoners and paid assassins carried on their heinous

[17] *Ibid.*, p. 129.

crimes for precisely this end. Today it is plainly not a matter of indifference to states whether friendly or antagonistic leaders hold power in neighboring states, nor are the technical difficulties of disposing of them any greater than in the past. However the civilizing influence of practical morality has made these acts ethically reprehensible and normally impossible of execution. Clemenceau put his finger on the core of "the German problem" for France and Europe when he declared there were 20,000,000 Germans too many. The expedient way of dealing with this problem would be through the decisive methods by which the Romans solved the Carthaginian problem once and for all. Yet there are moral restraints that for all practical purposes rule this out, although in the exchange between Stalin and Churchill at the Teheran Conference there are hints of another conception of international politics in which the same moral restraints do not operate. Churchill reports of Stalin:

"The German General Staff, he said, must be liquidated. The whole force of Hitler's mighty armies depended upon about fifty thousand officers and technicians. If these were rounded up and shot at the end of the war, German military strength would be extirpated. On this I thought it right to say: 'The British Parliament and public will never tolerate mass executions. Even if in war passion they allowed them to begin, they would turn violently against those responsible after the first butchery had taken place. The Soviets must be under no delusion on this point.'

"Stalin however, perhaps only in mischief, pursued the subject. 'Fifty thousand,' he said, 'must be shot.' I was deeply angered. 'I would rather,' I said, 'be taken out into the garden here and now and be shot myself than sully my own and my country's honour by such infamy.' "[18]

Finally, it is redundant to say that the American theologian

[18] Sir Winston Churchill, *Closing the Ring* (Boston: Houghton Mifflin Co., 1951), pp. 373-74.

Reinhold Niebuhr has influenced thinking on international morality. Niebuhr is persuaded that men and states cannot follow their interest without claiming to do so in obedience to some general scheme of values. Two very grave moral and practical questions have continued to trouble him and have led him to make a series of distinctions regarding the national interest. First, he has asked whether a consistent emphasis upon the national interest is not as self-defeating in national as it is in individual life. Or, put in other terms, does not a nation concerned too much with its own interests define those interests so narrowly and so immediately (as for instance in terms of military security) that the interests and securities, which depend upon common devotion to principles of justice and upon established mutualities in a community of nations, are sacrificed? Secondly, nations which insist on the one hand that they cannot act beyond their interest claim, as soon as they act, that they have acted not out of self-interest but in obedience to higher objectives like "civilization" or "justice." Applied to the conduct of contemporary American foreign relations, this means we claim more for the benevolence of our policies than they deserve and arouse the resentment of peoples already inclined to envy our power and wealth. Thus national interest is imperiled at one time by the hazard of moral cynicism and at another time by moral pretension and hypocrisy. In earlier writings Niebuhr has dealt with the first of these questions and more recently with the second. In the evolution of his thinking, moreover, he has come to view them as parts of a single problem, involving our continued ambivalence toward the moral issue, claiming at one moment that nations have no obligations beyond their interests and at the next moment that they are engaged in a high moral crusade without regard for interests.

To mention one difference among the four theorists, Niebuhr along with Morgenthau has been most consistent in stressing the peculiarities and uniqueness of collective morality. He notes the ferocity and intensity of the struggle among groups, when compared to the rivalry of individuals, stemming from the tendency of collectivities like the nation to express both the virtue and selfishness of their members. This tendency is strengthened by the passing of any widely accepted view as to the proper end of man. One consequence of modern mass society had been to thwart the attainment of personal security and the satisfaction of basic human aspirations, especially for particular groups. Frustrated individuals strive to fulfill themselves vicariously by projecting their ego to the level of the national ego. In mass society, collective attainments offer possibilities of self-aggrandizement that individual pretensions no longer serve. At the same time, appeals are made to the loyalty, self-sacrifice, and devotion of individuals in the group. In this way, social unity is built on the virtuous as well as the selfish side of man's nature; the twin elements of collective strength become self-sacrificial loyalty and frustrated ambitions and aggressions. From this it follows that politics is the more contentious and ruthless because of the unselfish loyalty of the members of groups, which become laws unto themselves unrestrained by their obedient and worshipful members. Group pride is in fact the corruption of individual loyalty and group consciousness; contempt for another group is the pathetic form which respect for our own frequently takes. The tender emotions that bind the family together sometimes are expressed in indifference for the welfare of other families. In international society a nation made up of men of the greatest religious goodwill would be less than loving toward other nations, for its virtue would be channeled into loyalty to itself thus increasing that nation's selfishness. The consequence for Niebuhr's political theory is his conclusion that "society . . . merely cumulates the egoism of individuals and transmutes their individual altruism into collective egoism so that the egoism of the group has a double force. For this reason no group acts from purely unselfish or even mutual intent and politics is therefore bound to be a contest of power."[19]

II. THE FOURFOLD LIMITATION OF INTERNATIONAL MORALITY

The insights and the wisdom of the four observers stand out most clearly against the background of four persistent problems or limitations lying at the roots of most of our modern confusion and uncertainty regarding principle and necessity. When we try to apply general principles such as those put forth by Butterfield and de Visscher, these limitations are present to confound us. The first problem or limitation results from the perennial tendency of states to see their national purposes as universal principles and ends. The second limitation stems from the effect of this spirit of national self-righteousness upon the resolution of international tensions and conflicts. The third limitation arises from the nature of collective morality and its apparent differences with individual morality. The fourth limitation derives from the fact that there are few if any absolutes in international politics.

To take the first limitation, the fundamental source and cause of what has been called nationalistic universalism rests basically in a profound yet simple human dilemma. We are never as moral as we claim to be. This is true of the parent who disciplines the child "for its own good" no less than of the powerful nation which works its will on less powerful states. Even when justice is the goal of a loving father it invariably becomes mixed with coercion, caprice, and injustice. The Athenian envoys to Melos, who were perhaps more transparently honest than some of their latter-day successors, said of a powerful rival: "Of all the men we know they are most conspicuous in considering what is agreeable honourable and

[19] Reinhold Niebuhr, "Human Nature and Social Change," *Christian Century*, Vol. L, 1953, p. 363.

what is expedient just."[20] Centuries later the historian Dicey found that in Western society: "Men come easily to believe that arrangements agreeable to themselves are beneficial to others."[21] With a few exceptions, nations have seen their cause and supremacy as equivalent to universal justice. Lord Wolseley maintained: "I have but one great object in this world, and that is to maintain the greatness of the Empire. But apart from my John Bull sentiment upon the point, I firmly believe that in doing so I work in the cause of Christianity, of peace, of civilization, and the happiness of the human race generally."[22] Or, in 1935 in an early phase of his writings, Professor Arnold J. Toynbee discovered that the security of the British Empire "was also the supreme interest of the whole world."[23]

Nor is American history lacking in comparable examples. It provides the story of President McKinley, who spent the night in prayer for divine guidance before deciding—as one might have expected—to annex the Philippines. Or President Wilson, who following the bombardment of Vera Cruz in 1914 assured the world that "the United States had gone to Mexico to serve mankind"[24] and who shortly before our entry into World War I identified American principles and American policies as "the principles of mankind . . . [which] must prevail."[25] We are reminded of de Tocqueville's words: "If I say to an American that the country he lives in is a fine one, aye, he replies and there is not its equal in the world. If I

[20] *The Complete Writings of Thucydides*, the unabridged Crowley translation (New York: Random House, 1934), p. 334.

[21] Albert Venn Dicey, *Lectures on the Relation between Law and Opinion in England* (2nd ed.; New York: Macmillan Co., 1905), pp. 14-15.

[22] F. B. Maurice and G. Arthur, *The Life of Lord Wolseley* (New York: Doubleday & Co., 1924), p. 314.

[23] Arnold J. Toynbee, *Survey of International Affairs*, 1935 (London: Oxford University Press, 1937), Vol. II, p. 46.

[24] Woodrow Wilson, *The New Democracy: Presidential Messages, Addresses, and Other Papers* (1913-17), edited by Ray Stannard Baker and William E. Dodd (New York: Harper & Brothers, 1926), Vol. I, p. 104.

[25] *Ibid.*, Vol. II, p. 414.

applaud the freedom its inhabitants enjoy he answers 'freedom is a fine thing but few nations are worthy of it.' If I remark on the purity of morals that distinguishes the United States he declares 'I can imagine that a stranger who has witnessed the corruption which prevails in other nations would be astonished at the difference.' At length I leave him to a contemplation of himself but he returns to the charge and does not desist until he has got me to repeat all I have been saying. It is impossible to conceive a more troublesome and garrulous patriotism."[26]

It should of course be obvious that every nation has its own form of spiritual pride, its own peculiar version. The American version is compounded, I would suppose, of several factors. The first derives from the role of the immigrant who had turned his back on the vices of Europe and was making a new beginning. Having shaken the dust of the old world from his feet, he was anxious to prove that none of its ancient failings were his failings. Their purposes, often sullied by ambiguities and compromises bound up with national existence in the cockpit of Europe, were not his purposes. Strikingly enough, his affirmations of moral purity—or, more specifically, those by which national leaders appealed to his virtue—seemed to be confirmed by early American social history. In the first phases of this history the frontier saved us from the acrimony of class struggle and later our superior technology gave new outlets to the ambitious and adventurous. Beyond this we were freed from international responsibility by the fortuitous coincidence of our geographic isolation and a European equilibrium of power which British policy and naval power was dedicated to preserve. In such a world, it was natural to assume that domestic policies were more important than foreign policy and that the alliances so prevalent on the European scene were an expensive and pernicious

[26] Alexis de Tocqueville, *Democracy in America*, Vol. II, the Henry Reeve text (New York: Vintage Books, 1954), p. 236.

nuisance. Even the Monroe Doctrine was seen more as a unilateral declaration and less as a weapon in diplomacy. These objective conditions have passed but the psychology they inspired lingers on, for instance, in the sweeping and indignant denunciations of the exercise of power by European states, followed abruptly by our own decision to use force unilaterally if necessary in the Middle East.

A second factor shaping the American outlook results from the fact that our prevailing philosophy of international relations has been a curious blending of legalism and rationalism. Law and reason are of course indispensable ingredients of an orderly life. They are precious fruits of the flowering of a free community and the good life. Ultimately peace becomes inevitable only when law and order prevail. However, the tragedy of much of our thinking has been to assume this ultimate end was either realized or shortly realizable and to tailor our words and sometimes our deeds to fit this mistaken assumption. American lawyers whose influence on our foreign relations has been immense have more than once confused the realities of municipal law with the hopes of international law. They have imposed on the international system burdens it could not bear. If the problem was war, it must be outlawed (the Kellogg-Briand Pact). If the peril was aggression, a legal formula proscribing and defining it was the goal— even though a few months ago a United Nations Commission gave up this task in despair. If states trembled in a state of insecurity, reassure them with security pacts heaped one upon the other! If a state threatened the peace, pass a resolution! All these acts, so frequently a positive force in organized and integrated communities, have on balance weakened the feeble system of international order, for pacts, declarations, and formulas at odds with the realities of international life tempt the lawless to reckless adventures and the law-abiding to a whole chain of emotional responses, beginning with self-righteousness and indignation, shading off into disillusionment and finally into despair.

If we have suffered from legalism, the price of liberal rationalism has been still greater. It has been said of the League of Nations and the United Nations that they represent an attempt to apply the principles of John Locke's liberalism to the machinery of international order. They carry into world affairs the outlook of a liberal democratic society. One rather acute critic has noted in some rational spokesmen the tendency to believe that there existed a card index of situations or events to be consulted for the appropriate and prescribed action whenever the event or situation turned up. There is a persistent temptation to value standardized procedures more than prudence, the perfection of machinery more than political wisdom. Four decades of experience in transplanting liberal rationalism to the world scene have taught that this approach, which logically is unexceptional, can be full of unforeseen difficulties. This is not the place to discuss these problems except to suggest that where prestige of states is involved, rational discussion is not always served by open forums. Mr. Lester Pearson has written of the problems of diplomacy in a "goldfish bowl." Moreover, responsible international conduct is not guaranteed by gathering together representatives of over eighty states differing widely in size, power, and political, economic, and cultural developments. States not affected by events and not required to sacrifice vital interests can more easily strike poses than those whose security is in jeopardy. Nations with limited interests in a question may band together to outvote states whose survival may be at stake. It would be helpful to know how often uninstructed delegates on matters of no concern to their government throw their votes capriciously to the support of a resolution for which they would be unwilling to accept direct national responsibility. It would be useful to discover how often states turn to the United Nations when they are unwilling or unable to evolve a viable foreign policy of their own.

To ask such questions is not to detract from the vital and constructive role of the United Nations. However, if this new international institution is to survive and grow, its members must face the hard facts concerning it. It provides a set of methods and procedures and embodies certain fundamental aims and goals. It can contribute only what its members bring to its affairs in the form of policies, resources, and loyalties. It will not in the foreseeable future be a substitute for foreign policy. When a nation's representatives are asked to state its policy for a certain area and they reply it will act through the United Nations, they have replied only to the procedural question. They can still be held to account for shaping a substantive policy. Former Secretary of State Dean Acheson in a statement to the House Foreign Affairs Committee declared:

"It will not do to say that the United Nations will determine policy, make decisions, and enforce them. The United Nations is not a supranational entity with a mind, a will and power. It is a forum, and no more than the nations which meet there. Nothing more comes out of it than is put into it.

"If a great nation, like the United States, looks to the United Nations to form American policy, instead of fighting in the United Nations for what the American Government believes should be done, then we have committed an unprecedented abdication of responsibility and power. We deserve what we get. If we believe we have exhausted our responsibilities when we join in the United Nations to pass resolutions which are defied, and which we have no intention of backing up, we have engaged in a most dangerous form of self-deception."

The second limitation on morality arises from the effects on international diplomacy of the dread conflict that rages today between giant organized systems of self-righteousness. The most profound and far-reaching change in the last half-century is not the technological revolution or even the revolt of three-quarters of the world's people against so-called colonial domination. Rather, it has been the fragmentation of a formerly cohesive international society into morally self-sufficient national communities. This change has brought civilization to the threshold of a twilight era in international morality. It has prompted Dean Roscoe Pound to say: "It might be maintained plausibly that a moral order among states was nearer attainment in the middle of the eighteenth century than it is today."[27] In the seventeenth and eighteenth century, and to a lessening degree up to the First World War, international morality addressed itself to a body of aristocratic sovereigns who spoke the same language, shared common cultural values, were bound by family ties, and, in a word, were members of the same club. Their goals were simple and limited. They might seek a piece of territory, a bit of glory or greater power and prestige. But the whole world was not their oyster and they accepted the fact that they were partners in an international order that "gentlemen" were pledged to preserve.

This aristocratic fraternity of leaders who preferred speaking with one another rather than with their own peoples has passed and in its place is a leadership responsible to the popular will. In consequence we witness the kaleidoscopic spectacle of a rapid and continuous turnover of diplomatists who must deal with one another. The popular selection of officials with all its potentialities for good has shattered the community of interests and the imponderable ties of loyalty and affection on which a crude but unmistakable personal international morality had been based virtually from the seventeenth century until the eve of World War I. In this era the morality of individual leaders was identical with the morality of states. Lest we too

[27] Roscoe Pound, Philosophical Theory and International Law, *Bibliotheca Visseriana* (Leyden, 1923), Vol. I, p. 74.

hastily dismiss the benefits that flowed from these ties, we need only reflect that Anglo-American unity has more recently been served by the comradeship of a Churchill and an Eisenhower and that the former's dream enunciated as early as his Fulton Speech in 1947 was perceived and carried forward by the President in the Summit Meeting at Geneva. It is also worth noting that following the Suez crisis in late 1956 the crumbling Anglo-American alliance was strengthened when the President's wartime colleague became Prime Minister Macmillan. Moreover, these examples are the exceptions that prove the rule. Contrast them with the task of Ambassador Lodge working in the United Nations without benefit of long contact and friendly relations even with some of our Latin American and European allies. Or note the effects upon imaginative thinking of the mass exodus from Washington following 1952 of some of our most experienced diplomatists, e.g., that remarkable group surrounding George F. Kennan and Paul Nitze in the Policy Planning Staff. Furthermore, you may recall that in the eighteen months from July 1945 to 1947, the U.S. had three secretaries of state and of all policy-making officials of the State Department i.e., under and assistant secretaries of state—in office as of October 1945 none was still in office two years later. One need not despair of democracy to confess that this phenomenon of the rapid fluctuation of personnel with its consequences both for continuity of policy and community of interests with the leaders of other nations whose membership is similarly in flux presents us with a major problem. Observing this trend, Hans J. Morgenthau writes that ethical rules have their seat in the consciousness of individual men. "Government by clearly identifiable men who can be held personally accountable for their acts is therefore the precondition for the existence of an effective system of international ethics."[28]

This factor of a passing international corps of leaders is but

[28] Morgenthau, *Politics among Nations*, p. 226.

a symptom of an infinitely more profound transformation of international society. The fabric of moral consensus which existed among approximately equal political entities has been rent by the rise of separate and self-contained moral systems which today take the form of national political religions. These changes have weakened to the point of ineffectiveness supranational moral rules of conduct and have endowed particular national ethical systems with universal validity. What is at stake today in the world conflict are systems of beliefs and ethical convictions. Gone is the era of the eighteenth century described by Gibbon in *The Decline and Fall of the Roman Empire* in which wars were "temperate and undecisive contests" which "cannot essentially injure our general state of happiness, the system of arts, and laws, and manners."[29]

Righteousness plainly has a place in an assessment of the behavior of states. Yet the patterns of history are more complex than this. For example, we are often told that Germany has invaded France four times within a century and a quarter. Who among us remembers that on the first occasion it was England and Russia which finally induced the German powers to join them in rolling back the tide of Napoleonic empire? Who recalls that on a second occasion France made clear that if it won the War of 1870, it had in mind in Belgium, Luxembourg, and elsewhere a more scandalous aggrandizement than Bismarck ever dreamed of? Who is aware that the crime of Alsace-Lorraine begins not in 1871 but with the aggressions of Louis XIV? Multiply these instances a hundredfold and the whole tragically complex pattern of history unfolds and calls for understanding of a kind that is blurred rather than clarified by national self-righteousness, which destroys the international order and the prospects for an accommodation of interests on the basis of mutual respect and trust.

The third limitation on the implanting of moral principle

[29] Edward Gibbon, *The Decline and Fall of the Roman Empire* (The Modern Library Edition), Vol. II, pp. 93-95.

has its origin in collective as distinct from individual morality, an issue on which the four writers place different degrees of emphasis. This is the other side of the coin from the self-righteousness discussed above. Religious ethics calls self-interest into question. Man must lose himself in order to find himself. At the level of organized communities, however, the problem of legitimate self-interest arises, inasmuch as political ethics takes self-interest for granted. A political leader cannot ask his people to sacrifice themselves. His first duty is to preserve the Constitution and he owes allegiance to the safety and well-being of the nation and of its generations yet unborn. Short of treason he cannot bargain away what he holds in trust. Moreover in another respect any equating of morality in individual relations with international morality is bound to be misleading. One of our great American Presidents who can hardly be dismissed for lack of moral fervor was Woodrow Wilson. In a lecture at Princeton he declared: "Morality is a great deal bigger than law. The individual morality is the sense of right or wrong of one man. The social morality must strike an average. This is where reformers make their tragic mistake. There can be no compromise in individual morality but there has to be a compromise, an average, in social morality. There is indeed an element of morality in the very fact of compromise in social undertakings."[30] In this same vein we recall the words of Cavour: "If we had done for ourselves what we did for the state, what scoundrels we would have been."

Reinhold Niebuhr has distinguished between moral man and immoral society. While he has subsequently modified the sharp lines of his dichotomy, he would hold, I believe, to the "hidden truth" which this distinction lays bare. Accordingly, those virtues of gentleness, magnanimity, love, and trust which

[30] Quoted by Raymond Fosdick in "Personal Recollections of Woodrow Wilson" in *Freedom for Man: A World Safe for Mankind*, ed. by Quincy Wright (University of Chicago, 1957), p. 7.

enrich the dimensions of our family life at its best and are possible in the more intimate communities in which we move and have our being, must be viewed with circumspection, reserve, and uncertainty on the world stage, where states through power and force press their claims and counterclaims. We may as moral beings deplore and renounce the evil portents of a massive armaments program, but who among us, if responsible for the nation's security, would have persisted in meeting Soviet power through compassion and the repudiation of force? Or who, confronted by the threat to Western civilization of the Nazi juggernaut, would have turned aside an alliance with the equally oppressive Russian communist regime? Burckhardt observed that "for every truth there is a balancing truth." Assertions such as those by Herbert Butterfield that the only morality is individual morality have to be seen in the light of the differences between the individual and the collectivity and the imperatives to which each must respond.

A fourth limitation derives from the proposition that there are few if any absolutes in international politics. Lord Acton warned that "an absolute principle is as absurd as absolute power." In foreign relations particularly, every attempt to conceive political ethics in absolute terms has floundered on the shoals of circumstance. This is because broad moral principles seldom if ever can be said to furnish a direct, precise, and unambiguous guide to action. For example, the noble injunction "Thou shalt not kill" has only a peripheral relevance when nations are suddenly plunged into total war. Moreover, less ultimate moral and political principles such as a belief in the common interests of, say, all the workers of Europe or of the world, scarcely deters British and German laborers from going to war against one another when their nations see their interests in conflict.

There is another absolute principle with which Americans in particular are familiar. In the aftermath of World War I, we blithely assumed that the creation of democratic regimes everywhere would remove the threat of conflict. This tempting illusion has since come home to haunt us. On one hand, it was illusory to believe we could play any more than a marginal role in shaping the evolution of other political systems beyond the jurisdiction of this nation. Not only is our power limited but, more fundamental, political institutions are matters of organic growth. The ways in which people move toward more enlightened government constitute the profoundest processes of national life. Nor are we persuaded any longer that we have penetrated the veil concealing the mystery of the absolutely best state for all peoples. The words of de Tocqueville written in 1831 about the United States have deeper meaning for us today: "The more I see of this country the more I admit myself penetrated with this truth: that there is nothing absolute in the theoretical value of political institutions, and that their efficiency depends almost always on the original circumstances and the social conditions of people to whom they are applied." In any event, the record is unmistakable that the trappings of democracy can be used for purposes as cruel and bellicose as those of autocratic regimes. One need only mention in passing the rise of totalitarian democracies; the ability of tyrants, for example in the Middle East, to manipulate democratic machinery and symbols to their own selfish ends; the pattern of ideological conquest evolved during the libertarian French Revolution and the annexationist dreams of the German liberals of 1848.

III. NECESSITY AND THE NEW BALANCE OF POWER

Historians looking back on the events of international politics following World War II will doubtless stress the massive concentration of influence and authority in two world powers, the United States and the Soviet Union. The novelty of this configuration may be seen by contrast with the seventeenth, eighteenth, or nineteenth centuries when numerous states of more or less equal power crowded the European landscape. The power of the Soviet Union so greatly over-shadowed that of any other European country that the whole of Western Europe buttressed by the United States was com-pelled to organize its military and economic resources to pre-serve the balance of power. In the same way, American power inspired an editorialist of *The Economist* (London) to say: "In any comparison of the potential resources of the Great Powers the United States, even before Hitler's war, far out-stripped every other nation in the world in material strength, in scale of industrialization, in weight of resources, in stand-ards of living, by every index of output and consumption. And the war, which all but doubled the American national income while it either ruined or severely weakened every other Great Power, has enormously increased the scale upon which the United States now towers above its fellows."[31]

This condition of two immensely powerful states, each commanding the homage and obedient cooperation of friendly if not client states, has obtained for the better part of the past decade. The objective basis on which the Soviet Union and the United States have founded their relationships has been what Winston Churchill described as a "balance of terror," not the mutual confidence and trust of moral con-sensus. Necessity and their respective power has induced the super-powers to follow policies of limitation and restraint as in Korea, Berlin, and Eastern Europe, even though the ele-ments that constitute the equilibrium of forces between them have continually shifted with advances in military technology. Bipolarity and the nature of Russian and American objectives have made possible a decade of uneasy peace, less because of morality than common sense. Harold Nicolson has observed: "Diplomacy is not a system of moral philosophy; it is, as Sir Ernest Satow defined it, 'the application of intelligence and tact to the conduct of official relations between the govern-

---

[31] *The Economist* (London), May 24, 1947, p. 785.

ments of independent States.' The worst kind of diplomatists are missionaries, fanatics and lawyers; the best kind are the reasonable and humane sceptics."[32] Soviet diplomats plainly have not been noted for their tact, but the best among them have shown a skepticism and common sense, a preference for policies of advance and retreat, and have earned thereby the grudging respect of Western statesmen like the present British Chancellor of the Exchequer, Captain Peter Thorneycroft: "The Russians are nothing if not realists."[33] Nonetheless, until recently these restraints have resided in the political judgment of the leaders of two mighty states who had reason to assume they possessed greater power and virtue than the rest of the world.

The new balance of power has altered the relationship between necessity and foreign policy and introduced novel limits and restraints on the actions of the two giants. The more than twenty nations which have emerged since the war and their friends in the Middle East, Africa, and Asia constitute a major force in world politics. Their ultimate power may be exaggerated by their strategic role in the United Nations, where they hold the balance of power, but their importance seems destined to increase in the future. Both Moscow and Washington have shown a consistent unwillingness to act without counting the consequences among the so-called underdeveloped countries. Beyond this the bipolar world has shown signs of crumbling on the edges of Soviet and American power and authority. Europe's crisis in October of 1956 had its roots in a rediscovery of national identity on that continent. For nearly a decade the postwar "Grand Alliance" between Europe and America was founded on mutual or identical interests. Both Europe's recovery and its security were guaranteed by American power, for its recovery was an outgrowth

[32] Harold Nicolson, *Diplomacy* (London: Oxford University Press, 1939; second edition reprinted 1955), p. 50.
[33] *Parliamentary Debates,* Vol. 408, February 28, 1945, p. 1458.

of the Marshall Plan and its security rested ultimately with our atomic monopoly. In this context it mattered little that certain concrete European interests in Asia and the Near East were sometimes at odds with American interests. Economic, political, and military necessity dictated that Europe stand with the United States or invite catastrophe and possibly national suicide. Ironically, the success of European recovery followed by the withdrawal of Marshall aid undermined this concert of power and the Russian explosion of an atomic bomb came perilously close to shattering it. At this point Europe, far from being reassured by our stockpile of bombs, trembled in fear at the thought of being pulverized by one side or the other; nations like France and Britain, whose postwar policies had often been subordinated to American programs, stirred, questioned their policies, and reasserted their sovereign rights on such matters as the fulfillment of rearmament pledges (the British White Paper is merely the logical culmination of these tendencies accelerated, perhaps, by diplomatic ineptitudes on both sides). Chancellor Adenauer called for a United Europe capable of standing upon its own feet in a world threatening to pass it by, and a speaker of the BBC Third Programme predicted: "It is no longer so foolish to think of Western Europe as a potential Third Force."

Simultaneously, the eruption within the Soviet Empire made it clear that unity of purpose in the East would no longer be taken for granted even under the shadow of the Red Army. On November 3, 1956, *The Economist* (London) commented: "By swift changes, the consequences of which are still incalculable, the peoples of Eastern Europe have ceased to be mere pawns on the political chessboard." Poland revolted for "Bread and Freedom," gained a new leader who symbolically enough had once been imprisoned for his "nationalist" tendencies, dismissed the Russian General Rokossovsky as Minister of Defense, and installed a national Communist regime. Nationalist sentiment again fanned the flames of revolt in Hungary, but Hungarians saw the control of events pass out of their hands. The historic consequences of these changes and their relationship to a more general upheaval are beyond prediction, but their effect on the two-power world seem plainly beyond dispute, even though recent months have witnessed at least the temporary consolidation again of Soviet authority.

More difficult by far is the question of the effect of these changes on international morality. At the risk of oversimplification I would suggest that the consequences are bound to be ambiguous. One effect of a multipower world will doubtless be to set restraints on conduct. The curious paradox of the present-day international realm is that great nations have never had more power, yet they have never had more trouble with the small nations they have the power to crush, and the voices of students and peasants in Poland and Hungary and rising national groups in Africa, Asia, and the Middle East are commanding more and more widespread attention. Injustice threatens most whenever great weakness is confronted by unlimited power. Perhaps this is why victorious nations wreak vengeance on conquered foes. This tendency has been allayed by the rise of competing centers of power, and out of the claims and counterclaims of a number of countries for influence and respect a rough and approximate justice may result. The ability of the smaller powers ultimately to use nuclear force theoretically might exert the same decisive effect on all use of force that now prevails in Soviet and American calculations vis-à-vis one another. Necessity might compel them to turn to the peaceful pursuit of their goals.

However, there is also something terrifying about the specter of twenty or more states brandishing absolute weapons. For example, possession of these lethal weapons by Egypt might have deterred the Franco-British-Israeli intervention but one or the other side might also have been tempted to use them with a tragically fatal and chain reaction effect. With the multiplication of the producers, the prospect of their use through an accident or in frenzy increases perhaps in geometric proportion. Moreover, there are risks as well as opportunities in the sudden catapulting of new and inexperienced nations to positions of unaccustomed prominence and world leadership. They will not always be right. Almost without exception they lack apprenticeship in the subtleties and uncertainties of world affairs. Their will, as expressed in the liberum veto of the holder of the balance of power in the United Nations, is not necessarily the embodiment of wisdom and virtue. In recent months the trend has become more pronounced to equate the positive law of the United Nations with moral law. In view of the structure of this body and its original purposes, this solution of the moral dilemma in foreign policy raises as many questions as it answers. Especially in the context of American attitudes on foreign policy, the tendency to covet popularity and gratitude, to seek a more intimate relation with other nations than is possible, to be too apologetic toward the underdeveloped countries, and to be forever on the defensive with those who hold up our more extravagant professions of principle to our practice—these recent changes in the balance of power and our instinctive responses are as much a cause for sober reflection as for dancing in the streets. It would be a fatal error if, beguiled by the new configurations of power, American philosophers and policy-makers should assume that because of our sympathy for the newer states, we had transcended for the first time in American history the inevitable tension between necessity and principle.

IV. NOTES ON A THEORY OF INTERNATIONAL
MORALITY

Whatever the limits of moral principles, there is need for the type of normative theories discussed at the outset of this chapter. The late Charles A. Beard in considering the role of

moral principle suggested that: "the mandate of moral obligation appears to be operative in three spheres which, on occasion, seem to overlap: (1) the nation itself, as something of
an independent entity; (2) the nation in respect of other
single nations and certain limited groups of nations; and
(3) the nations as one unit in a larger whole made up of many
diverse units forming what is commonly called the community
of nations."[34]

It may be useful, taking this conceptual scheme as our clue,
to consider three possible layers or dimensions of international
morality. Scholars relating these three levels of morality
might uncover new insights on the relationship of principle
and necessity. A concluding note on one possible theoretical
framework for approaching these tantalizing and awesome
problems may be in order.

The core of this threefold concept is found in the moral
content of the national interest. Whereas it is obvious that
the first duty of a nation's foreign policy must be to safeguard
its territorial integrity and the interests of present and future
generations, it should also be clear that the moral values of
any society are so protected and defended. The nation-state
is both the problem-child of international relations and the
highest effective expression of a genuine moral consensus in
large communities. More progress has been made in creating
freedom and order and opportunities for the individual, say,
within the United States, than in any foreseeable international
community. Moreover, nations can in practice usually give
moral content, however modest, to their national self-interest
while the international interest is more vague and ill-defined.

The moral dignity of the national interest finds expression
in various spheres. The interests of a nation's people in its
basic values and common welfare transcending sub-national
loyalties are an antidote to crass materialism. The mere existence of a citizenry that takes its history and tradition seriously

[34] Charles A. Beard, *The Idea of National Interest* (New York: Macmillan Co., 1934), p. 401.

assures that a nation's reputation shall not perish nor its will to stay alive be destroyed. The sense of membership and of partnership in a common enterprise with ancestors who have gone before and heirs who are to follow gives moral stamina and political vitality to a society. Moreover, national attachments are the one sure and sound basis for transcending partisan political loyalties. In a period of crisis in British politics, Winston Churchill counseled his fellow conservatives: "We are Party men but we shall be all the stronger if in every action we show ourselves capable, even in this period of stress and provocation, of maintaining the division—where there is division—between national and party interests."[35]

In general a more tolerable relationship is achieved between nations who speak in their national interest than those who claim to speak for the whole world. Hence states, while asserting the moral integrity of their interests, ought never to see them too exclusively as ends in themselves. World patterns are too complex and variegated to reserve all virtue to a single state or course of action. The periods of greatest decline in international morality have come when national purposes have been presented as pure and unsullied goals for acceptance or rejection by the rest of the world. There is an important area in foreign policy where national interests must be asserted confidently and with pride and courage. Indeed, Americans sometimes run the risk, having proclaimed our virtue and indulged in all manner of pretentious talk, of alternately feeling shame over the fact that we are a great power with a noble tradition and shrinking when not everyone loves us. Our actions will be more honored and esteemed if we are somewhat more humble about equating them with final and absolute virtue. They can be justified as necessary and proper steps without casting them in the form of crusades and filling the air with the most extravagant claims.

[35] Winston S. Churchill, speech to "Conservative Annual Conference," October 14, 1949. Reprinted in collected speeches *In the Balance*, p. 329.

A second dimension is the converse of the national interest. The one thing which saves the idea of the national interest from itself is its essential reciprocity. To the extent that nations are in earnest not alone about their own self-interests but in their recognition of the application of similar criteria by others, the national interest as a guide escapes any temptation to conceal real designs for world aggrandizement. Edmund Burke declared: "Nothing is so fatal to a nation as an extreme of self-partiality, and the total want of consideration of what others will naturally hope or fear."[36] After a nation has determined its own objective interests in terms of its national security, it has an obligation to draw back, as it were, and appraise coolly and realistically the interests of its neighbors. In this way alone can nations decide if their interests are compatible or can be adjusted. There is no other basis for true coexistence. It is as tempting as it is hazardous to treat other peoples as pawns in the struggle to preserve one's own national interest. There is a tendency to treat other nations as means instead of as ends embodied in their own national purposes. Yet particularly in relations with those societies in Asia and Africa which have most frequently been treated as instruments to be used and exploited by others, their claims upon international society to accord them means of national recognition and personal self-respect make such a tendency well-nigh fatal. It is essential that every nation pursue wisely its own best interests, but the pathway for each nation must not be strewn with the remnants of the interests of others that were forgotten in its headlong drive to attain national security. Among nations with decent intentions there must be a reciprocal process of recognizing each other's vital interests and avoiding collisions and conflicts *insofar as* it is possible through the compromise of divergent interests. Interests are capable of being compromised; principles can never be made

[36] Edmund Burke, "Remarks on the Policy of the Allies with Respect to France" (1793), *Works* (Boston: Little, Brown, & Co., 1889), Vol. IV, p. 447.

the object of bargains. Yet if nations are to survive somehow they must find ways of compromising their differences while at the same time protecting and safeguarding their interests. As it is the essence of politics that individuals possess the capacity to compromise their differences, the art of diplomacy merely raises this process to the level of nations and founds it upon a structure of multiple national interests. Conflicts which seem at the time to present to the parties a clear case of right and wrong, almost without exception have appeared to future historians, less blinded by passion and loyalty, as something infinitely more tragic than good men fighting bad. The real pattern of conflict and war is one of minor differences hardening into intractable political divisions, of men faced by terrible dilemmas and of nations eventually driven by the inner dialectic of events to wars that no one desired. The difference between a struggle between good and evil and actual struggles in world politics in which every party in some way is at fault but is unable to disengage itself from the tragic predicament of fearing others but never comprehending their counter-fears is the difference between the substance of "heroic" and "revisionist" or scientific history. In this predicament, each party has a sense of its own insecurity but never imagines that its own righteous efforts could have anything to do with the insecurity of others. After each military conflict, the minds of the early or "heroic" historians are locked in the combat expounding their own nation's cause. Their judgments are generally the kind that stem from self-righteousness. Subsequently, it remains for "revisionist" historians to rewrite the narrative in terms of the mutual fear of each side for the power of the other. In their histories of conflict the revisionist schools have frequently proved that we have muddied the waters and darkened our minds about the true nature of a struggle when it has been interpreted in terms of certain accidental characteristics. In the present crisis between East and West, for example, historians may show

170

that the ideological aspect of the struggle was accidental in comparison to the more profound and underlying political struggle. In this tragic predicament, the one source of relief from the struggle can come from the accommodation of conflicting political interests. The first step in this process is to discover what are the vital interests of the foe. The one escape from this human predicament is the patient quest of mutually compatible national interests if they are found to exist. A firm and steady endeavor to find out what are the interests of the other party to a crisis provides any nation with some basis for predicting its action and in the same way of anticipating the faithfulness of its allies.

There is a form of political morality that stems from a decent regard for the interests of others. While it is not always the same as the private ethics enjoined by the great religions, it nonetheless is expediency grounded in morality. In the writings of philosophers from the Greeks to Edmund Burke, it is identified as prudence or practical morality; in guidebooks to diplomacy like Richelieu's *Political Testament*, it appears as expediential morality. It has been considered the lubricant by which the smooth workings of international society are made possible and in modern times as the cement without which the sturdiest alliance will crumble. It is too much to expect that nations will show gratitude or lasting affection for one another. Generosity is as likely to produce envy, resentment, and contempt as good will, for no government based on popular support can afford to acknowledge the full scale of its dependence on others. But there are other personal factors that are not inconsequential. Diplomats, as has been said, are men sent abroad to lie and deceive in the interests of their country. But, as Harold Nicolson points out, they must also return to negotiate another day. If a diplomat or nation is known to be habitually retrograde in the observance of obligations, it can hardly look forward to long and effective diplomatic commerce with others. Winston Churchill measured this dimension of international morality in these words: "There is, however, one helpful guide, namely for a nation to keep its word and to act in accordance with its treaty obligations to allies. This guide is called *honour*. It is baffling to reflect that what men call honour does not correspond always to Christian ethics. . . . An exaggerated code of honour leading to the performance of utterly vain and unreasonable deeds should not be defended, however fine it might look."[37]

A final or third layer of international morality comprises general principles like opposition to tyranny, or community, or values embodied in the United Nations Charter. Men seem obstinately to reject the view that state behavior at some point is not a fit subject for moral judgment. One sign that this principle is accepted as relevant is the apparent compulsion of political actors to justify their needs in moral terms. Hypocrisy is the tribute vice pays to virtue. Beyond this there is a striking dialectical movement of expediency and morality which has its impact on international politics. Moves in practical politics must be articulated in such a way as to pay tribute to moral principles. However limited and particular, acts of political expedience must seem to carry forward aims of justice and the common good. Thus political morality in these modest terms forces the statesman who would justify expediency with ethics to choose his measures so that on some points at least the practical and moral march hand in hand. "It is political wisdom to act successfully in accord with the interests of state. It is political and moral wisdom to choose the most moral of several alternatives through which both expedience and ethics may be served." The margin which separates cynicism from this form of wisdom is frequently narrow indeed, but by it the statesman is saved from a fatuous "moralism" or the despair of unqualified expediency. It is the essence of moral judgment to transcend the limits of expediency and narrow self-interest in this one sense at least.

[37] Winston S. Churchill, *The Gathering Storm* (Boston: Houghton Mifflin Co., 1949), pp. 320-21.

Principle in this final sense is an ultimate objective, not an immediate guide to action. It is a lodestone of moral conduct, not a mere ideological rationalization by which practical steps are legitimatized. Principles in this sense are concepts held by statesmen whose reach quite self-consciously exceeds their grasp. Whereas their implementation in practice is dependent upon considerations of the national interest, they shine in the firmament of political philosophy as objective standards of political behavior. In any full and complete political system there must be room both for philosophy and action, yet there can be no more serious error than to confound these two conditions. The realms of ideals and practice are not the same, yet it is equally false to imagine they can never meet. If the vertical dimension be conceived as of the line of ideals, it does intersect at certain points in history the horizontal dimension of political practice. In this respect principle in relation to contingencies and necessity has a role to play.

CHAPTER 5

THE PROBLEM OF ISOLATIONISM AND
COLLECTIVE SECURITY

———◆●◆———

The Citizens of the United States cherish sentiments
the most friendly, in favor of the liberty and happiness of
their fellowmen on that side of the Atlantic. In the wars
of the European powers, in matters relating to themselves, we have never taken any part, nor does it comport
with our policy, so to do. It is only when our rights are
invaded, or seriously menaced, that we resent injuries,
or make preparations for our defense.—MESSAGE OF
PRESIDENT MONROE TO CONGRESS, DECEMBER 2, 1823

———◆●◆———

LARGE-SCALE social ideas, like far-flung empires, often have
their birth less in closely reasoned philosophies than in a burst
of popular passion or a fit of absent-mindedness. Of course it
is comforting to modern intellectuals to assert that major
political concepts and doctrines result from rational analysis
rooted in historical consciousness. We are all sufficiently the
children of the Enlightenment to cling stubbornly to the view
that history is the result of unfolding truth and that institutions stem from controlling ideas or are the long shadows of
a great man's philosophy. We fondly believe that a good
political idea will outlast a bad or faulty one. Writ large,
this principle may be true, yet it may also be true that "emotion, not intellect, is the dynamic of history." Historians
beholden to this second approach insist that massive social
forces carry men along and that philosophies or ideas become
mere rationalizations to account for experiences. One must
hasten to add that any simple determinist viewpoint challenging the creative and originative role of ideas is equally

174

fraught with ambiguity and peril. For example, large portions of mankind have apparently accepted the maxim that circumstances control the lives of men and ultimately their ideas. Whereas traditionally men held that ideas ruled the world and served as guides to action, today ideas are viewed as, at best, ideologies. In the Soviet world the doctrine of dialectical materialism has challenged the independent role of ideas, whereas in the West the religion of progress has prevailed. The historical fruits of these doctrines give no occasion for rejoicing that modern thought has unraveled the endless dilemmas that arise in relating ideas to social action.

It may, therefore, be appropriate that today we are witnessing a reexamination of certain major approaches to recent international relations and to the ideas underlying them. This inquiry causes us to ask whether our established truths are quite as firmly rooted as we had supposed. Some of our wisest observers question whether we hold too passionately and unreservedly to faith in the multiplication of security systems or emergent international government or less ambitious experiments like NATO, SEATO, and the Baghdad Pact. They urge us to explore today the foundations of collective security as it emerged from the Paris Peace Conference in 1919 in the same way that during the 1930's and early 1940's we questioned the supremacy both for theory and practice of "splendid isolation." This is a legitimate intellectual endeavor provided we apply standards of comparable rigor to the competing trends we explore. One way of doing this is to examine these major tendencies in the light of history and of some of the more basic conceptions of international relations and to test the assumptions and picture of the world which lie at the roots of isolation and collective security historically and, to the degree they persist, up to the present.

I. ISOLATIONISM: IDEA, IMPULSE, OR INTEREST?

America's foreign relations over the years are no exception to the cardinal rule that objective conditions largely shape and govern a nation's external relations. For approximately one hundred and thirty-four years from the Treaty of Paris in 1783 until World War I, the United States was relatively immune from the European struggle for power. We sometimes forget that in 1783 at the moment of victory in the struggle for independence, the Continental Congress reduced the army to a strength of eighty privates. On the signing of the Constitution, the demands of the western frontier had increased the number to five hundred. As late as 1837, Abraham Lincoln could speak of the impregnable status of the national domain even "in a trial of a thousand years" with the entire military potential of Europe, Asia, and Africa marshalled by a Napoleon. Indeed, not more than four decades ago an American President provided for the abolition of the army's staff division for war plans on the grounds that we did not contemplate involvement in war. This singular good fortune resulted from a convergence of at least three factors: America's geographical position and remoteness from Europe, the European balance of power, and the absence of strong and hostile neighbors. Even so, it must be noted that the United States fought two wars with its only powerful neighbor, Great Britain, and went to the brink with several others. These misfortunes inspired the kind of caution reflected as late as June 2, 1937, by Secretary of State Cordell Hull, who told four members of the House of Representatives who visited him in connection with the application of the Neutrality Act to Germany and Italy: "This is not our war. We must be cautious. We must be quiet."[1]

What, then, can we say about isolationism? Is it or has it

[1] Quoted in *Survey of International Affairs*, 1938 (London: Oxford University Press, 1938), Vol. II, p. 17.

ever been a carefully worked out philosophy or idea of international relations? Or is it primarily a national impulse reflecting the deeply felt but inchoate needs of the people? Or can we associate it with certain interest groups striving to assert and to rationalize their claims? Perhaps all three conditions are true, but if we examine the roots of isolationism the emphasis will probably fall more on one than on the others.

One way of encompassing our problem and fencing it in may be by enumerating the elements of isolationism as they are writ large in recent American history. One ingredient is undoubtedly the role of immigrant groups. They had shaken the dust of Europe from their feet and had crossed the Atlantic in the spirit of a "chosen people." They shared the intellectual and emotional tradition of men who have come out from a house of bondage into the "promised land." For them the dogma that they were not as other men was less an audacious paradox than an unquestioned truism. Their faith was reflected in a holy mission embodied in a century and a half of experience that served to confirm to a remarkable extent their underlying creed. Moreover, sacred sentiments and hallowed traditions stand above and beyond discussion, self-criticism, and compromise. In this, we shall discover, isolationism and collective security have something basically in common.

The immigrant in American life becomes a particularly crucial factor if we accept the view that proclamations of isolationism increasingly were founded more upon an attitude and frame of mind than on any clear conception of America's international situation. Immigrants held to the common conviction that their new country was *alter orbis* and that it behooved them to demonstrate unquestioning fealty to their new sovereign. They were prone to accept the sometimes historically relevant description of Europe as a region of "ambition, rivalship, interest, humor, or caprice." Power politics was an invention of Western Europe that Europe's heirs on the shores of North America were expected to spurn.

A second factor which nurtured an isolationist outlook was the continuing appeal of an essentially libertarian and anti-militaristic view of America's destiny. A succession of extremely able philosophers and writers found nonaggressive and abstentionist terms of reference to describe the nation's mission. Thus John C. Calhoun conceived that Americans would "do more to extend liberty by our example over this continent and the world generally, than would be done by a thousand victories." Protesting against the tendencies inherent in the Spanish-American War, William Graham Sumner wrote: "Expansion and imperialism are a grand onslaught on democracy . . . [they] are at war with the best traditions, principles, and interests of the American people."[2] Sumner saw European power politics as diametrically opposed to American ideals and heralded the Spanish-American War as the end of our cherished liberties. Indeed the notion that isolation is the one means of preserving democracy runs as a continuous theme from the views of the Founding Fathers to Senators William Borah and Robert A. Taft. It is clearly among the fundamentals of isolationist thought.

A corollary of this libertarian doctrine has been the emphasis on economics over politics. John Adams declared that he would lay down as a first principle of foreign policy that "we should calculate all our measures and foreign negotiations in such a manner, as to avoid too great dependence upon any power of Europe . . . that the business of America with Europe was commerce, not politics or war."[3] The term "treaty" itself was used in an early period of American history less often as an indication of a political bond than in a *traité de commerce*. Franklin spoke of exchanging "commerce for

[2] "The Conquest of the United States by Spain," *Essays of William Graham Sumner* (New Haven: Yale University Press, 1940), Vol. II, p. 295.
[3] Letter to Secretary Livingston, Paris, February 5, 1783, *The Works of John Adams*, ed. by Charles Francis Adams, 1850-56, Vol. VIII, p. 35.

friendship" and is reported to have offered the French agent in Philadelphia *un commerce exclusif*. In the early days of the Revolution the colonies were dependent upon foreign aid and the greater part of their gunpowder came from across the seas. In March 1776 Adams sketched out what he conceived as a proper form of alliance with France based upon the following formula: "1. No officers from her. 2. No military connection. Receive no troops from her. 3. Only a commercial connection; that is, make a treaty to receive her ships into our ports; let her engage to receive our ships into her ports; furnish us with arms, cannon, saltpetre, powder, duck and steel."[4]

In seeking to replace an international order of politics among nations with one of commerce between states, the colonists were following eighteenth-century thought. They had learned from the *philosophes* the tradition that was to become one of the pillars on which isolationism was to rest—though one must hasten to add that this tradition supported equally well at least one internationalist strain of thought. We must look to this tradition, however, to understand the objects of government and of foreign policy at the founding of the Republic. They were solely and simply to protect the individual in the exercise of certain rights. The nation's soil must be safeguarded from military or political intrusion and citizens must be protected and assisted when their activities, which were normally commercial, religious, or cultural, spilled over national boundaries. These two functions—promoting national security and private American economic activities abroad—were all that flowed from the original objects of American society. This libertarian view was put forth in the 1920's again by men like Senators William Borah, Hiram Johnson, and George Norris. There were, to be sure, a limited group who gave expression in a spirit of missionary zeal to

[4] John Adams, *Works*, Vol. II, pp. 488-89.

the spread of "republicanism" as early as the Greek Rebellion in 1820-1821 but in the first century or more of our history, liberty and isolation were commonly joined.

A third element, and perhaps the most basic, is the expansionist program which carried Americans westward across a vast continent that was virtually empty but enormously rich. From the French wars of the eighteenth century to the close of the nineteenth century, the American purpose was to open up a continental territory, to consolidate it within the Union, and to make it as invulnerable as possible against other powers. The struggle to secure a new continent officially ended only in 1890 with the close of the last of our thirty-seven wars with the Indians. Diplomacy opened the way for a series of successes that make all the more remarkable popular disdain of negotiations. To mention but a few notable successes: the Jay Treaty, the Louisiana Purchase, the Florida Annexation, the acquisition of Texas, the Oregon boundary settlement, the Treaty of Guadalupe Hidalgo, the Gadsden Purchase, the annexation of Alaska, and the establishment of American rights in an isthmian canal.

Ironically, the true believers in a policy of taming the continental domain are today called isolationists. Yet the memory of their struggles against foreign powers, the wilderness, and the Indians should make it plain that if they stood for anything in practice it was not pacifism or withdrawal. The words of our early leaders—Washington, Adams, Monroe, and their successors—must be viewed in historical context. When Washington urged political separation from Europe, he was painfully aware that his new nation was surrounded by unfriendly foreign powers. To assure a free hand for expansion to the West, his successors frequently quoted the words of his Farewell Address: "The great rule of conduct for us in regard to foreign nations is in extending our commercial relations to have with them as little political connection as possible." Moreover, it was to bring about the evacuation of the last frontier post held by British soldiers on American soil and to assure the opening for settlement of the Ohio Valley that Washington defended the unpopular Jay Treaty. Expansionists in eighteenth- and nineteenth-century America wished to isolate the continental domain and the Western Hemisphere, to conquer it not as an empire but as "a new domicile of freedom," and to accomplish their ends not in response to domination by others but with freedom of action. The expansionist impulse carried Americans westward to the Pacific, where at the mid-nineteenth century they paused at the "water's edge."

It is curious how the expansionist urge has characterized the programs of both political parties in the United States. Even present-day Republicans, who until recently clung to isolationism, have been imperialists and interventionists in Asia. Their political predecessors, having presided over the settlement and development of the west, consolidated the Union under Lincoln, saw the frontiers disappear, and were responsible in 1867 for the purchase of Alaska. They annexed Hawaii. They conquered the Philippines. They have provided their share of demagogues who exploited the aspirations of those looking westward to the promised land. The fervor of this expansionist program toward Asia reduced the energy which could be directed to participation in European affairs. In Louis Halle's words: "While the image of Europe has traditionally aroused in us a cherished sense of escape, the image of the Far East has tended, rather, to invite our proselytization." Some of our friends abroad have suggested that the Far East historically has offered opportunities of dominion and influence denied to us in Europe.

Alongside the expansionist tradition there is also an anti-expansionist view respecting our course of empire to the west. It reflects itself in the "little United States" line of thought deriving from Hamilton; in the arguments, albeit constitutional, against the Louisiana Purchase; in certain Whig attitudes on the Mexican War, and in the polemics against expansion in 1812. It may give us a clue to another and partly contradictory source of isolationism, namely, a reluctance to embrace the full powers of the Executive Office. C. B. Marshall suggests that isolationism "was the logical and prudent condition of U.S. foreign relations in the epoch of creating a nation from the potpourri of ethnic origins and filling out a continental range, and represented a realistic appreciation of the conditions of power during those decades."

By referring to these three elements of isolationism—the role of immigrant or ethnic groups, the libertarian traditions, and westward expansion—we have of course hardly made contact with the central problem of the existence of a theory of isolationism. In one sense it is futile to talk of a theory of isolationism, for the term is charged with emotion and has increasingly acquired pejorative connotations. Isolationism and the mythology surrounding it suggest inaction, passivity, lethargy, and withdrawal. Is it any wonder that those who espouse isolationism prefer to be called nationalists, continentalists, or even "America Firsters"? If isolationism is seldom if ever professed but rather ascribed or imputed to objects of attack, a coherent, self-conscious, and self-critical theory seems almost beyond reach. Isolationism is not a theory but a predicament, we are told. Or, it is useful "only insofar as it indicates the misunderstanding of an ideology, serves as a point of departure for investigation, and contains in its connotations certain suggestive half-truths."[5]

These criticisms and impressions suggest that whereas isolationism may be either an impulse or the reflection of interests or interest groups, it is surely not a theory. Before we accept this judgment, however, we should perhaps look somewhat

[5] Alfred Weinberg, "The Historical Meaning of the American Doctrine of Isolationism," *American Political Science Review*, Vol. XXXIV, No. 3, June 1940, p. 539.

further. It may be that we shall find a deposit of ideas, beliefs, and values that can be analyzed and assessed.

The historian Alfred Weinberg has written: "In all seriousness, isolation is not a theory of American foreign policy. Isolation is a theory about a theory of American foreign policy."[6] Who coined the word? If we view isolation in strictest terms, Washington can hardly be called its father. He warned against too much *political* connection, but this scarcely inhibited him from agreements respecting commerce and trade, nor did it stand in the way of completing an alliance with France. Following Washington, few of his successors harked back to an avowedly isolationist course, although Seward spoke of the first President's counsel as one of isolation if "superficially viewed." For the most part not the advocates of a policy of self-limitations but their opponents seeking to discredit them made a doctrine out of isolationism—criticizing, for example, those who opposed crusades like mid-nineteenth century support of revolutionary liberalism of Europe. The reserve of the isolationists was exaggerated and made into a weapon of political warfare.

Perhaps the core idea of isolationism is what has been called "national reserve" or "a deliberate and more or less regular abstention from certain political relationships." It is an attempt to isolate a state from entangling foreign relations. Plainly, such a concept is not an American invention. It has its parallels in the "Little England" movement in the nineteenth century, certain Australian attitudes, and, far broader, in the universal human desire to think first about things nearest home. It amounts to the nonjuridical side of sovereignty. It finds expression wherever sovereign states seek maximum self-determination or freedom of action. Its American version, however, has accented aspects that are not everywhere stressed. Take, for example, nonentanglement. Ideally, in a world

[6] *Ibid.*

devoid of conflicts, self-determination might entitle a state to freedom from all alien interference. In the real world, it oftentimes requires treaties of mutual aid or alliances designed to safeguard independence itself. Because of America's geographical detachment, the place of alliances seemed distant and remote. Gradually this antipathy and suspicion of treaties spilled over into resistance to every source of entanglement, including policies, designed to promote commerce which might lead to political contacts or to parallel but independent foreign policies of two or more states. Nonentanglement was possible for a country in the Western Hemisphere but with rare exceptions for nation-states squeezed together in the heart of Europe it would have destroyed independence and with it all "freedom of action." What would have happened, for example, to the states making up a coalition against Napoleon if they had maintained that sovereignty involved freedom from all entangling alliances? Certain basic assumptions underlying America's approach to foreign policy, such as confidence in our self-sufficiency, a belief in the divergence of our interests from those of others, and a sense of moral and political superiority, gave a unique flavor to American isolationism. There was a residual deposit of ideas, about which we shall have more to say later, which formed the theoretical basis of our isolationism. But, instead of bringing these concepts to the surface, giving them their due, and adapting them to changing circumstances, both friends and foes of isolation saw fit to erect such temporary expedients or instruments of isolationism as "nonentanglement" into ends or absolutes in themselves.

There are other examples of ideas and policies that may have served the basic idea of reserve and freedom of action but are scarcely equivalent. Nonintervention became such a doctrine for some American makers of policy who defined it *in extremis* to mean any trespass upon the external or internal sovereignty of others not warranted by a life-or-death defense

184

of our most vital interests. Underlying this was a fear of counter-intervention and an obsession with the perils of being caught up in the swift currents of international life. International law and its rules respecting intervention figured less prominently, for in one sense American policies of nonintervention have been *sui generis*.

The problem of a theory of isolationism is therefore weighted down with difficulties and uncertainties. There is a central idea that supports all the partial insights we have mentioned. It is in effect the concept Washington enunciated when he spoke about retaining "command of our fortunes." Its servants are policies of "reserve." Yet this idea has expressed itself in a variety of creeds and dogmas which include "noninterference and nonparticipation in European politics," "avoidance of joint action," "insulation against entanglement," and all the other principles cited above. Moreover, these limited concepts became sanctified and encrusted with tradition until they were no longer conceived as "counsels of prudence." They hardened into iron rules for conduct. The manifold ingredients making up isolationism prevented the isolationist from looking for consistency and opposed the crystallizing of a perceptive theory. It made isolationism a "happy hunting ground" for politicians and invited fierce and impassioned debate instead of reasoned analysis. Writing of the so-called theory, one scholar has noted: "Because this interpretation is a poor theory, misrepresentative even if taken only semi-literally, it has placed the discussion of American foreign policy in a bad predicament of obfuscation, not without its influence upon national decisions."[7]

In consequence we are likely to find the mainsprings of isolationism in the play of national impulse and of interest and ethnic groups. This is a theme that runs through the inquiries by Samuel Lubell, and it is one which in its myriad complexity deserves the careful analysis and attention he gives

[7] *Ibid.*

to it. Our purpose here is merely to suggest that as a theory isolationism was deficient not because it lacked certain residual truths but as a result of the way in which these truths were restricted and exploited in political practice. Consequently anti-European and more particularly anti-English sentiment—most notably expressed by the Irish, the Germans, and the Swedes—was more important than any rational set of isolationist ideals. Thus isolationism as a whole has not been a constant force nor a stable doctrine with a unique ideology. It has fluctuated in response to given situations and reflected ideas and attitudes of differing groups which espoused it as suited their interests. Moreover, these ideas tended to calcify, making difficult the rapid shifts and adjustments of policies that were required.

There was a final weakness preventing the emergence of a rational theory of isolationism that would do justice equally to the uniformities, ambiguities, and complexities of international life. This weakness may be illustrated by a reference to the late Senator Robert A. Taft. If any isolationist or neo-isolationist might have been expected to leave an enduring legacy of isolationist theory, it would be a man of Taft's intelligence and integrity. Yet one looks in vain for consistency and coherence in the foreign policies he embraced. Prior to World War II, he held to a policy of neutrality, maintaining that we had nothing to fear from Germany or from the deterioration of the European situation. He predicted that the outcome of a war in Europe would have no bearing on American security; we could easily defend ourselves. Yet the logic of his position was undermined by his support for substantial and ever-increasing defense costs and was eventually destroyed by his championing of aid to Britain. (He insisted he had favored a loan to Britain, Canada, and Greece amounting to two billion dollars before lend-lease "was ever introduced or invented.") This in spite of repeated denials that American security was bound up in any way with that of

England. The touchstone of Taft's foreign policy before World War II was his fond hope that the United States be left alone.

Beginning in 1944, Taft became one of the most enthusiastic supporters of a new international organization. Moreover, he demanded that a "United Nations" be capable of solving disputes by judicial process. At the same time he favored the veto and challenged any diminution of sovereignty. If in this unhappy state of affairs disputes proved not to be susceptible of judicial solution, he preferred that we isolate ourselves from them. He appeared to assume that the cause of justice would be strengthened more by our doing nothing than by our doing the best we could in an unsatisfactory situation. These internal conflicts and inconsistencies reached a climax as Taft became the leader of the opposition. During Truman's administrations he was endlessly critical but rarely constructive. He was against the size of defense spending, whether eleven or forty billion dollars were involved. He opposed increase of European defense forces on grounds that the Soviet Union might be provoked, but favored a more decisive Far Eastern military campaign on grounds that there could be "no possible threat" to Russia "from anything we may do in China." John P. Armstrong sums up his excellent study of Taft by noting: "His [Taft's] ideas fit no recognizable pattern; there is neither a consistent body of ideas bearing directly on the problem of foreign policy nor a progression from one position to another."[8]

Yet if Taft's ideas on foreign policy were inconsistent, it can be argued that what he had to say about the domestic consequences of foreign policy had a coherence, a consistency, and almost a rigidity in its application. Whereas for many of our historic Western writers and statesmen the "primacy of

[8] John P. Armstrong, "The Enigma of Senator Taft and American Foreign Policy," *The Review of Politics*, Vol. XVII, No. 2, April 1955, p. 221.

foreign policy" over domestic policies and consequences was widely accepted, for Senator Taft the direct opposite was true. He took his stand for a strong legislature and a maximum of personal and economic freedom. He directed his wrath against big government, a strong executive, and high taxes. When he questioned lend-lease it was mainly in terms of the power it assigned the President. He opposed compulsory military service, not because world political conditions made it unnecessary but out of concern that it might destroy democratic government. He came to attack President Truman's decision in Korea, not because he questioned the soundness of such a policy but because in his mind it represented a usurpation of executive power.

Mr. Armstrong concludes: "Senator Taft's ideal was the preservation of the late nineteenth century American political and economic system to which he attributed this country's greatness. He saw it almost as an absolute around which all else turned. Conscious, first of all, that any active foreign policy would seriously interfere with the attainment of this ideal, he approached every proposal in a hostile manner. Dumbfounded, as he contemplated the domestic consequences of each new policy, he was psychologically unprepared to inquire into either its soundness as a policy or the conditions with which it was supposed to deal. Merely for him to have acknowledged the existence of a serious threat to American security would have entailed compromising his stand against Big Executive government, for international crises have a way of tending to reduce the role of Congress to that of a ratifying body, and of serving to increase the powers of government."[9]

If this can be said of a political leader with the extraordinary intellectual endowments and acumen of Senator Taft, it must be obvious that the theoretical foundations of isolationism are impoverished indeed. In a word, the problem of isolationism has been that, lacking roots in an enduring theory,

[9] *Ibid.*, p. 229.

it has taken root in ad hoc strategies and policies cast in the form of principles such as nonintervention and nonentanglement. Like plants artificially preserved long after they have withered and died, these policies as time has gone on have been confused with the theory in itself and come to claim the homage, devotion, and loyalty that broader precepts should command. The deposit of political truths that surrounded isolationism in an era when it formed a viable foreign policy was in consequence obscured and concealed from those who rushed in to supply a new theory. Perhaps partly because of the excesses and rigidities of isolationists, the proponents of collective security lost sight of the changeless truths underlying this ancient creed and in so doing perpetrated a new philosophy rooted less in impulse than theory—but a theory distorted, exaggerated, and ultimately enfeebled by its own excessive rationalism and utopianism. When we have held this new theory up to the mirror of reality, we shall in conclusion return to the lessons of isolationism seen in relation to the meaning of collective security.

II. COLLECTIVE SECURITY AS IDEA AND REALITY

From one standpoint it is a truism to say that collective security is something new under the sun. In past eras, especially in the eighteenth and nineteenth centuries, war was conceived of as a duel in which contestants should be isolated and restrained by the rest of international society. When nations engaged in armed conflict their neighbors sought to localize the struggles and alleviate war's poisonous effects. However shortsighted their actions in not meeting the conflict directly and turning back aggression at its source, the nations pursuing these policies were sometimes successful for varying periods of time in preserving islands of peace in a warring world.

On August 8, 1932, however, Secretary of State Henry L. Stimson proclaimed that the modern state system was entering a new era in which warring powers were no longer entitled to the same equally impartial and neutral treatment by the rest of society. He announced to the New York Council of Foreign Relations that in future conflicts one or more of the combatants must be designated as wrongdoer and added: "We no longer draw a circle about them and treat them with punctilios of the duelist's code. Instead we denounce them as lawbreakers.[10]

This is the cornerstone of the almost universally recognized theory of collective security to which most Western statesmen profess loyalty today. It is said that Stimson's memoirs, *On Active Service*, have become the bible of the Department of State, and in Britain we have the word of *The Times* (London) that collective security "indeed, is the view to which this country, like most others, is committed by its membership in the United Nations."

It is important that we ask at the outset, What is collective security in theory? What are its precepts and main tenets? What, in simplest terms, is the philosophy of collective security? The rock-bottom principle upon which collective security is founded provides that an attack on any one state will be regarded as an attack on all states. It finds its measure in the apparently simple doctrine of one for all and all for one. War anywhere, in the context of Article 11 of the League of Nations, is the concern of every state.

Self-help and neutrality, it should be obvious, are the exact antithesis of such a theory. States under an order of neutrality are impartial when conflict breaks out, give their blessing to combatants to fight it out, and defer judgment regarding the justice or injustice of the cause involved. Self-help in the past was often "help yourself" so far as the great powers were concerned; they enforced their own rights, and more besides. In the eighteenth and nineteenth centuries this system was

[10] Henry L. Stimson and McGeorge Bundy, *On Active Service in Peace and War* (New York: Harper & Brothers, 1947), p. 259.

fashionable and war, although not eliminated, was localized whenever possible. In a more integrated world, a conflict anywhere has some effect on conditions of peace everywhere. Disturbance at one point upsets equilibrium at other points, and the adjustment of a single conflict restores the foundations of harmony throughout the world.

This idea of collective security is simple, challenging, and seemingly novel. It would do for the international society what police action does for the domestic community. If the individual is threatened or endangered in municipal society, he turns to the legitimate agents of law enforcement, the police. The comparatively successful operation of this system has meant relative peace and tolerable harmony for most local communities. Through the action of police or "fire brigades" on a world scale, collective security has as its goal two comparable objectives. It would prevent war by providing a deterrent to "aggression." It would defend the interests of "peace-loving" states in war if it came, by concentrating preponderance of power against the "aggressor." These two ends have been goals of both the League and the United Nations.

This doctrine of collective security bears little resemblance to the march of events from 1919 to 1960. The real issue concerning collective security from the beginning has had little to do with charters or precepts or institutions. Consequently, the past forty years have witnessed in rapid succession two tragically destructive wars which the historian Arnold Toynbee compares to the double wars of the Romans and the Carthaginians and the two struggles of the Peloponnesian Wars which wrecked Hellenic civilization. Their cause must be sought less in the doctrines of the time than in the apparently irreconcilable clash between the foreign policies of certain major powers.

Collective security in practice has been hampered by three persistent problems, all stemming from one fundamental source. In a word this source is the fatal divorce of the theory from political reality. First, if peace is to be maintained, there must be some minimum consensus regarding the territorial arrangements that are to be preserved. The peace-enforcement agency must have a peace to defend. Following World War I, the new international organization was founded simultaneously with the establishment of peace but, as had been true with the Holy Alliance, the nations most responsible for implementing the peace soon found that they gave it a different content. For France the status quo or peace required that Germany be kept in a state of continuing inferiority. French predominance on the continent was considered vital to the status quo. Britain by contrast was prepared for concessions to Germany aimed at creating a balance between France and Germany. When France hesitated in applying sanctions against Italy in the Ethiopian crisis, it did so because of the hope of maintaining Italy as a counter to increasing German strength. Following the Second World War, the relation between international government and the peace occupies an even more precarious state. The weight of thought on the timing of a peace conference had favored its postponement until passions cooled and more reasonable negotiations were possible. This was the lesson of Versailles, it was said, and on this Cordell Hull, members of the Commission to Study the Organization of Peace, and James F. Byrnes all spoke with one voice. We see now that this approach has been no more successful than the approach at Versailles and the absence of a status quo imperils the United Nations no less than the divergence between France and England as to the meaning of interwar status quo weakened and helped to destroy the League of Nations.

Second, the strength of international organization for the foreseeable future must rest upon the frail reed of a collection of separate national interests sometimes compatible but oftentimes conceived of as divergent with one another. Perhaps the most stubborn mistake in our thinking about international organization has been to assume that states through reason and persuasion could be made to see that their selfish national interests could always be served best by embracing something called the international interest. Leaders have appealed to the great powers to take "the long view," as Senator Arthur H. Vandenberg did when in a speech before the Senate on January 10, 1945, he examined the Russian claim that it must have a circle of friendly states on its borders to give security against German aggression. He replied: "The alternative is collective security . . . which is better in the long view, from a purely selfish Russian standpoint: To forcefully surround herself with a cordon of unwillingly controlled or partitioned states, thus affronting the opinion of mankind . . . or to win the priceless asset of world confidence in her by embracing the alternative, namely, full and wholehearted cooperation with and reliance upon a vital international organization."

In all honesty the historian must add another leaf to Senator Vandenberg's handbook. He and other American statesmen, while raising this standard for others, have not infrequently both in word and deed appealed to another less lofty if more attainable political goal. Indeed few have been as transparently candid as Senator Vandenberg in expressing the hope that American spokesmanship at the peace table be at least as loyal to America's own primary interests as Mr. Stalin is certain to be in respect to Russia and Mr. Churchill to the British Empire. The Senator appeared to invoke a second rule of thumb when he warned that no one is going to look out for us unless we look out for ourselves. In fact, the view that American statesmen have been free from concern for immediate strategic interests is both mischievous and untrue.

Some of the best Western thinkers were constrained to warn at the founding of the United Nations that the primacy of the individual nation-state and its interests was still a reality. Thus J. L. Brierly cautioned: "In any case we must this time avoid the mistake which the Covenant made of assuming that every state's interest in the maintenance of international order was equal to that of every other, and also that every state's interest would be the same without regard to the region of the world in which order might be threatened or broken."[11] These moderate words were drowned out by the overwhelmingly predominant view that the brave new world in effect demanded of all men that national purposes be supplanted by world interests in which all equally have a stake.

By hindsight, wiser and more informed observers would feel that Professor Brierly perceived more clearly the true nature of present-day international society than did many of his contemporaries. We note, for example, that Britain has been prepared to defend her international responsibilities in the Middle East more readily than other states because for England these resources have been a matter of life and death. In Korea, the U.S. saw further communist expansion as a threat to its long-run interests in Asia. Some years ago Paul Henri Spaak in an address before the Foreign Press Union declared: "There must be a hierarchy in international obligations. The nations of the continent cannot be asked to consider with the same realism and sincerity of judgment affairs which directly concern them and events which are taking place thousands of kilometres away in regions where they have neither interests nor influence. Indivisible peace, mutual assistance, and even collective security are general ideas whose practical effect must be clearly explained and clearly limited."[12]

Despite these facts which in 1945-1946 were disparaged as fictions, there is truth in the maxim that peace tends to be indivisible, especially in an atomic age. War feeds on itself

[11] J. L. Brierly, *The Outlook for International Law* (Oxford: The Clarendon Press, 1944), p. 87.
[12] Quoted in *Survey of International Affairs*, 1936, pp. 354-55.

and like a contagious disease will spread unless it can some-how be quarantined. In this sense all states have an interest in checking even small wars before they fester into big ones. Collective security when conceived of as the successor to peaceful settlement when conciliators have failed in their task can be a way of meeting this problem. However, those who are preoccupied with sanctions and enforcement may sometimes be unaware that what is most needed is a poultice to draw the infectious poison from a conflict, not a sword drawn in punitive action. The friends and extreme spokesmen of collective security sometimes display a lamentable tendency to wait until a breach of the peace occurs and then pounce vengefully on the offender as if he were no more than a wicked child. Sometimes minor wars may lead to all-out conflict, but again they can through reasonable precautions be localized. Unhappily for the dogmatists there can be no "one" remedy. Sometimes intervention may be called for; again "hands off" may be needed. The chief trouble with the theory of collective security is that in seeking a generalized and normative pattern, it assumes too cavalierly that nations with needs and interests will act as policemen whether or not they see their own interests threatened. If we demand that nations act wholly in a disinterested and international way, in effect we ask them to cease to be nations.

Third, international government can give reality to collective security only when authority within the organization is commensurate with that outside. It is tempting to view international institutions in such formal terms that the dynamic role of the foreign policy of member and nonmember states is obscured. An approach which recognizes the politics of international organization is confronted at almost every point with the need to relate decisions within the peace structure to those in the outside world. The League foundered and failed less because of an imperfect constitutional system than because the centers of power in world politics never corresponded with the locus of authority at Geneva. Earlier in the nineteenth century, the Holy Alliance failed because the Concert of Europe lost contact with an objective political situation created by states whose interests were at odds with the aristocratic regimes of Europe united under an ideology of legitimacy. At present it is difficult to see how a United Nations can preserve the peace if leading centers of power are excluded from its decision-making agencies. To some extent the shift in power from the Security Council to the General Assembly reflects the emergence of countries like India whose voice must be reckoned with despite absence from the Council. But as Germany and China take an increasing part in world politics, an age-old problem which confounded the two earlier experiments in organized international action will doubtless become more and more troublesome. Beyond this, the United Nations has the curious effect from time to time of inverting these relationships by putting into the hands of a small group of states with comparatively modest power and responsibility in the world the fate of important nations. The Arab-Asian bloc presently holds the balance of power in the United Nations and can determine the content of resolutions that sometimes strike at the heart of the vital interests of other powers while safeguarding India's vital interests in Kashmir and Egypt's control over Suez. It remains to be seen how long this situation can continue before it evokes a reaction, particularly when one great power plays one game when its vital interests are at stake while the West accepts other rules of the game. Moreover, it is interesting to speculate whether the United States can be as magnanimous with its own vital interests as it has recently been with those of others.

Conclusions

Looking back over the past forty years, we can say that isolationism and collective security as major trends in America's foreign relations have shared certain qualities in common. Neither has been in itself a cure nor substitute for war. Neither proved adequate to forestall the great calamities from which we have suffered. Neither had any absolute value and each has influenced the shape of the other in American practice. To this we may add that one or both appear to have suffered from a high rate of obsolescence. Take as an illustration the validity today of two cardinal assumptions that underlay collective security. First, it was assumed that the anticipated hostile act with which the world would be confronted would be an overt military one, clearly identifiable as aggressive. Aside from the problem of defining aggression, for which no international body has discovered a satisfactory formula, it becomes ever clearer that the military threat is not necessarily the gravest issue confronting the world today. Instead, perils creep in upon us in manifold ways, including that of "concealed aggression," through which forces that are ostensibly domestic in nature seize power, as in China. With the revolt of peoples in underdeveloped countries and the rapid pace of demands for social change, the military problems of our day have to a considerable degree been superseded by economic and political threats.

A second basic assumption of collective security provides that "the combined military strength of the members and their effective coordination will be adequate to deter or meet aggression." In practice the organization of preponderant military power is difficult if not impossible to come by. Moreover, the importance of a mere collection of allies in a grand coalition is relative to a host of other factors. These include the level of armed strength of the members, the extent of their military coordination, the degree of unity between them and prospects for their resolution and political morale in time of stress. The number of countries arrayed against an aggressor is not a negligible factor. But with respect to deterrence it is hardly an absolute. There hangs over a coalition a law of diminishing returns. It appears to be true that the wider a coalition, the more difficult become the problems of harnessing armed action to a single strategy, preserving secrecy and suddenness of decision, taking advantage of bluff and surprise and rapid maneuver, and showing restraint. Proponents of collective security, in arguing that an aggressor aware of the number of powers arrayed against him would swallow his evil designs, have overlooked the inherent weaknesses that go hand in hand with the strengths of any massive coalition. Indeed, it is entirely possible when all is said and done that the military and political posture of a single leading power in such a coalition, rather than its scope or magnitude, may prove the principal deterrent. Furthermore, as conflicts proliferate on a wide geographic front, the interests of states whose destinies are intimately bound up with the welfare of the region involved may be more decisive than the vague and essentially negative obligations undertaken by states in global security arrangements. As Asia, Africa, and the Middle East enter world politics more actively as subjects—rather than as objects, it may be a fair question to ask whether concern with regional centers of power buttressed by friendly states outside the area is not more important than the search for universal collective systems. If so, collective systems like SEATO and CENTO may be open to the gravest question.

This assumption of collective security presumes an integrated world community in which aggression, right and wrong, and law and violence can be simply and unambiguously determined. Yet, in the international realm as it is, nations rarely if ever contend over what the law is. Historically they have gone to war over what the law ought to be or how certain legal and political arrangements should be interpreted. If this has been the case in the comparatively homogeneous world which revolved around Europe as its center, is it not infinitely more true when international society is in a constant state of change and flux with some peoples emerging from a colonial status, others sinking back into a state of virtual dependence, and with new forms of nationalism being continuously and boisterously asserted. In this kind of world an absolute and inflexible defense of collective security would be as unreal as the earlier appeals for the outlawry of war. Both are heard as anguished cries of protest against the intolerable existence of the world. Naïvely construed, collective security becomes a futile attempt to freeze a status quo that refuses to be frozen, as well as an obstacle to the processes of peaceful change.

Isolationism has in turn its peculiar perils. Its apparent stress on the primacy of the national interest and the right of a state in a troubled world to retain control over its own destiny is for the foreseeable future a valid and neglected truth. Yet the national interest for isolationists is identified traditionally with the emotions and impulses of particular ethnic groups or of chosen economic or intellectual elites within the nation. Seldom has the American isolationist proceeded from an objective appraisal of our vital interests, the distribution of power in the world, or the threats to American security. This may be true again today in the various inter-service disputes involving Admiral Arthur W. Radford and some of his successors. Someone responsible for foreign policy, looking dispassionately at the continuation of conflict in the world, might conclude that wars in some form are inevitable. He might decide, however, that an exception could be atomic or hydrogen conflicts. Preparing in part for the worst through some emphasis on new weapons, he might at the same time insist that conventional military forces should be kept in a state of readiness to meet limited conflicts. In truth, both prudence and recent history in Korea and Indo-China lend support to this approach. We may ask then whether the type of neutrality which insists that American military preparations should be designed exclusively for the absolute struggle is not in a sense a latter-day version of isolationism. Is the one-shot approach to global conflict a case of having everything rather than nothing to do with the world and having done with it as quickly as possible? Can we define neo-isolationism as isolationism turned inside out? Is it a matter of isolating the making of decisions in foreign policy from the endless pressures and contacts of other sovereign states, rather than insulating the Western Hemisphere as in the past? Is it having everything rather than nothing to do with the world—but on one's own terms?

In the final analysis perhaps isolationism and collective security threaten to mislead us because of their dismissal of politics with its uncertainties, its limited actions, and its tactics of advance and retreat. The one boasts a heritage, kept alive by the passion of ethnic minorities striving valiantly to prove their Americanism, which identifies politics, compromise, and adjustment in diplomacy and alliances with the decadence and corruption of Europe. Despite the rich intellectual resources devoted to its defense, isolationism has failed to supply a lasting and viable theory of international relations. It has sacrificed its command of certain residual truths by clinging to the form rather than the substance of freedom of action within limits. Command of one's fortunes in a nation as in a family can never be absolute. It requires a recognition of certain mutualities of interests without sacrificing what is essential. Isolation gives us no theory of international politics because in fact it has been indifferent to international politics with its uncertain terrain, its dilemmas and tragic compromises, its ambiguities, half-truths, and shades of grey, and its inevitable stress on abhorrent terms like power and national interest.

But for different reasons, collective security has failed us, has left us with problems it could never solve, and has preserved and increased the gap already existing between theory and practice. It has approached foreign policy dogmatically and legalistically rather than pragmatically. While isolation provides no theory, collective security gives us a philosophy so abstract and idealized as to provide little guidance in practice. To make collective security effective even in the most modest way, the policy-maker in any instance would have to ask a series of questions: Is overt military aggression the main thing to be feared? Are the methods prescribed to counter it ones likely to be disruptive to the power of resistance to other forms of aggression? Is it possible to define acts of aggression in a manner agreed to by all the members of the coalition? Is the status quo to be preserved by collective security capable of and worth preserving, or is it likely to come apart at the seams despite all efforts?

When such questions are answered in each emerging case the value of collective security can be gauged. Clearly the moral is that collective security as a means of achieving world peace is no more an absolute than arbitration or disarmament or the outlawry of war. Its positive value may sometimes be very great, but this will depend on a whole series of specific variables which cannot be brought under the control of any fixed theoretical concept. It is unhappily the case that however persistently men may seek for some blanket code of procedural rules, compliance with a code would automatically do away with such realities as the immense variety of the human family, the inescapable conflicts of its members as they seek influence and power, and the fact that human behavior is only partially calculable by man himself, by reason of the fact that he lacks both the means and the moral courage fully to understand himself.

If collective security is insufficient as a theory of international relations, it may nonetheless have its place if applied judiciously and with immense reserve and self-restraint. It can be a means of organizing and making legitimate the network of mutual interests of a "free-world" coalition, especially if the task of preserving the tenuous ties among them is taken seriously. This calls for the best arts of statecraft and diplomacy, arts which antedate collective security by centuries.

Perhaps the supreme paradox of American foreign policy today is the necessity placed upon us to seize and employ the essentially utopian instruments of collective security in a brutally realistic power struggle. Its agencies furnish a political framework through which the broad coalition of the free world can be strengthened and a more stable equilibrium of world power be restored.

For every concrete policy the value of policies for the consolidation of the "free world" must be measured coolly and dispassionately against the effects on our ties with the neutral and uncommitted nations. In certain cases they may yearn more for economic aid or political recognition than mutual guarantees. Thus an empirical and pragmatic approach as against a legalistic and punitive view of collective security finds uses more modest and limited than the ardent advocate assumes.[13] It is but one variable among many. It aims at the institutionalizing of force but perhaps must settle for the facilitating of a more stable balance of power. Today's realities are such that it should be played in a minor key as against economic growth, peaceful change, and the harmonizing of differences. Tomorrow's facts could call for new estimates and insights. Until then, perhaps we should safeguard and preserve the recurring truths we find at the heart of isolationism and collective security, however inadequate, until we have a more inclusive and recognized body of theory for American foreign policy.

[13] A few writers early warned against the legalistic approach, among them Alfred T. Mahan in *Armaments and Arbitration* (New York: Harper & Brothers, 1912), p. 99, who said: "Law lacks elasticity, not merely because it itself, at least in international relations, may be correct as a general proposition, yet cannot always be applied satisfactorily to a particular case. In some instances a different instrument is required. A political impasse must be met by a special provision, by measures which shall proceed on a basis not of strict legality, but of evident necessary expediency; in short, by diplomacy rather than by law."

CHAPTER 6

THE AMERICAN DILEMMA

————————•◦•————————

> While there is battle and hatred men have eyes for
> nothing save the fact that the enemy is the cause of all
> the troubles; but long, long afterwards, when all pas-
> sion has been spent, the historian often sees that it was a
> conflict between one half-right that was perhaps too
> wilful, and another half-right that was perhaps too
> proud; and behind even this he discerns that it was a
> terrible predicament apparently beyond the wit of man
> to resolve.—HERBERT BUTTERFIELD

————————•◦•————————

FIFTY YEARS from now Americans looking back upon our
foreign relations will judge us as we judge our forebears. It
may not be completely idle to speculate for a moment on the
possible character of their judgment. Will they say that we
lived in an age of greatness that flourished as America slowly,
hesitatingly, but unflinchingly, assumed a position of world
leadership? Will they say that as we grew stronger, our
wisdom, responsibility, and justice deepened; or will it be
true of us as of the great powers of the past, whether the
Roman Empire, Greek Republic, or French State, that we
were corrupted by power, enfeebled by perplexities, internal
dissension, and uncertainty, and destroyed by our loss of the
capacity to act within the limits of our power? What will they
say about the intellectual climate, about the spirit in which we
approached our problems, about the philosophy of foreign
relations of the people and their intellectual and political
leaders? How will they judge the courage of those in authority
and the responsiveness of the great mass of goodhearted but
half-informed ordinary men and women? What will they

think of our devotion to moral principles or our qualities in that realm the ancients called practical wisdom? Will it be the judgment of history that our fateful position as an island of plenty and prosperity in a global sea of poverty and insecurity tempted us after numerous encounters with our hapless but ungrateful friends to withdraw to the safe haven of the American continent? Is it possible that the baffling pace and bewildering complexity of world problems will exceed the capacities of human resources for coping with them, keeping them in check, or solving them in at least a provisional way? Or, will human resourcefulness and ingenuity find new ways of encompassing our difficulties? Can we discover the moral resources for acting when we cannot foresee the consequences of our actions, for choosing between practical alternatives weighed down with ambiguities and imperfections, and for guiding the people to accept the things they might do if they had the grasp and knowledge that their leaders possess? I am emboldened to think that these are the crucial issues and the standards by which we shall be judged, not our professions of high principle, ringing affirmations of devotion to institutions like the United Nations, or the flaunting of appeals to the moral conscience of mankind. I am impressed that in facing the future we confront some baffling and almost impossible choices among alternatives that are far from clearly and logically most desirable. Moreover, we must reach our decisions in realms where we have had the least success in the past.

I. THE STATE OF THE AMERICAN MIND

It would be reassuring to say that America in its time of challenge from the brutalities, complexities, and uncertainties of the external world had put its own house in order and organized its thoughts and ideas. A democracy for more than a century and a half with successes that outdistance the fondest hopes of the Founding Fathers, we are endlessly tempted to maintain that our free institutions are secure, our rights safe-guarded, and our conception of domestic and international politics clear and sure. Our accomplishments in every realm pay tribute to American inventiveness; we are a positive people with faith in the future and in man as the measure of things, including the God who is seen in the image of man. As a successful people we easily grow impatient with the failings on one hand of nations whose greatest achievements are presumed to lie in the past or, on the other, of newly emerging states who are painfully groping toward a better life. From the throne of the world, we look to Europe and Asia not as equals but as peoples to be understood, however compassionately, each in their own less fortunate terms. We approach our problems not with the fresh curiosity and wonder of the young child but, ironically at the dawning of our leadership, with the fixed doctrines of the self-made, older man. We speak to Europeans in the condescending tone of greater morality. We see Europe as a civilization whose past greatness is beclouded by imperialism, colonialism, and power politics, sins from which we assume we are free. Europe is like the aging father who has had his chance while we as the aspiring and buoyant youth seek with our virtues to crowd out all his ancient and unhappy failings. In much the same spirit, the misery, poverty, and exploitation of underdeveloped regions are expected to yield to the command of our material resources, for we view the world's economic problems in the light of the relative equality that has been attained in American economic life. Their economic and political development sometimes appears to be more our goal than the will of the local peoples.

This brief commentary of course exaggerates the American outlook and singles out certain tendencies that are less than the whole of American thinking. I have deliberately over-stated, and not for a moment would I leave an impression that this viewpoint is dominant for all. Notably since World

War II, American foreign policy has cut loose from the moorings of "splendid isolation" and consciously embraced the firm ties of partnership with peoples in Europe and Asia. We have bilateral security arrangements with more than forty nations and our loyalty to the United Nations is beyond dispute. We point to the Marshall Plan as an act of almost unparalleled generosity. Yet the tendency of seeing ourselves as morally and spiritually, if not geographically, apart from the other nations of the world is always present, though hidden beneath the surface, ready to erupt or appear. It affects our approach to problems like colonialism, diplomacy or the use of force, and influences the trend toward a too sanguine point of view about prospects of charting the future. The brutalities, complexities, and uncertainties of foreign relations escape us because of the state of the American mind, and we falter particularly in the realm of means, where discriminate judgments, not higher instincts, are at stake.

Not the least of our problems arise from the facts of power and force. For more than a century, America has proved itself singularly inept in coming to terms with force. Beginning as early as 1840, there were organized expressions of public feeling proclaiming a deep-seated suspicion of an approach to our problems by diplomacy or force. The "banning the bomb" approach did not await the ultimate weapon. The "peace movement had as its goal the elimination of force through procedures like arbitration or some other form of moral suasion. Because arbitration was the most plausible of various peace movements, we may pause to examine it, however briefly. Significantly, it was the first of the movements to receive governmental sanction. It had served nations well at the turn of the century on issues that had not proved amenable to traditional diplomacy. Settlements like the Alabama Claims case and Bering Sea fisheries dispute were fresh in the public mind, and it was not surprising that the question should be asked why, if settlements like these had been possible, should the same principle not be applied to all outstanding differences. It was forgotten that states customarily reserve to themselves decisions on matters where vital interests are at stake. The United States itself had refused arbitration on the issue of the sinking of the *Maine,* which touched off the Spanish-American War, and no thoughtful person could have imagined the United States Senate agreeing in advance to bind itself to arbitrate problems involving the Monroe Doctrine or our strategic interests in Panama or the Caribbean.

However, at the turn of the century at both Hague Conferences the United States delegation pressed for a universal arbitral system. The most important result of the first Hague Conference was the creation of the Permanent Court of Arbitration, which through its selection of panels of judges to serve in individual disputes promised to serve a useful purpose. However, after 1932, in only two cases did the states draw on the resources of the Permanent Court. It came to be supplanted by the Permanent Court of International Justice or the International Court of Justice, which were primarily successful in cases of a relatively noninflammable nature. Other arbitration treaties were negotiated; for example, no less than eleven were signed between November 1904 and February 1905. However, in the Senate they were hedged about with restrictions, and Theodore Roosevelt was prompted to say: "Of course it is mere nonsense to have a treaty which does nothing but say that there is no power of enforcing, that whenever we choose, there shall be another arbitration treaty."[1] Because of these objections the agreements remained in limbo, without senatorial action having been taken. Despite the vigorous efforts of men like Elihu Root and President Taft, they were either not ratified or if ratified they remained essentially dead letters. The most elaborate and extensive arrangements were the so-called Bryan Conciliation Treaties negotiated with thirty countries, of which twenty-one were

[1] George F. Kennan, unpublished "Notes for Essays," 1951-52, p. 67.

ratified, providing for conciliation commissions to investigate disputes not susceptible of settlement by diplomatic means and defining a cooling-off period during which the investigation would be carried on. The commissions were envisaged as permanent bilateral bodies to which the respective governments would appoint officials.

For the historian the most striking feature of these treaties was that over a period of forty years not a single one was invoked or used in any way. In the period between the wars, an immense body of contractual obligations was evolved in which statesmen assured one another of their resolve not to use force or break the peace. From 1899 to 1933 a total of 97 international agreements for arbitration and conciliation had been negotiated and ratified. It is impossible to appraise or conceive in any satisfactory way the amount of energy and talent that went into this enterprise. Yet, aside from certain private disputes that scarcely had international significance, only two outstanding international problems were arbitrated and ironically no general arbitration treaty was necessary in either of these cases. One was the North Atlantic Fisheries dispute between the United States and Great Britain involving interpretation of the provisions of a ninety-year-old treaty. The other concerned the question of sovereignty over the island of Palmas and arose from a dispute between the United States and the Netherlands. These two cases comprise the entire return on the prodigious efforts of American leaders and in particular Secretaries of State Bryan, Kellogg, and Stimson.

It should also be noted that events which threatened to shatter the fabric of international society were taking place simultaneously with the efforts at legislating arbitration. At the time of the first Hague Conference, Russia was extending its influence into Manchuria; the final stage of the battle of the Marne coincided with the signing of four conciliation treaties in Washington; and the attempts by Kellogg and

Stimson took place as Hitler's star was rising in Germany, the First Five-Year Plan was unfolding in Russia, and the Japanese were pushing into Manchuria. It would be difficult to show that these events were affected even in the slightest by this approach to the problem of force. More dramatic were the efforts at disarmament and, climactically, at the outlawry of war, but the fanfare and moral enthusiasm surrounding them were in no sense commensurate with their usefulness as restraints on power.

Today, in the aftermath of World War II, force once again has confounded the policy-makers. The early postwar treaties were conceived of as means by which wartime partnership could be extended into the peace. Yet the disparity between Western power and the force in being of the Soviet Union, especially in its distribution in Europe, played havoc with attempts at erecting a viable peace. The only crime of Yalta was the failure to recognize soon enough the intimate connection between power and peace—a failure for which we all are at least partly responsible. If this failing were not deeply embedded in our contemporary national character, we might have been less willing to see the basis destroyed for a settlement of the Suez crisis, where we subsequently had to carry on negotiations with Colonel Nasser more from weakness to a degree which since then has steadily increased.

The problems of power have obviously been magnified by the sharp rise in the magnitude of force. Nearly four decades ago the Right Honorable Herbert Asquith observed that science was beginning to "lisp the alphabet of annihilation." Today the dangers are daily borne in upon us not only of mutual devastation in war but also of radioactive poison in peace. In the hydrogen era our approach to the problem of force has been curiously reminiscent of earlier days. The number of words and proposals devoted to a generalized attack on the disarmament problem perhaps exceeds attention to any comparable problem. Whereas before World War II the approach was one of erecting a system of fixed legal and arbitral procedures culminating in broad over-all legislation outlawing war (the Kellogg-Briand Pact), the postwar design has called for almost endless exchanges with Soviet delegates within the United Nations and outside, all looking toward the banning of the use of force or at least limitation of certain of its forms. The call for cessation of tests is a more recent variation on this common theme.

The dread disease that has tended to paralyze American thinking on the problem of force has its roots in at least three conditions of the American mind. We have assumed that force could be dealt with in the isolated compartments of disarmament conventions or arbitral treaties divorced from the harsh realities of power in the outside world or from viable strategic doctrines evolved to meet mutual interests and needs. We have favored a legal over a diplomatic approach. We have preferred to think in absolute rather than discriminate terms and to see force as a single-edged weapon that might be drawn only in a violent cause, forgetting its second edge, which could be used to deter aggression. In consequence, perhaps there is no area of international life where success has been more fleeting and where the best efforts of men supremely endowed have been greeted with more modest achievements. Only the strong currents of the prevailing American approach to world problems and the yearning for over-all formulas have kept afloat this mode of dealing with force.

II. ROOTS OF THE AMERICAN DILEMMA

You will have gathered from my comments that I fear even more the unsettling effects of our way of viewing international problems than their substance and perplexing if not insoluble nature. For one thing there is little we can do to change the outside world and the existence and recurrence of trouble. It promises to be with us always in much the way that irritations and frustrations are a part of our personal life. Most of us learn to take the good with the bad in daily life but are distressed when we find that international society is brimming over with ambition, greed, injustice, and selfish interests. Not many of our personal problems can be solved unequivocally and most of us walk the thin knife's edge that separates certainty from uncertainty, security from insecurity, and hope from despair. The fabric of international life is at least as variegated and perhaps more resistant to tidy answers and neat resolution. Moreover, sweeping and decisive solutions to problems on the world scene are almost always a subtle blending of some broad plan of action and particular interests, passions, and enthusiasms. They are propositions that doubtless would be valid if the world were cast in our image and if others were as fair-minded, progressive, satisfied, and law-abiding as we are enabled to be. But there are still massive differences in wealth, power, and national values and our standards are not those which others automatically embrace. This lends an air of pretentiousness to our claims that states should abide by the precepts that profit us more than them.

I see the roots of the American dilemma especially in four corners of our national and international life. They involve the politics, colonial viewpoint, morality, and democratic diplomacy of the United States. The first dilemma arises from the problems inherent in marshalling domestic support for our programs while at the same time putting our best foot forward in the eyes of the rest of the world. In rallying a consensus in support of policies, we say things to ourselves that from the standpoint of other peoples might better be left unsaid. In this the United States is of course not unique, and we do well in reflecting on this fact to curb our impatience with other world leaders. Nehru, for instance, prides himself on the fact that above all he is a national leader; his assertions on international problems ought never to be divorced from the

Indian political context, where a free society restricted in the resources it can turn to its foreign affairs struggles to maintain itself in an essentially hostile region of the world. The American experience is, however, made especially poignant because we are a vast sprawling continent of great diversity of political and religious belief, with a constitutional system in which power and responsibility are broadly diffused, although less in foreign affairs than for the conduct of national government. Thus we speak in many voices, some raucous and strident, as we seek to persuade one another of the right course to follow. Moreover, the language of domestic politics is not the language of political theory. It means to unite as many as will join to support policies or programs. It looks to a common denominator that can more often be found in moral generalities or in broad principles than in specific directives of strategy that, like military policies, must be cast as practical alternatives that circumstances may effect. It prefers militant slogans to qualified truths and a crusade to public conversations on problems.

It is a permanent part of the landscape of international relations that American foreign policy must draw its support from a union of the viewpoints and interests of the experts, the public, and our friends and allies. No American statesman can ignore one point on the triangle without courting disaster, nor can he unduly stress one, however vital, at the expense of the others. Following World War II and until 1950, American policy was acceptable to the authoritative views of experts, to the national mood, and to the intellectual foundations of coalition diplomacy. This day has passed, and since then the demands of these groups have tended increasingly to go their separate ways. One writer in 1956 went as far as to say: "Today when the nation's foreign relations are vulnerable to the criticism of experts at home and abroad, they enjoy such broad endorsement and acceptance at all levels of American life that they have become almost untouchable."[2] We know that the predicament of any administration in the conduct of American foreign policy is that in shaping wise programs of action it cannot afford to lose touch with people or with their chosen representatives. This was the tragedy of President Woodrow Wilson that President Franklin D. Roosevelt vowed not to repeat. He chose to work especially on preparation for the United Nations through a Secretary of State who was a graduate of the Congress and through bipartisan delegations who accompanied him to major international conferences. In much the same spirit, Secretary of State John Foster Dulles is said to have observed that his predecessor Dean Acheson had succeeded in all but one important respect and that had proved his undoing: he had failed to protect his flanks in the Congress. For a time, Mr. Dulles appeared to have profited by Mr. Acheson's mistake. He had neutralized the Right wing of his party partly by isolating some of its members from the rest of their colleagues and partly by joining those who might otherwise have opposed him. He pursued a policy of advance and retreat which from the standpoint of domestic politics was provisionally sound but as it was accentuated confounded our friends abroad and alienated the internationalists in the Democratic Party. Hence, without fixing praise or blame, we can say that the present administration, by stressing one side of the triangle involving its most sensitive domestic relations, has aggravated its foreign relations, some would say almost beyond repair.

No purpose would be served by minimizing the incredible complexity and difficulty of relating the national interest to the demands of national politics and reconciling them both with the legitimate aspirations of our allies and friends. We are bound to suffer and cause offense even with those states

---

[2] Norman A. Graebner, *The New Isolationism: A Study in Politics and Foreign Policy* since 1950 (New York: The Ronald Press Co., 1956), p. 239.

to whom we are bound most closely by geography, history, and common traditions. An editorial in *The Economist* (London) on November 17, 1956 observed: "Between us and the Americans it is, in a sense, a tale of two inferiority complexes: ours because we harp upon prestige, without recognizing that prestige can only be earned by our success in managing our affairs and in gaining the respect of others and cannot be bolstered by words and gestures; theirs because by ill-timed criticism and an indifference to their allies' interests they still work off the last traces of their long-gone colonial (and isolationist) status." These fears and anxieties of course beset other policy-makers as well as our own. If there is any way out of this dilemma, it is probably through the voice of a strong and wise President, responsive to the broad mandate given him by the people but courageous in his choice of the means of serving the national interest. In foreign policy, of all fields, the President must lead, for only he sees the broad picture and has available the detailed map that a continuous intelligence process fills in. He must act as the wisest and most reasonable citizen would act if he had all the facts at his command. He must first determine the requirements of the national interest and then interpret them to gain public consent. It would be folly to leave this to the people, even though conceivably on some issues they might be wiser than their leaders. Some of our European friends have been tactless enough to suggest that this leadership has frequently been lacking of late. The pro-American London *Economist* declared on November 17, 1956 (p. 596): "Mr. Eisenhower suggested that, once the immediate causes of friction had been disposed of, then the U.S. would be ready with constructive proposals for the future. But to many observers what matters now is the present; they may be forgiven for feeling once again that the President is failing to exercise the responsibilities of his office."

The events in Indo-China in March and April 1954 called

into play the interests of three parties: the experts, the public, and friends and allies. As the fortress of Dienbienphu was besieged, General Paul Ely, French Chief of Staff, called for allied intervention in behalf of our ally. The administration first maintained that the fall of Indo-China would be like tipping over the first in a row of dominoes, a theory reminiscent of the justification of our Korean policy in 1950. If one vital area in Southeast Asia succumbed to the communists, others would be likely to follow as the wildfire of communist successes engulfed the whole area. Secretary of State Dulles, in his address to the Overseas Writers in New York on March 29, 1954, called for the internationalization of the Indo-Chinese war. He warned that the "imposition on Southeast Asia of the political system of Communist Russia and its Chinese Communist ally, by whatever means, would be a grave threat to the whole free community. The United States feels that the possibility should not be passively accepted, but should be met by united action. This might involve serious risks. But these risks are far less than those that will face us a few years from now, if we dare not be resolute today." Vice President Nixon told newsmen in Washington that the loss of Dienbienphu would be catastrophic. Senator Knowland expressed the view that the free world had reached "the jumping off place" where it stood in danger of losing all Southeast Asia. President Eisenhower himself put forth the theory of the dominoes. During April, however, this hard view began to respond to pressures from domestic quarters and from one of our allies. On April 7, 1954, the President was quoted as saying at a press conference "we simply cannot afford to lose Indo-China." In the strongest statement of all, Mr. Nixon on April 16 advised the American Society of Newspaper Editors: "If, to avoid further Communist expansion in Asia and Indo-China we must take the risk now by putting our boys in, I think the Executive has to take the politically unpopular decision and do it." This speech was a bombshell and political reactions no less violent. Four days later the Secretary said it seemed unlikely that American troops would be used in Indo-China, and on April 28 he promised that American troops would not be sent to Indo-China or elsewhere if the administration could help it. What were the reasons for the shift in policy? It must have had something to do with the British reluctance to join in the united action of an air strike to relieve embattled Dienbienphu. Furthermore, it doubtless bore some relation to the sharp reaction to Nixon's speech of April 16, especially by Republican editors. In any event, despite strong feeling within the administration, the counter-pressures of public opinion and the reactions of our allies carried policy-makers away from intervention. For present purposes this episode in American foreign policy is crucial not for its wisdom or its folly but because it illustrates the peculiar pressures of making foreign policy by triangulation.

The second American dilemma stems from the colonial problem which reaches beyond America's national life and touches conflicting interests at work throughout the world. Since the Second World War, the colonial issue appears at the top of every agenda for discussion of American foreign policy. Responsible officials are encouraged to make proclamations and to throw America's weight behind popular revolutions. In this setting it is tempting to take general and sweeping positions and to express an American doctrine on the rights of peoples everywhere to independence and self-government. This is particularly true because Americans' own experience is so rich in lessons and apparently pregnant with meaning. The fruits of attempts thus far to propound a dogma should serve, however, to give us pause, for the record of America's efforts to align itself squarely with either colonial or anticolonial powers is sprinkled with as many failures as successes.

Nevertheless, Americans face new situations today and demands crowd in upon them for new and more vigorous policies. We are reminded that Senator Vandenburg with his emphasis on Europe and Western unity never disparaged the rights of colonial or former colonial peoples. Nationalism is on the march in Asia, the Middle East, and Africa, and Americans implore one another to identify their country with these movements rather than to appear to stand athwart their pathway. Unhappily, the colonial problem is less tractable than those exhortations suggest. For at the same time as the fight is waged to end old imperialisms, a new and more demoniac expansionism threatens. To meet it, some feel that America must cleave to trusted friends and allies with whom it has interests and military bases in common, striving to preserve a more stable world balance of power. Yet, in itself, this is not likely to be enough. The present equilibrium of power will be upset unless America can join with new forces in the so-called underdeveloped areas. We may say, therefore, that the United States faces the triple challenge of stemming the tide of Russian imperialism and world communism, uniting the other Western states, and drawing closer to non-Western peoples only recently emerging as independent states. In a manner of speaking, policy-makers must keep three balls in the air. This is the unenviable task of American statesmanship.

The pathos of our present position may be illustrated briefly from recent events. First, there was the statement on Goa recognizing Portugal's authority in the tiny enclave in India, prompted doubtless by the zeal of European officers in the State Department to display a sense of community with Portugal. This provoked deep resentment in India and perhaps throughout much of Asia. Next came the expression of "sympathy" for Greek feelings in the Cyprus dispute by the United States Ambassador to Greece, Cavendish W. Cannon, which unleashed a torrent of British protest. Then the Dutch voiced dismay at Mr. Dulles' warm and friendly comments during a visit to the Indonesian Republic. More recently, the

United States aroused its European friends by appearing to take sides with Egypt, and Middle Eastern friends, by reassuring Turkey against Syria and Russia. Taken together, American efforts to cement ties of community and good will with one side in the colonial struggle threatened or ruptured the bonds of unity with the other. Possibly the one exception was Ambassador Dillon's speech supporting France's search for "liberal solutions" of her problems in North Africa, and even this was challenged by the moderate Tunisian nationalist leader Bourguiba.

Perceiving these problems, can we say anything about this perplexing picture that will offer some guidance to the juggler or policy-maker of whom we have spoken? Are there guidelines or principles we can enunciate to spotlight a few of the darker corners of this colonial problem? Perhaps there are. First, we must start with the presumption that the colonial problem is fraught with dilemmas with which America must learn to live. Nor will dogmas for or against colonialism waft them away. Solutions must be worked out case by case; and as, for example, Tunisia is not identical with Algeria nor Ghana with Southwest Africa, policies must be shaped to meet individual needs. Second, timing is of the essence. The statement supporting Indonesia stirred up a hornets' nest because of Dutch-Indonesian tensions at that time over the trial of a former Chief of Dutch Military Intelligence charged with plotting to overthrow the Indonesian government, the conflict over Netherlands New Guinea, and the unilateral abridgment by Indonesia of certain financial and economic treaties. Third, if any general solution can be found it rests in the coordinating of mutual interests, not in the wholesale sacrifice of one set of interests to another. In North Africa, French, American, and African long-term interests appear to coincide as respects "liberal solutions." Similarly in other regions, the goal should be the harmonizing of interests. This calls for a judicious balancing of claims. Fourth, it is one of the ironies of history that force may be necessary to preserve colonial arrangements, not in order to perpetuate them but that their orderly liquidation may be achieved. Fifth, it will not do to call every conflict of view between America and its European allies a colonial issue. On October 2, 1956, in what one commentator called a Freudian slip that betrayed the main lines of American thinking, Mr. Dulles noted that Britain and America were at odds over Suez on the question of the "shift from colonialism to independence." He treated Suez as an issue between the "colonial powers" and "the powers which are primarily and uniquely concerned with the problem of getting their independence as rapidly as possible." Walter Lippmann was prompt to point out that Egypt could hardly be considered a colony, especially as it sought to expand its national power. A British journal observed: "The American desire to keep the goodwill of the Arab states is good sense . . . but it will defeat itself in the end if, in pursuing it, the Americans think in anti-colonial conventions which are current. . . . In that way they will merely seek to please everybody, committing their strength to the support of local weak men, and overlooking that the conflicts which trouble the region, being real conflicts, require solutions of substance which are bound to give offense to some."[3] Finally, conflicts of interest—as in the past between Britain and India or the Dutch and the Indonesians or the French and North Africans—may be swept along by powerful historical movements until one side emerges supreme. Here it may be necessary for American policy-makers to choose sides and in this way inevitably give offense. These facts need not preclude prudence and restraint today in Algeria and tomorrow in the Belgian Congo.

A third dilemma has its roots in the moral problem. The question of right and wrong is continuously raised in international relations, as in all the other social orders. Nations as

[3] *The Economist* (London), December 8, 1956, p. 853.

individuals either seek to do, or claim to have done, what is right. The nature of Western values as embodied in American culture assures that, far from being an exception, America persistently aspires to justice and to the goal of international order. We are pained when we are told that some aspect or another of national conduct cannot be justified in broader international terms, yet Americans may take comfort from the fact that historically this has been among the most baffling philosophical problems. The question is whether an action shall be called good if it serves the group of primary loyalty or whether it must serve a more inclusive purpose. Political morality as distinct from pure law or justice answers this question in terms that give it a unique flavor. It looks for the point of concurrence between the particular and the general value or interest, rather than calling for the sacrifice of the part to the whole. Politics can count on a residual egotism or self-interest which represents the creative potential of individuals and groups. The nascent international community must guard against extreme forms of parochial loyalty that claim too much and reserve to themselves the right to suppress and overwhelm weaker neighbors. Short of this, however, the larger community is able to harness, beguile, and deflect the more limited national purposes, even though it cannot easily transcend them. In Reinhold Niebuhr's discerning words: "The individual or the group may feel called upon to sacrifice an immediate value for the sake of the more ultimate or general interest. But the community cannot demand this sacrifice as its right." Nor, one might add, can another sovereign state.

The American credo of political morality, especially in recent years, has been more pretentious and less modest than this. It has oftentimes called upon others to sacrifice local advantage to some nobler and higher cause. Some of the past statements from French, Israeli, Egyptian, and British leaders on the Suez crisis have thrown a dash of political realism on the standards that the United States sought to impose. Justice and international order are properly considered the broad framework of political morality, but their relative emphasis in any decision and the particular content they should receive can never be determined in advance. The values of community and order are frequently in tension with the principles of justice, which are liberty and equality. In the fall of 1956 at Suez, the international order suffered a threat to the peace. At the same time three of the nations invoked the principle of justice, which in equality calls for giving each man his due, including his right to survival. If the national community cannot assure a tolerable measure of justice, even though as a despotism it maintains order, in the long run its authority tends to erode. Similarly, if the international order lacks the power and prestige to safeguard all its members, they will be tempted to seek justice in other ways. There is an indefiniteness in political morality resulting because "various and frequently contradictory values are involved in political decisions and the preference which is given one value and end over another, must be determined by historical contingencies rather than fixed principles. There are fixed principles and norms in the political realm, but there is no fixed principle for relating the norms to each other. It is possible to define as 'bad' only those situations in which one or more norms are completely wanting. . . ."[4]

America's policy-makers by contrast look for shortcuts to the moral problem. They talk a great deal more about promoting the impact of morality than about determining its content. They seize on the most readily available expressions congenial to their tastes and interests, like "majority rule" and "the will of the United Nations." The workings of political machinery are invested with all the trappings of a religious exercise and political pronouncements are equated

[4] Reinhold Niebuhr, unpublished manuscript on "Theory of International Politics," p. 11.

with the glorification of God. Repelled by all the talk of "missions" and "crusades," one of our most sensitive critics has said: "I would rather *be* moral than claim to be it; and to the extent we succeed in lending moral distinction to the conduct of our affairs, I would rather let others discover it for themselves." The deep pathos of the moral problem calls more for Christian humility than for a moralistic self-righteousness, which can win few friends abroad and serves only to lower the currency of moral principles.

The final American dilemma is an outgrowth of the special relationship of diplomacy and democracy within the West in general and this country in particular. In diplomacy, the choice of methods and techniques is no less vital than clarity about objectives. Democracies sometimes assume that the demands of coherence and consistency in diplomacy fall less heavily upon them than upon other states. In part this goes back to a prevailing outlook about democracy and foreign policy.

The first two decades of the twentieth century witnessed the flowering of a philosophy of international politics that was unambiguously simple, straightforward, and capable of engendering widespread popular appeal. This philosophy looked in a spirit of buoyant optimism to democracy and national self-determination as the twin sources of international peace and order. The creation of popular regimes on the Anglo-American model everywhere throughout the world was heralded as a sure corrective to the harsh conflicts that for centuries had wracked international life. New nations brought into existence at the will of a self-conscious community of peoples would dissolve the rivalries and frictions that had always led to conflict among contiguous social groups. The faith of modern Western *homo sapiens* in man's potentialities for unending progress found its expression on the international scene in the assurance that a brave new world merely awaited the fulfillment of these goals.

It is ironic that this illusion based on an excess of faith in essentially divine-right *vox populi* has in the recent past been rudely shaken on numerous fronts. The phenomenon of totalitarian democracy, unknown in the nineteenth century, has not only left political rivalries and conflict intact but has heightened and made virtually irreconcilable the disputes among the new collectivities. Inflamed public passions playing on statesmen have made moderation and compromise more difficult of attainment. National leaders by pandering to popular passions have often reduced the alternatives open to responsible makers of foreign policy. Nationalism has not led to more peaceful relations among peoples who rested content with their political status but has bred the most embittered antagonisms between new nations and their former colonial masters or between non-Western states and their erstwhile exemplars in the West. National self-determination and democracy can hardly be said to have ushered in a new era; and our more serious observers find deep anguish in the steep and sudden decline of influence and self-confidence of the Western democracies. The West succeeds in engendering resentment and suspicion more often than it earns respect. Yet many students and statesmen insist on talking in bated breath about the causes and conditions of our decline. The bulk of those who assume leadership in intellectual and political life are singularly inhibited when it comes to diagnosing the source of our ills. It is commonplace to respond to a critical evaluation of the conduct of foreign policy in a democracy by pointing the finger of scorn at nondemocratic societies that are still more obviously the authors of our most recent historic catastrophes. The key to this difficult problem is surely not loss of faith in democracy. It is rather a deeper awareness of the methods of diplomacy.

Democratic diplomacy, like all diplomacy, must adhere to certain sound principles and rules. It must prove its consistency with the diplomatic tradition and the imperatives of effective negotiation. Majority votes in multilateral conference or dialectics, invective, or propaganda may hold a certain fascination for the spectators of world affairs. But more often than not their effect is to sow international distrust and to increase rather than alleviate world conflicts. The first principle worth noting is that diplomacy and foreign policy historically have not been considered identical. Foreign policy has been viewed as the legislative aspect and diplomacy as the executive aspect of managing foreign relations. Diplomacy has called for experts with freedom of action; policy is a matter for the most responsible branches of government, including at some point the legislature. Diplomacy is not the framing of policy but rather its execution. It is no more a point of focus for public attention than is the execution of the national budget as distinct from its authorization.

The Oxford English Dictionary states that: "Diplomacy is the management of international relations by negotiation; the method by which these relations are adjusted and managed by ambassadors and envoys; the business or art of the diplomatist." This definition suggests a second principle. The test of diplomacy is not the vindication of some abstract moral principle or the rewarding or punishment of virtuous or evil forces. It is rather the most effective accommodation of state relations that are sometimes in harmony but other times in conflict.

Third, diplomacy calls for an intimate knowledge of the mechanics of negotiation, for endless patience in the use of numberless expedients in working out agreements, and for consummate skill in adjusting national proposals and making them acceptable at home and abroad without sacrificing vital objectives.

In recent years many serious writers have questioned whether or not diplomacy has measured up to the standards inherent in these principles. Looking back on the interwar period, Hugh Gibson, who has few peers among twentieth-century American diplomatists and observers, wrote: "What we have come to call diplomacy in the course of the past twenty years has failed to achieve results and has led into all sorts of disasters. But it wasn't really diplomacy. It was the usurpation of diplomatic functions by politicians and inept amateurs; it was the new method of having the negotiation of infinitely complicated world problems handled by politicians, amateurs, and adventurers; the forcing on the world in critical times of new and untried methods; publicity stunts and hurried personal discussions between the political leaders, who should stay at home and be the heavy artillery in reserve rather than trying to direct operations on hurried visits to the front-line trenches."[5] These words have even greater relevance today than they had a little more than a decade ago.

For nearly four centuries the statecraft of Europe had certain salient features. It sought, in theory at least, to mitigate and reduce conflicts by means of persuasion, compromise, and adjustment. It was rooted in the community of interests of a small group of leaders who spoke the same language, catered to one another as often as to their own people, and played to one another's strengths and weaknesses. When warfare broke out, they drew a ring around the combatants and sought to neutralize the struggle. The old diplomacy, so-called, carried on its tasks in a world made up of states that were small, separated, limited in power, and blessed, ironically enough, by half-hearted political loyalties. Patience was a watchword; negotiations were often as protracted during war as in peace. It was taken for granted that talks would be initiated, broken off, resumed, discontinued temporarily, and reopened again by professionals in whose lexicon there was no substitute for "diplomacy."

Today not one of these conditions any longer prevails, and the search for new formulas in diplomacy has gone on apace.

[5] Hugh Gibson, *The Road to Foreign Policy* (Garden City, New York: Doubleday & Co., 1944), p. 63.

The first and most novel pattern to crystallize after World War II found expression in the United Nations and in what is called "popular diplomacy." It looked to international forums and to majority votes in the General Assembly as a substitute for tortuous paths of traditional diplomacy. It must be said that this choice was expressed more rigorously in practice than in the United Nations Charter, which emphasized talks among the parties to a dispute before an issue was placed on the agenda. Popular diplomacy reflects the faith in parliamentary procedures, in the rule of the people, and in straightforward, rational, and open discussion. It is jointly the product of an age of rationalism and an age of popular government. It translates into global terms supreme political attainments of free people within the democratic state. Popular diplomacy, despite the role of the Great Powers in the Security Council, marks a swing of the pendulum to diplomacy by all the peoples of most of the nations. It is the antithesis of secret diplomacy by a concert of leaders of the preeminent countries.

Because popular diplomacy is the keyboard on which much of our postwar diplomacy has been played, we are able to make a modest estimate of its success. To use Lester Pearson's phrase, we find that the problems of "diplomacy in a goldfish bowl" are more intractable than we had supposed. Publicity has been both a virtue and a vice. It has kept the spotlight of public opinion on world affairs, but it has encouraged the actor in world politics, in striking a pose, to take inflexible positions from which it is difficult to retreat. Majority votes on Korea have demonstrated who controlled greater support; they have, however, allowed conflicts of interest to remain untouched or have actually contributed to their increase. When this new pattern of diplomacy has worked, it has been savored with more ancient techniques, as with the private diplomacy of Mr. Ralph Bunche in Palestine and of Mr. Philip C. Jessup on Berlin, and the "quiet diplomacy" of the Secretary General.

These successes, however noteworthy, have failed to arrest

226

the sharp swing of the pendulum to another type of international diplomacy. The Eisenhower administration has espoused personal diplomacy as a means of correcting the excesses of public negotiations. The first Geneva Conference, the United States-Canadian-Mexican Conference at White Sulphur Springs, and the meetings with India's Prime Minister Nehru and with Prime Minister Macmillan of England illustrate a new and emerging pattern. It is a pattern based upon the President's partiality "for talking things out rather than negotiating things out" in an atmosphere of genial informality. It reflects the view that some of the roots of conflict will dissolve when leaders from other nations, sitting across a table from Mr. Eisenhower, become persuaded of his good intentions. The personal touch of a famous personality has been placed on the scales of world diplomacy.

The two novel approaches—personal and parliamentary diplomacy—are at opposite poles of the spectrum. One emphasizes public speeches, mass assemblies, and resolutions emerging from open forums; the other stresses informality and man-to-man conferences free of protocol, agendas, and advance preparation. (At White Sulphur Springs the Canadians on the eve of the conference did not know the topics to be discussed.) Yet these new patterns, so divergent in conception and design, share one thing in common. They constitute a revolt against traditional diplomacy.

For diplomatists historically the first rule has been that negotiations are essential when national interests are in conflict. Since such conflicts arise from causes more basic than personal hostility, personal amiability in itself can hardly resolve them. Sir Harold Nicolson has argued: "Diplomacy is the art of negotiating documents in a ratifiable and dependable form. It is by no means the art of conversation. The affability inseparable from any conversation . . . produces illusiveness, compromises, and high intentions. Diplomacy, if it is ever to be effective, should be a disagreeable business, and one recorded in hard print."[6]

The trouble with approaches that set aside the lessons of the past is that history has a way of returning to haunt us. Both popular and personal diplomacy have their place, especially if safeguarded against their excesses. The best way of doing this is to remember that foreign policy has a memorable tradition, not all of which is folly in the present. This is perhaps the one means of escaping the final American dilemma.

III. CONTEMPORARY PROBLEMS AND THE AMERICAN DILEMMA

Having said that the United States stands in the predicament of facing tangled dilemmas instead of clear-cut alternatives in international life, Americans nonetheless are forever tempted in approaching immediate contemporary problems to search for hard and firm solutions. For each emergent crisis, we all have our answers to settle things once and for all. Our leaders hold authority partly by virtue of their ability to engender hope. For this positive thinking, they are required to pay the price of lack of awareness of the tragic element in international politics. We look, for example, at the Middle East as an area in which law and order can be vindicated and where through an American doctrine the unhappy past can be set right. We expect that the recent prestige we have earned through the sponsorship of virtue in the United Nations will make the Arabs and particularly Colonel Nasser more reasonable and amenable to long-term commitments on oil and movements through the Canal. It seems taken for granted that a judicious sprinkling of aid will put the Arabs in a cooperative frame of mind. All this as Russian influence continues to seep in, Nasser extends his sway, the Arab League contends with Iraq, and no peace for the area is in sight.

[6] Harold Nicolson, *Diplomacy* (London: Oxford University Press, 1950, second edition), p. 101.

228

Another approach to these problems not notably in evidence in Washington in recent months takes us back to the political realists about whom we talked at the beginning. They urge us to look to the historical roots of a problem and remind us that Soviet aspirations in the Middle East date back before the Bolshevik Revolution. Shortly after 1917, Moslems were brought together in a congress at Baku and exhorted by the Russians to strike out on a *jihad* or holy war against British imperialism. These attempts were no more than a modern expression of Russia's age-old dream of access to the warm waters of the south. Again during the abortive negotiations of Russia and Nazi Germany in 1939-1941, Molotov specifically insisted on Russian control of the Black Sea Straits. Following the war, the Soviets probed southward toward Iran and Turkey, but fear of war and economic exhaustion with its limiting effects on what could be offered restricted these attempts. Now the situation has changed, the Russians have more prizes in their diplomatic bag, the thermonuclear stalemate has reduced the chances of atomic war, and the discussions of the Afro-Asian powers at Bandung and after inspired the belief that a neutral third force could be used to deprive the Western powers of their control over oil. The Arab-Israeli dispute was made to order for Russian intrigue, despite the fact that both Russia and the United States had been godparent to the Israelis at the United Nations. It speaks for the flexibility of the Russians in this crisis that they have welcomed to their fold some of the world's most reactionary potentates. They have extended warmest friendship to countries where the mildest agitation for socialist reform is a punishable crime. Before the Czech arms deal with Egypt, the United States as the sole source of arms to the area rationed the supply so as to avert an explosion. With Russia's intervention, the West faced the unhappy choice of admitting her to the "ring of suppliers" or of leaving her to expand her influence alone. Had she been admitted, she would have gained the right to determine matters in a region that hitherto was considered a Western preserve. The West preferred to resolve this dilemma by doing nothing at all, and today for the first time in centuries the Soviet Union sits astride the region, having triumphed in its essential goals. We should perhaps remind ourselves that Russia's stake is in continuing the chaos and tension and in maintaining frontier violence. If Israel were annihilated, that would remove the only interest that links Russia with the Arab world. At this point, the balance sheet of Suez for the Russians is favorable in the form of substantial gains in popularity and prestige. While the United States made efforts to rally the United Nations, scarcely any Arab doubts that the Anglo-French forces were decisively halted primarily by the Russian ultimatum. The loss of Soviet equipment was a comparatively small price to pay for such gains in power and prestige. British and French power in the area has been reduced to the vanishing point and what began for Nasser as an ignominious military defeat has ended in a major political triumph that he as a nationalist leader can scarcely ignore.

In this context, despite our brave words and doctrines, it will not be at all easy to halt, contain, or dislodge Russia in the Middle East. In such a contest, the Soviets have one great advantage; none of their vital interests is at stake. They have stepped up trade with some of the Arab countries, but none is really essential. Middle Eastern oil is for them a dividend and not, as for Western Europe, a necessity. With the second Baku field and Rumanian production, Russia estimated it had exceeded 100,000,000 barrels of oil in 1958. It therefore aspires less to influence in the Middle East than to the denial of Western authority there. This fact confronts our policymakers with one of their severest tests. The American answer has been made in the form of the Eisenhower Doctrine whereby approval has been given to the President's authority to use American forces in the Middle East to prevent aggression. In this way we have rounded out our alliances and stretched a Western trip-wire across a region formerly outside it. The political supports for this arrangement are of course far flimsier than in Europe, where there was little doubt that protection would be accepted. However, some Arab countries apparently fear Western protection more than they do communism and the Levantine world lacks the cohesiveness we associate with Western Europe. Also, we are constrained in our aid by the fact that the Arabs, while potentially neutral in the East-West conflict, are belligerents in a struggle with Israel. This has occasioned the view that "So long as this state of mind prevails, their gratitude for American bounty may at any moment be swamped by an arms delivery from Russia. Bargainers by temptation, they say they must 'turn to Russia' unless the American help materializes. But there is no hope that it will serve its purpose unless the giver himself turns bargainer—which is the real, immediate necessity—and stipulates that only genuine neutrality is worth support, that neutrality is indivisible and that if governments want help to be neutral towards Russia, they must display neutrality towards Israel too."[7] This nettle must be grasped, but there are few signs that the present administration is prepared to press forward in showing the Arab governments that they have as great a stake as we in seeking for stability and preserving their ties with the free world and that we and our friends in Europe can live without them as well as they can live without us. This calls for some form of suasion, the use of American economic and political power, perhaps through alternatives to the Suez Canal and of Middle Eastern oil like new pipelines, faster tankers, and perhaps even wider international authority. Once this condition of strength has been reached, then prospects will increase for an over-all improvement or settlement. But the situation calls for time,

[7] *The Economist* (London), December 8, 1956, pp. 850-51.

patience, and great effort—commodities not always in full supply.

The same kind of pattern faces us in Europe. We may have to accept and even encourage a unified Western Europe whose policies are bound to be independent of ours and may sometimes clash irreconcilably. Similarly, on the opponent's side of the Iron Curtain, Eastern Europe shows at least signs of having uprooted the myth of the political and economic solidarity of communist regimes. Much of the unsoundness of Stalinism in the satellite countries is now coming out in the wash. The Russians have perhaps failed to perceive the full implications of the liberalization movement they started, involving the exchange of political pawns for political partners. In Hungary they were caught by surprise and the best they could muster was a tragic expedient, not a step in a calculated program. The incentives to hold Eastern Europe are no less potent than in the past—strategic advance positions both for defense and attack. Indeed, radar increases the importance of a cordon sanitaire rather than eliminating it. Yet bloodshed in Hungary cancelled at least three years of uninterrupted progress in the Communist Party with popular fronts and coexistence. They left the Russians suspended between the tragic need to use force and the consequences for their over-all role of recourse to overt force and violence. Unhappily this predicament is not a Russian monopoly. The same predicament is illustrated graphically by the dilemmas of the thermonuclear age. If American leaders had occasion to learn anything from over two centuries of national experience, it was that foreign policy divorced from strength is likely to be impotent. Following two world wars, the United States dismantled its military establishment as an earnest of its peaceful intentions and goodwill. In both cases, aggressive forces bent on expansion seized on these acts to press forward into areas defenseless against their power. Both Germany and the Soviet Union imposed their will upon helpless nations that fell within their zone of control. The lesson this taught Western leaders was that weakness could be no substitute for security, that policies harnessed to power were more likely to succeed than those drawing strength alone from high ideals and noble expectations. The Low Countries in World War I and the Baltic States in World War II succumbed not because they were lacking in morality but because they found no means of securing their national frontiers.

The West has carried this discovery into the atomic and thermonuclear age. It is possible to argue that such peace as we have known since 1945 is the outcome of "a balance of terror." There are signs that the Soviet Union more than once marched up to the brink, threatening to engulf Greece and Turkey, Iran, and Berlin, only to march down again when it met resistance. Conversely, where resistance proved ambiguous, uncertain, or divided as in Egypt, Syria, and in the Far East, the spread of the Soviet sphere of influence flowed across boundaries that had long marked the limits of Russian power. Is it any wonder, then, in recent days faced with further Russian blandishments and technological advances, that the military regeneration of the West has become the rallying cry? Or would our conduct not rather be surprising if, abandoning the lessons of a half century and heedless of the risks, we turned to embrace a program of unilateral disarmament or destroyed our military ramparts without counting the costs. Today's spirit in a nation arousing itself from complacency, stirring as from a long sleep to sudden consciousness of its peril, testifies to deep and latent faith among the people that any radical change in the military and technological balance of power must be redressed. Our policies reflect the belief that history has something to teach. We have learned one lesson well but have we learned all that the past and present have to tell us? Is there more to history than the truth that aggressors must be resisted, that we must match every advance in the destructiveness of a foe, and that this in the present world must be virtually an end in itself?

There are indications that one reading of history in fact is not sufficient for every purpose. The nature of the Soviet threat is partly military and imperial; it is also peculiarly an economic and political challenge calling for other responses than pure force. Those who advance this latter theory point to the Soviet technical assistance program pledging $1,500,-000,000 to the underdeveloped areas. They also note evidence of successful Soviet penetration without Russians ever firing a shot. The scene and the tactics of Russian imperialism have shifted. Subversion, infiltration, and indirect aggression defended as appeals against anti-colonialism, anti-interventionism, and anti-Westernism have put the West on the defensive perhaps on its weakest front. Ultimate weapons in these areas are bound to have ambiguous effects, for their use against great numbers of agrarian peoples spread over vast areas seems doubtful strategy at best. Moreover, crises that have passed without their deployment in Indo-China, Korea, and Egypt serve to reinforce such doubts. Because they neither possessed nor saw the relevance of these terrible weapons, the newer nations have led the movement for their outlawry.

However, the contradictory reactions in the newer states to thermonuclear devices is best seen in the effects of sputnik. In the same countries that urge us to disarm, American prestige and virtue suffered a grievous blow when the Soviet Union launched the first satellite. Despite continuous criticism of America throughout Asia and Africa for its materialism and preoccupation with purely technological and military advance, confidence in American policy was judged by these standards. One is reminded once more of Europe's and Asia's response when the United States through the United Nations held the line in Korea. Then our sharpest critics, including some in India who had found us rigidly anti-communist and obsessed with the military threat, applauded the successful deployment of American power, particularly until the fateful crossing of the thirty-eighth parallel. Therefore, even in parts of the world where heaviest stress has been placed on moral and political solutions, the exercise of power by East and West has con tributed to national prestige and seemed almost to create moral valuations of its own. We endlessly assume that the strong are more virtuous or the virtuous are stronger. This is but one example of the kind of problem for which the modern technological outlook is singularly unqualified, namely, the central issue of political morality. Most discussion of this theme runs to one or the other of two extremes. Either too much or too little is claimed for ethical principles. Both secular and religious thinkers alternately deny that morality influences politics—"politics is a dirty business"—or affirm that virtue is the sole criterion. A well-known evangelist affirms that a certain Nationalist Chinese leader could never have tolerated corruption because "he prays three times a day." Another present-day religious movement imagines that all our personal and political problems could be wafted away through "positive thinking." One is reminded of William James's comment that the trouble with religious people was that they were forever lobbying for special favor in the courts of the Almighty. However, secular thinkers who espouse doctrines of commercialism and cynicism, progress and success, or militarism or nationalism are no less blinded to the essentials of the moral problem.

The irony of the American capacity to deal with contemporary problems is that neither of the twin sources provide a deeper understanding of these problems. The first source has its roots in historical experiences still fresh in the minds of many who were caught unprepared by the events of the period between World War I and II and who carry a sense of guilt for this failure. They atone for this guilt with strident affirmations about the facts of power. For the most part, power is seen as a comparatively simple phenomenon of which the military element is overwhelmingly the most important part. Both Democratic and Republican American Secretaries of State during much of the present decade have viewed power not as the endlessly complicated relationship of two living organisms with goals and objectives both comparable and fundamentally unique. Rather, they approach power as men might approach a problem in physics to be weighed on the simple scales of relative military preparedness and forces potentially in being. Yet in farflung corners of the world, American influence and power can scarcely be measured in these terms. Its existence there is as much a result of spiritual and intellectual forces as of military conditions. There it becomes a subtle phenomenon made up of intangibles like prestige, the capacity to exert strength implicitly, not explicitly, and the ability to exercise authority without being put continuously to the test. Sometimes favorable territorial arrangements, or a nation's alignment with movements of greatest public promise, or solid economic ties of mutual benefit are far more a source of power than raw naval or military strength.

Because these aspects of America's position in the world are more complicated and impalpable in nature, our national leaders and their most responsible critics have had little to say about them. In part this has stemmed from the bankruptcy of the moralistic tradition in American thinking. This is the second source that underlies America's understanding of its problems. There are moral elements in every power struggle but by claiming that these elements stood alone and supreme the moralistic tradition has served to enfeeble and destroy our capacity of dealing with these problems. Moralism continues to deny the persistence of self-interest, the clash of contending groups and forces, and the need for power as the minimum precondition of international agreement. The moralistic tradition calls essentially for an all-or-nothing approach. Either we renounce totally the exercise of force in, say, the Middle East or through total disarmament, and couch foreign policy in unqualified moral terms, or we send increasing numbers of arms to this unhappy and troubled region, make threatening proclamations, and intervene overtly in every local dispute. Thus American policy remains suspended between the towering moralism of Suez and the harsh and unsubtle blandishments that go back to the Eisenhower Doctrine. Such an approach has no room for more limited and proximate moral and political actions. Its moralism is as absolute as its stress on military power. Both take root in the twin sources of the American outlook: a severely military view of power and a utopian moralism that offers few criteria for measuring the moral aspects of any problem.

Most tragic of all, the naïveté and lack of realism attending earlier discussions of morality in foreign affairs prompt us to view the present crisis with an alarming matter-of-factness. We see nothing disturbing about the use of limited nuclear weapons which exceed in magnitude the bombs at Hiroshima and Nagasaki nor even the prospect of our striking the first blow. The sharp and outspoken reactions of our NATO allies at the December 1957 Paris Conference was at least partly a judgment of the official American state of mind. We were criticized not only for being too rigid but for our insensitivity to the threat of their annihilation. There is irony in Europe's reaction, for not infrequently American policy-makers are criticized for being indifferent to all but the moral component of foreign policy. It is said that we endlessly moralize upon the need for virtue in international life, whether embodied in systems of law and order or in resounding international proclamations, without being ready to make the sacrifices upon which international security must be based. The gap between the Stimson Doctrine and our capacity to exert American power in the Far East in the 1930's is a case in point. Nevertheless, there are signs that both the administration and its most influential critics have seized on one phase of our present weakness, our failures in military preparedness—a failure for which all of us are partly to blame. In this crisis it is fitting and proper that private citizens and public officials should take the lead in calling for a rededication of our national strength and treasure to the restoration of American power. This is so because there has been or will shortly occur a radical shift in the military balance of power threatening the West and ourselves with total destruction. The prescriptions for meeting this threat run the gamut from calls for a national effort comparable to that following Pearl Harbor to more precise increases in the defense budget estimated from $3,000,000,-000 to $8,000,000,000 annually. If these proposals for resolving the national will against an ever more powerful and unscrupulous foe are appallingly grim, the mortal dangers we face are yet more forbidding.

Moreover, the call to greatness in these proposals is itself an act of moral dignity and nobility of purpose. A democracy with all its strengths suffers from certain inescapable weaknesses. The picture it gives to the world must frequently be one of indecision, of uncertainty and wide divergence of views, of raucous debates and fervent exchange as we say things to one another that dismay outsiders. It has no single political doctrine—no democratic manifesto—that can readily be exported for immediate application to all the baffling and frustrating experiences of friends abroad. The ultimate truths of democracy are stated best in the crucible of experience when free men faced with stubborn realities prick out solutions through the thrust and counterthrust of open discussion. Perhaps our gravest peril through much of the past decade has arisen from the clogging of the channels of public discussion and the peculiar inhibitions placed upon us by the national mood. Now that the air has cleared, men with ideas have come forward again, and reasonable and fair-minded people around the world, if they are not blinded by passion and prejudice, must eventually be impressed by the process of free opinion grappling with unprecedented problems and issues. No price tag can measure this achievement.

However, one of the persistent difficulties we face in convincing ourselves and our neighbors of the changeless truths of democracy has roots in the origin and growth of democratic values. Communist values are preordained by historical materialism and by the high priests of Marxist-Leninist creeds. Democratic values, while anchored in what the Founding Fathers called the Higher Law, are forever evolving and in the process of becoming. Their historic formulation must be sought in part in a single constitutional document but perhaps even more in the gloss on this document—the interpretations of statesmen, jurists, and legislators in time of crisis. The process by which democratic values become living realities in a pluralist society is a free people's most precious treasure. It also remains a mystery to those who have not experienced its worth. Perhaps this is why the present crisis seems so pregnant with meaning and opportunity. Great leaders like Lincoln in the Emancipation Proclamation, Jefferson in the Declaration of Independence, and Roosevelt in the Four Freedoms have delved deep into the family of values that comprise the woof and warp of American life, raised up certain "self-evident truths," ordered and related them to fit the problem, and by deed no less than word laid the basis for the enduring articles on the scroll of our American faith. This is the matchless opportunity to which another American President may respond. Leadership that draws its strength from the fires of moral and intellectual courage can rally men to do their utmost in education, science, and diplomacy.

There is another dimension of the present crisis that is moral in character. A nation's prestige is in part the result of its power. It is also, however, the product of its reputation for justice, and justice in world affairs includes more than a towering dedication to law and order. It also involves respect for the interests of others, compassion, humility, trust, re-

239

sponsibility, and sympathy for men struggling with problems that are not our problems. It includes the search for a common purpose, of a goal however distant at the end of the arms race, and of reflection on those political terms which might bring men safely through that frightening tunnel we call peace by thermonuclear terror. The breakdown of American leadership is doubtless due to the lag in American military policies, and calls for urgency here are essential. But even if we hold our own in this area, we shall lose the struggle if we have nothing to offer in the political and economic realm.

No reasonable man of course can believe that the end of the Cold War is in sight or that this offer or that by itself will lead to a detente, nor should anyone think we could negotiate a lasting settlement from our present position of weakness. But if we talk only of new strategic doctrines, new tactics for the use of ever more absolute if tactical nuclear weapons, and new bases for IRBM's on the soil of unwilling allies to be triggered only when they see survival threatened, not we but Europe will assume future leadership, as has already been apparent on at least one occasion in the acts of our most trusted ally, Mr. Adenauer of Germany. If American policy remains suspended between a rigid, inflexible military posture and total and unattainable schemes for complete disarmament, our allies in frustration and despair will take matters into their own hands and negotiate terms that may be in their selfish interests but that will destroy that web of mutual interests, so painfully nurtured since the war, which can hold Western civilization together.

This is why political morality demands the wisdom and courage to pursue an intelligent, accelerated arms program at the same time we seek limited political solutions to concrete problems. It can never be satisfied with an anti-missiles effort which leaves no room for exploratory talks on the problem of Central Europe. The art of asking questions at appropriate diplomatic levels, for example, through our Ambassador in

Moscow or at sub-summit levels, must never be allowed to become a casualty of the present conflict. Private, patient diplomacy at the source of a festering tension is more likely to bring relaxation than global approaches at the summit. "It is idle to reason or argue with the Communists," Mr. Winston Churchill observed in a speech to the House of Commons on January 23, 1948. "It is however possible to deal with them on a fair, realistic basis and in my experience they will keep their bargains as long as it is in their interest to do so, which might, in this grave matter, be a long time, once things were settled." In any case, if the art of diplomatic conversations could be recovered and practiced not merely in highly publicized conferences, we might discover what possibilities exist for disengagement in Central Europe, for some kind of a lowering of temperature in the Middle East, for a recognition that neither side any longer can attain military predominance or paramouncy and therefore that we must learn to live as equal powers not liking or trusting one another, always fearful of rash and heedless acts, but no longer committed to that hopeless policy of unconditional surrender which has informed our actions in Germany, the Far East and Middle East and that will sooner or later carry us over the abyss. The concrete measures that might reverse this frightening trend would be political in nature. The decision to act in this way, however, is a moral choice of men secure enough in the final triumph of their cause to take the domestic and political risks of which greatness is born.

There is an Asian saying that "justice must not only be; it must also be seen to be done." It of course is possible that every present criticism of American foreign policy may prove misplaced and that both the frantic dedication to more and larger bombs and to more absolute moral principles may some-day be seen as part of wisdom. At the very least, however, the peoples of other countries not only in Asia but Europe as well show a profound anxiety with what Americans say and

241

do. This may be nothing more than the envy and suspicion of the weak for the strong. However, this condition in itself calls for some reflection. It reminds us once more of Edmund Burke's warning that: "Nothing is so fatal to a nation as an extreme of self-partiality and the total want of consideration of what others will naturally hope or fear." Europe and Asia may only be asking for greater partnership in the fateful decisions of the days ahead. They have this right even as they have the right to carry forward their own social and economic development. We recall the explanation of a learned judge in a country once under British control: "You gave us justice, roads, hospitals, the British peace, but you took away what we now value more, our self-respect." It is an illusion to think that our allies, faced with the total destructiveness of new weapons will with energy follow our lead if they doubt our intentions or feel we are morally weak.

But even if we stood alone, the task of foreign policy would be much the same. It would call for vigor and public courage in rallying American military strength. It would insist, however, that the chances of a free people using this strength or surviving its use in a thermonuclear struggle would depend very closely on whether they grasped fully the moral and political aspects of the crisis. And in diplomacy, this calls for an awareness that "the best is often the enemy of the good." The best opportunity for political solution is one that may never come. Accepting the uncertainties of the moral and political realm, American foreign policy might escape the final illusion that we are or can become so strong and virtuous that we need not be ever vigilant to reasonable prospects for compromise and adjustment in the cold war.

PART THREE

PEACE AND POLITICAL REALISM

EPILOGUE

ALL OF US share the temptation of allowing the jet stream of events—Iraq, Lebanon, Cuba, Berlin—to overwhelm our thinking and to shape public opinion. To the extent that foreign policy is a practical down-to-earth endeavor, this contact with the real and the concrete is probably a sign of national health. Americans, however, are predisposed as a practical people to close their eyes to the broad trends and movements of history despite the forewarnings that are sounded by strong leaders in public and private life.

This was evident in the years surrounding World War I when President Wilson cried out for programs that would reflect America's international responsibility. His optimism and even naïveté should not obscure his more enduring legacy. He endeavored valiantly, though without any immediate success, to rouse the public conscience to an awareness that abstention and isolation had lost their relevance, that the United States henceforth would be, for better or worse, a major factor in everything that transpired in world affairs. If Wilson conceived of world responsibility both too narrowly and too idealistically, if he assumed that the League and the United States in the League were ready to shoulder more burdens than proved possible, he at least caught a glimpse of the dawning of a new era and expressed this fearlessly.

President Franklin D. Roosevelt stood at another turning point in world affairs. The rise of nazism had not been contained in Europe, the world balance of power was being shattered, and only American power, affirmed and asserted, could preserve Western civilization. As the conflict with nazism drew to a close, Roosevelt prepared the way for the United Nations.

It fell to President Truman to initiate policies aimed at

245

resisting another threat to Western civilization. The Marshall Plan, the Truman Doctrine, and NATO were the tripod on which resistance to Soviet expansion was based. The era from 1946 to 1955 was one of building up counter-forces as the most dependable means of holding back the Russian advance.

Obviously one period of history spills over into the next, and the years from 1955 to the present are both a continuation of the past and a preparation for a new era. At Geneva, the Soviet Union and the United States recognized in effect the nuclear stalemate. However popular it has become to speak of the 1955 summit conference as symbolic of broken promises, illusions, and false smiles, history's hard lesson is that world politics at Geneva began to turn a corner, whether for better or for worse. To be sure, foreign policy has been more complicated since that time. Events in the non-Western world have gained in importance as the struggle between East and West has multiplied points of conflict. Cultural and intellectual barriers show signs of relaxation as the Soviet and Western worlds compete in this field. In recent days, the scene of the Cold War, spurred by the Russian ultimatum over Berlin, has shifted once more to the diplomatic arena as the foreign ministers embark on the arduous task of preparing, if possible, for a summit conference. The last three or four years have thus been a transitional period.

It may fairly be asked in this context what is the overriding objective of Western policy or what ought it to be? I would answer unreservedly and unashamedly, "peace." Admittedly, such an answer begs many questions; it leaves a host of troublesome issues in the realm of means with which statesmen through the centuries have grappled. All men cry peace but the stubborn task remains of perceiving the narrow road that leads to peace. History teaches that peace has rarely if ever been earned through surrender, weakness, or appeasement. Instead, the great eras of peace are marked not by absence of conflict and tension but by their control. Rivalries were checked, power kept in balance, and wars were confined within geographic and technological limits.

These lessons from the past are partly if not wholly valid in a thermonuclear age. The one thing that has changed is the disappearance of predictably temperate and indecisive conflicts about which historians wrote in an earlier century. Every limited war threatens to erupt into total war, wiping out broad sectors of national societies, and every conflict in which the stakes are high enough is likely to intensify to the point of mutual annihilation. A French political realist, Professor Raymond Aron, can write: "Humanity has entered an unprecedented phase in which the great powers are, for the first time in history, preparing for a war they do not want to fight. How long can peace be preserved by the threat of a suicidal war?"[1]

Most informed realists, idealists, legalists, and moralists would agree that there was something fundamentally novel and unprecedented in the present era calling for men's highest ingenuity if civilization is not to perish. At this point, however, agreement ends as each man's favorite ideas are called into play to prevent the apocalypse. Rationalists and idealists proclaim that new technological advances unlocking the deadly secrets of nature will reason awaken in men. They believe that as nations and governments learn that total destruction can accompany open conflict, they will eschew war, thus transcending their ancestors, who failed to set aside less lethal instruments of force. At an opposite extreme, those who see relations among states as little more than protracted conflict and who espouse the theory of inevitable war can read only doom in the future. They doubt that war can be limited or conflict averted and are tempted therefore by doctrines that call for striking the first—and hopefully the fatal—blow. Intermixed with these utopian and catastrophic forms of

[1] Raymond Aron, *On War* (New York: Doubleday & Co., 1959), Preface.

247

thought are moralistic and legalistic trends and approaches. Moralists yearn for a universal change of heart—a transvaluation of values—prompted by the worldwide human predicament. Legalists expect that the world rule of law will be achieved in much the same way that a common enemy united the thirteen original colonies. Other approaches are denounced as fatalistic for they have been tried and found wanting. These answers are, of course, familiar to anyone acquainted with the history of international thought. They were the answers put forward when gunpowder, mustard gas, and civilian bombing threatened earlier societies. We err by assuming that they are revolutionary and novel, and that political realism is archaic and static. The dialogue between these contending approaches is deeply embedded in all history.

If we accept this fact, the examination of peace and political realism becomes more amenable to calm and reasoned discussion. The unhappy and misleading identifications alternately of realism with war or appeasement can be held up to the searchlight of truth and its concepts measured against realities as expressed in contemporary world politics.

First, political realism is fatalistic only in assuming that politics of a particularly intense and unrestrained character is a necessary concomitant of present-day international society. Its fatalism falls short of assuming that war is inevitable; indeed, its main preoccupation is the search for reasonable, if limited, measures for the prevention of war. It accepts the actors on the international scene for what past and present world politics shows them to be—men striving in the first instance at least for their nation's security and influence. I am reminded of a similar problem—that of understanding economic behavior. In a particularly illuminating essay, Professor Frederic C. Lane of Johns Hopkins University has written:

"Most men most of the time have been occupied in making a living. The values that existed for them, not merely as aspiration or as ideas to be talked about, but in action and as qualities of personal character, were those embodied in the daily activities by which they made their living. If bullying and fawning, arrogant command and servile obedience were the rule in economic life, that is the way men were—that is what society was like. Other themes—religious aspiration, artistic feeling, and creative intellectual vigor—reward endless historical investigation for their own sake, even when they have no discernible connection with social organization, but historians interested in justice, freedom, or any other qualities of social life have reason to give primary attention to the human relations entered into during the processes of production and distribution."[2]

The parallel with the processes of the international system seem too obvious for comment.

Secondly, political realism holds to the past only in the most general philosophical sense. Change is indeed the first law of history, and no event repeats an episode that belongs to the past. Both communism and nazism are threats to Western civilization, but the ingredients that compose these threats are almost infinitely varied. Nevertheless, in terms similar to those of the economic historian or economic theorist who sees "arrogant command and servile obedience" recurrent in economic behavior, the international theorist expects in the politics of nations ambition and rivalry and the conflict of "national wills" in the struggle to maintain and to change every status quo. The realist invokes the past not to repeat its successes or failures but to gain what light he can on the means by which rivalries were composed in an orderly and peaceful way.

Thirdly, political realism is wedded to particular institutions or forms only to the extent that they are present in the problems confronting policy-makers. The realist is conserva-

[2] Frederic C. Lane, "Economic Consequences of Organized Violence," *The Journal of Economic History*, Vol. XVIII, No. 4, December 1958, p. 417.

tive in believing that living institutions and problems constitute a challenge more than equal to his best insights and imagination. Wholly fictional arrangements or ideal blueprints for peace are worthy of someone's attention but real issues in the present are more than enough for testing his mettle. If choices are made in international relationships on the basis of national interests, the realist considers this an appropriate target for study and action even though he might wish that the basis for action were broader and more enlightened. Hence, nationalism today, however shortsighted or misguided, is worthy of analysis and evaluation not only in the East-West struggle but among "fledgling states" vigorously asserting their newfound status.

Finally, in the broad realm of contemporary policy, realism has no choice but to face problems on their merits. If, at one moment, the building up of the elements of power is the task of statesmen seeking a deterrent to Soviet Russia's "new imperialism," this process must be seen as part of political reality. If, at another point, the elements of power reach such magnitude and intensity that new techniques of accommodation are called for, the realist must not flinch from discussing the course of changing diplomatic and economic encounters. Politics among nations occurs on a moving front determined by the pressures nations and the forces of history bring to bear on one another. At one point, maintenance of the international order or a precarious equilibrium of power may be the paramount goal. At another point in time, the development of new means of destruction may give higher priority to world peace. These conditions set the framework within which statesmen and, at one stage removed, international thinkers must do their onerous and thankless work.

As American foreign policy in the post-1955 phase of its history looks for new formulas and techniques to achieve world peace, the great mass of ordinary men and women can take heart that the problems confronting them are both new

and old. Diplomacy, which for a generation or more is certain
to be the historic instrument by which mutual annihilation must
be forestalled, has an ancient tradition compounded of wisdom
and folly, success and failure. The chief virtue of political
realism and its main contribution to peace lies in the unqualified emphasis it would place on these techniques and methods.
In this sense, political realism enjoys an intimate and permanent relation to peace and to the survival of mankind.

SELECTED READINGS

Acheson, Dean, *Power and Diplomacy*. Cambridge: Harvard University Press, 1958.

Aron, Raymond, *A Century of Total War*. New York: Doubleday & Company, Inc., 1954.

Bailey, Thomas A., *A Diplomatic History of the American People* (6th ed.). New York: Appleton-Century-Crofts, Inc., 1957.

Beloff, Max, *Foreign Policy and the Democratic Process*. Baltimore: Johns Hopkins University Press, 1955.

Bowles, Chester, *Ideas, People and Peace*. New York: Harper & Brothers, 1958.

Bowles, Chester, *The New Dimensions of Peace*. New York: Harper & Brothers, 1955.

Brinton, Crane C., *The Anatomy of Revolution* (rev. ed.). New York: Alfred A. Knopf, Inc., 1953.

Butterfield, Herbert, *Christianity, Diplomacy and War*. London: Abingdon Press, 1954.

Carr, Edward H., *The Twenty Years' Crisis, 1919-1939: An Introduction to the Study of International Relations* (2nd ed.). London: Macmillan & Co., Ltd., 1940; New York: St. Martin's Press, Inc., 1946.

Cobban, Alfred, *National Self-Determination* (rev. ed.). Chicago: University of Chicago Press, 1948.

Craig, Gordon A. and Gilbert, Felix (eds.), *The Diplomats, 1919-1939*. Princeton: Princeton University Press, 1953.

Dahl, Robert, *Congress and Foreign Policy*. New York: Harcourt, Brace & Co., 1950.

De Schweinitz, K. and Thompson K. W., *Man and Modern Society: Conflict and Choice in the Industrial Era*. New York: Henry Holt & Co., Inc., 1953.

Dennett, R. and Johnson, J. E. (eds.), *Negotiating with the Russians*. Boston: World Peace Foundation, 1951.

Dunn, Frederick S., *Practice and Procedure of International Conferences*. Baltimore: Johns Hopkins University Press, 1929.

Earle, Edward M. (ed.), *Makers of Modern Strategy: Military Thought from Machiavelli to Hitler*. Princeton: Princeton University Press, 1943.

Gathorne-Hardy, Geoffrey M., *A Short History of International Affairs, 1920-1939* (4th ed.). London, New York: Oxford University Press (for the Royal Institute of International Affairs), 1950.

Halle, Louis J., *Civilization and Foreign Policy*. New York: Harper & Brothers, 1955.

Halle, Louis J., *Dream and Reality: Aspects of American Foreign Policy*. New York: Harper & Brothers, 1959.

Hallowell, John (ed.), *Soviet Satellite Nations: A Study of the New Imperialism*. Gainesville, Florida: Kullman Publishing Co., 1958.

Hankey, Sir Maurice, *Diplomacy by Conference*. New York: G. P. Putnam's Sons.

Hill, Martin, *Immunities and Privileges of International Officials*. New York: Columbia University Press, 1947.

Herz, John, *Political Realism and Political Idealism*. Chicago: University of Chicago Press, 1951.

Jennings, William Ivor, *British Commonwealth of Nations*. Hutchinson's University Library. New York: Rinehart & Co., Inc., 1948.

Kahin, George McTurnan, *The Asian-African Conference, Bandung, Indonesia*. Ithaca: Cornell University Press, 1955.

Kennan, George F., *American Diplomacy, 1900-1950*. Chicago: University of Chicago Press, 1951.

Kennan, George F., *Realities of American Foreign Policy*. Princeton: Princeton University Press, 1954.

Kennan, George F., *Russia, the Atom and the West*. New York: Harper & Brothers, 1958.

Kertesz, S. C., *Diplomacy in a Whirlpool*. Notre Dame, Indiana: University of Notre Dame Press, 1953.

Kissinger, Henry, *Nuclear Weapons and Foreign Policy*. New York: Harper & Brothers (for the Council on Foreign Relations), 1957.

Mallory, W. H., *The Political Handbook of the World, 1958*. New York: Council on Foreign Relations.

Marshall, C. B., *The Limits of Foreign Policy*. New York: Henry Holt & Co., Inc., 1954.

Morgenthau, Hans J., *Politics among Nations: The Struggle for Power and Peace* (2nd ed.). New York: Alfred A. Knopf, Inc., 1954.

Morgenthau, Hans J. and Thompson, K. W., *Principles and Problems of International Politics.* New York: Alfred A. Knopf, Inc., 1950.

Morgenthau, Hans J., *Scientific Man vs. Power Politics.* Chicago: University of Chicago Press, 1944.

Mowat, Robert B., *Diplomacy and Peace.* London: Williams & Norgate, Ltd., 1935.

Nicolson, Harold, *The Evolution of Diplomatic Method.* New York: The Macmillan Co., 1955.

Nicolson, Harold, *Diplomacy* (2nd ed.). London, New York: Oxford University Press, 1950.

Niebuhr, R., *Christian Realism and the Political Problem.* New York: Charles Scribner's Sons, 1954.

Niebuhr, R., *The Structure of Nations and Empires.* New York: Charles Scribner's Sons, 1959.

Osgood, Robert E., *Limited War.* Chicago: University of Chicago Press, 1957.

Padelford, N. J. and Lincoln, G. A., *International Politics.* New York: The Macmillan Co., 1954.

Pearson, Lester, *Democracy in World Politics.* Princeton: Princeton University Press, 1955.

Satow, Sir Ernest M., *Guide to Diplomatic Practice.* Vol. 2. London, New York, etc.: Longmans, Green & Co., 1957.

Schwarzenberger, Georg, *Power Politics* (2nd ed.). London: Stevens & Sons, Ltd.; New York: Frederick A. Praeger, Inc., 1951.

Sprout, Harold and Sprout, Margaret (eds.), *Foundations of National Power* (2nd ed.). New York: D. Van Nostrand Co., Inc., 1951.

Toynbee, Arnold, *The World and the West.* New York: Oxford University Press, Inc., 1953.

Van Royen, William, *et al., The Mineral Resources of the World.* Vol. 2 of *Atlas of World Resources.* New York: Prentice-Hall, Inc., 1952.

Wight, Martin, *Power Politics* (new ed. due). London: Royal Institute of International Affairs.

Wriston, Henry, *Diplomacy in a Democracy.* New York: Harper & Brothers, 1956.

INDEX